What reviewers say about Gay L. Balliet's Books—

Touched by All Creatures

"Eminently readable. Will be welcomed by everyone who enjoyed James Herriot's efforts."

—Booklist

"Balliet is a worthy successor to James Herriot. *Touched by All Creatures* is a book that readers will return to again and again."

—Midwest Book Review

"The wonder of animals and the earthy, humane details of doctoring them shines through."

—Publishers Weekly

"Genuine . . . quickly draws readers in."

—School Library Journal

"Every bit as eccentric, loveable and heart-tugging as [James Herriot's] Yorkshire chronicles."

—Sunday Tribune Review

Lowell: The True Story of an Existential Pig

"A lot of animal and pet books cross my desk, but this is one of the few I can heartily recommend. It's touching, funny and quite enlightening."

—San Jose Morning News

"Like James Herriot's books, Balliet's *Lowell* reads more like a riveting novel than a 'pigography.'"

—Sunday Star-Ledger

". . . another delectable trough's worth of vets-at-home and vets-on-the-road anecdotes [with a wide range of philosophical and psychological speculation."

—Publishers Weekly

Lions & Tigers & Mares ... Oh, My!

Gay L. Balliet

RDR Books
Oakland, California

Lions & Tigers & Mares . . . Oh, My!

RDR Books
4456 Piedmont
Oakland, CA 94611
Phone: (510) 595-0595
Fax: (510) 595-0598
E-mail: read@rdrbooks.com
Website: www.rdrbooks.com

ISBN: 1–57143–105-5

Library of Congress Catalog Card Number 2004090912

Edited, designed, and produced by Richard Harris

Cover photo by Fella Studios, Inc. of Northampton, PA

Distributed in Canada by Jaguar Book Group
c/o Fraser Direct, 100 Armstrong Way, Georgetown, ON L7G 5S4

Distributed in the United Kingdom and Europe by Roundhouse
Publishing, Ltd., Millstone, Limers Lane, Northam,
North Deven EX39 2RG, United Kingdom

Distributed in Australia and New Zealand by Wakefield Press (Aust) Pty.
Ltd., 1 The Parade West, Kent Town, Adelaide, South Australia 5071

Printed in Canada by Transcontinental Printing

To my husband Edgar

In memory of
Merry Shadowfax
"Fax"

Your stall is so empty.
Never another like you, like your ride.

We miss you Lillie, Al, Milton, Bruce, Jean, Whitey, Larry,
and Sonny & Cher—good souls.
And Ricky, mole detective
And Wendy, wrinkly nose—
Family members we'll miss forever.

CONTENTS

One World

THE DAY I MARRIED MY VETERINARIAN HUSBAND was the day my family, which had formerly been comprised of only my parents and me, began growing to panoramic proportions. Included in our band were Edgar, me, and the individual animals we owned and loved. Compared to our family of today, however, it was a small community, indeed.

Life quickly settled into a varied routine of tending cows, horses, elk, deer, and other assorted large animals. By day we roamed the countryside tending the animals, laughing and sharing coffee and jokes with the critters' owners. By night we burrowed into our home in the woods alongside our animal family of cats, horses, pigs, and fish.

What I didn't realize those first few years was how abruptly and dramatically my concept of family would change one day. No—the feeling that life held something larger for me didn't happen in the beginning, when we were more concerned with making a living and paying our bills. We were so intent on making a go of providing quality large animal veterinary care and emergency services to animal patients in the Lehigh Valley, the heart of the Pennsylvania Dutch country, that I failed to see the larger picture.

The revelatory seed within me was slow to emerge, seemingly impervious to our life's "weather." At times it threatened to shrivel and die, but it was a hardy seed, though exceedingly retarded in its growth. Then in one special moment that seed's coat cracked open, and a pedicle emerged. When the kernel finally split, I felt an elation hard to describe and equally hard to validate. Today the flower resembles some ancient, prehistoric lotus. The aroma permeates the very air, and the crisp edges never fade—the color always brilliant.

Like our work, our travels revolve around animals and nature. It seems we can't get enough of a good thing. Edgar and I enjoy scuba diving in tropical climes. Diving, we luxuriate in the marine life: the eagle rays, stingrays, sharks, and the smaller tropical fish like blennies, parrotfish, wrasses, tangs, and angelfish. If we aren't diving, we're hiking the cloud forests and volcanic regions of Costa Rica, or riding horses through the rainforest watching for a glimpse of a sloth lounging high in a tree or tracking howler monkeys in the canopy. Within the fold of nature, we embrace a primitive world in which far "curiouser" animals reign.

Back in landlocked Pennsylvania, doctoring and befriending the animals offers a different approach to nature and her creatures. Here we doctor and care for animals of the home, the farm, and the zoo, and we have become friends with many more—our own pets and those of our friends and clients. My husband's veterinary practice specializes in large and exotic animals, and I, when I am not busy pampering my animal "children" at home, tag along on his rounds to assist him and enjoy the world so many people have largely forgotten, taken for granted, or dismissed.

Both of these worlds—the tropical paradise and the farm—need to be conserved, protected. Edgar and I care for each animal patient as a valuable member of our world. For us, tending animals so vulnerable and so appreciative is an equally unique adventure as is the one we experience on vacation. While we help many different varieties of creatures in our veterinary practice—buffalo, horses, llamas, tigers, pigs, elk, deer, and wolves—every day is different and unique in our appreciation of all animals—wondrous and wee.

Of course, our veterinary life has a few drawbacks to it, such as the endless hours of driving and dealing with reckless drivers, the emergency calls in the middle of the night, the routine office chores such as answering the phone and scheduling appointments, paying drug and lab bills, ordering supplies, and so on. But the hands-on part of being a veterinarian and his assistant renders the negative parts little more than petty annoyances. When we turn down the driveway of a Pennsylvania Dutch farm and stroll into the milking parlor, equipment in hand, we enter a sweet and sour-smelling paradise where milk chocolate originates and breakfast cereal ends. Times like this, and others, like sneaking into the monkey cage at the Trexler Game Preserve and persuading a tiger to let us examine her eyes, are our escapes from the jaded life of the shopping malls and all the vices of a materialistic society with its human noise and "all that cal."

Here in eastern Pennsylvania the seasons are so different from one another, but each is influential—inviting and tiring at the same time. For example, Edgar and I both relish the winter's first snowfall. It marks an occasion for play, for celebration. Expecting to be snowed in, we drive to the grocery store and help outstrip the market's supply of milk and bread along with other excited folks anticipating the first blizzard. We empty the toilet paper shelves and skip merrily into our protective home as the first few flakes begin to fall. We take hikes in the falling first snow. We kiss in it. We bundle up our own horses and pot-bellied pigs against its frost and hoar, and we do it with enthusiasm, expecting something out of the norm: crystalline, sound-deadening snow, nature's ice tears.

We revel in the extreme weather, but by the third snowfall, we no longer run in gleeful hysteria to the grocery. We hole up before the woodstove instead of bundling up for a hike, and we find ourselves a bit apathetic to winter's beauty, which seems not as lovely, not nearly, as the season's first snowfall.

Likewise, we relish Pennsylvania's summer until the end of August when the sweat glands are drained dry and the prickly heat is at its worst. Then we dream of crisp fall leaves, autumn's penetrating rain, and hoarding toilet paper again.

At home, we are often alone—away from noisy crowds, fast food joints, demanding electronic technology, e-mail, the phone, TV, and the retail industry. Certainly our real experience tending animals—so palpable—is more endearing and enduring than any virtual existence in a box. Calls with Edgar may find us in the boondocks, on the side of a mountain at a home without neighbors, in the woods, or on a buffalo range in a wildlife preserve where human habitation is restricted. But we are never really alone, for an animal and its anxious owner await us. At the Dutch farms we are separated from the outside world, yet we are privileged to enjoy the company of animals and their honest human companions. At work on a cow with mastitis or a lame horse, we find ourselves alone, appreciatively alone—with the patient and her owner.

This is the life we cherish and celebrate.

And celebrate we did one summer's end. In appreciation of our clients, Edgar and I invited a couple hundred or so for a get-together at our farm. We planned the event for outside, setting up tables and chairs beneath the canopy of our woods. If it rained, we could always entertain in the indoor riding arena, but I was hoping for nice weather so that we could all enjoy one of the last days of summer. Edgar graciously suggested a caterer, and I suggested we call up "Caribbean Spice," a steel-drum band we had heard months before at a wine-tasting function.

For much of the summer I'd been busy weeding and primping the perennial garden, which overflowed with a profusion of pink coneflowers, rose and ivory hibiscus as round and as large as a child's face, yellow daisies with chocolate centers, curly dianthus, and Russian purple sage. Luckily I didn't have to weed the vegetable garden, since there wasn't much left to it—compliments of my four pigs, Ivy Mae, Annie Louise, Lowell and Lucille, who made a habit of "harvesting" the crops at 6 AM every morning. And when I wasn't in the garden or edging the lawn, I was crafting centerpieces, making chocolate pig candies, and arranging last minute details with the caterer.

The day before the party I had broken the last pig candy from its mold when I decided that the day was far too nice to be inside cooking. I had enough candies for the guests to take home anyway. So, I pulled on my running shorts and shoes, grabbed a headband, and headed out the door.

In minutes I was heading down the driveway and onto the grass path that circled our woods. Each lap around our property was about a half mile, so on a good day I went around about six times. On the way I met any number of the barn cats stalking butterflies or lounging on the cushy green trail, which Edgar kept mowed to a crewcut. With every daily run I came upon some wild critter going about his or her business: the groundhogs munching the alfalfa on the far side of the path; squirrels chattering as they frantically collected nuts for their winter storage chests; iridescent dragonflies, blanched moths, and Monarch butterflies skimming and fluttering to wherever insects go. As I chugged along my course, the air was alive with the sounds of crickets and seven-year locusts, the complaints of crows, and the shrieks of hawks on the hunt.

I was on my last lap, and glad to be, too—always glad to be done with the dreaded daily run—and thinking whether I had everything in order for the party, when I came around the point of the woods.

Suddenly in the middle of the path about thirty feet ahead, a figure stood as immobile as a tree stump.

I stopped dead. My mouth dropped open.

The large figure, caught in the shade of an overhanging tree, twitched her head toward me, sniffing. It was a doe.

I smiled. She was beautiful— her coat the color of chestnuts, her back straight, her legs long and fragile-lean, her ears erect, and her face delicate with large black patent-leather eyes.

I stood, trying to catch my breath, amazed. Often we spied deer walking through our woods. But when we saw them, we were usually in the house and the deer at a distance. We would only

catch brief glimpses of them as they grazed the woodsy underbrush, stepping gingerly behind the big oak and ash trees. Here was a deer up close.

I didn't make a move.

The doe sniffed again, but the breeze was coming out of the west, and I was downwind. Nevertheless, she could obviously see me; I was as exposed as she. She was trying to verify with her nose what her eyes were telling her was true: a human was near. Suddenly with her left hoof, she stomped the ground once, paused, then hit it twice. Then she snorted, sniffed, and stomped again.

There was no use trying to be coy, I thought. She knew I was there. I said in a soft voice, "Hi, Beautiful. Nice day, isn't it?"

She stood still, her ears tuned toward me.

"You don't have to be afraid. I'm not going to hurt you. You can go back into the woods, and I'll just turn right around and go home." I smiled, so entranced was I with the still, graceful figure of the deer. She had likely been born and raised by her mother nearby, probably in the 500-acre Catholic Seminary property that adjoins ours. While we carried out life in our smaller woods, feeding the animals each morning, having breakfast, going about our chores, and setting out on the road to do vet calls, she grew up combing the forest only a quarter mile away in search of berries and brush, keeping a constant watch for predators like coydogs and wild dogs. I imagined the deer and me living much different yet parallel existences.

"It's okay," I repeated softly. "You don't have . . ."

With that the deer bolted, flying as with wings, her white tail straight and bobbing with each leap. The next second she was away over the nearest hill, the force of fear impelling her back into the safety of the seminary's forest.

My arms dropped limply to my sides, and I sighed heavily. Why was the deer so afraid of me? I had never done anything to scare her or hurt her. Looking at the horizon with only a ghost-image of the deer disappearing over the hill, I felt strangely empty. I looked at the ground. Then I looked back to the top of the hill over which the deer had vanished in sheer terror.

And at that moment the kernel of revelation that had been growing inside me cracked open. My stirring seed burst open to reveal a pedi-

cle more strange and splendid than any domesticated flower, more pro-
found than any philosopher's stone. Atop its stalk hung a pregnant,
pendulous bud unlike any I had ever seen—filled with a blossom at
once surreal and inviting—a bloom that would startle and change the
way I looked at the world forever.

Suddenly a crow cawed overhead, shocking me from my stupor.

Why had the deer sensed me as a danger, a threat no less horrific
than death? Surely when the doe came upon my housecats cruising our
small woods, she didn't run as though the fires of hell were lapping at
her heels. She probably never ran from a groundhog or squirrel or fox
or any other creature of the woods. And while I wasn't a woodsy critter, I was another being just the same—one that meant no harm.
Perhaps she didn't like my patriotic runner shorts or my headband that
seemed to cut my head in two. But, to my mind, I was not an alien; I
was just another animal with slightly different physical and mental
qualities.

In fact, that's how the marine and land iguanas, the fur seals and the
sea lions had regarded Edgar and me in the Galapagos Islands when
we'd visited there. They had no fear of humans. We were different
beings: upright and stumbling over the rocks on two feet, but the
Galapagos creatures didn't run or hide from us. The sea lions stretched,
yawned, and barked at their beach buddies lying beside them, but
when we approached, they lifted their heads, looked, and lay back
down with nonchalance and boredom. We could walk amongst them
without their feeling disturbed or threatened. It seemed they regarded
us as one of their own kind. At the time I thought it was cute. Now I
realized that the exotic seed had been planted within me in the
Galapagos.

Why should the creatures in our woods feel differently toward us
than did those in the Galapagos? Yet, as the doe had run, so did the
squirrels, the groundhogs, and the chipmunks whenever we happened
upon each other in the woods. But the seed that burst into bud inside
me questioned why one of nature's creatures would fear another of
nature's creatures—a human? Apart from fearing me as a predator, was
I not a part of this world, too—born from it, surviving in it, and sharing significant DNA with its other inhabitants? Wasn't I just another
being sharing the Earth?

As a human, I am simply an extension of nature. My species evolved from it; my prehistoric ancestors originated from it, survived it by instinct and intelligence, and struggled and enjoyed life amid it. My species has evolved from the animals, from nature; therefore, I, all of us humans, are a part of it. I never took a logic course in school, and, to be sure, this is as logical as I get. But it made absolute sense to me as I stared, slump-shouldered, over the hill. Like the mythical figure who was birthed from sea foam, I am a part of the natural environment and the world of domestic creatures as well. I am kin to all critters.

The revelation that I was related to all life on Earth, that each human or animal is part of the larger family of beings, had been stirring within me for years. The moment with the deer had crystallized the idea and ripened the seed. I and every other person, I now realized, are simply part of the whole—a segment of the family of beings with whom we share the same world and time frame. And it follows that as part of a family, neither the human nor the animal should exploit or fear the other.

But there was a problem with my enlightenment. The deer hadn't seen things my way. She had viewed me as an alien and had fled for her life.

That day, instead of running, I walked back home. I passed Spinny, one of the gray tiger barn cats out hunting, and I said "Hello. How's your day going, Spin Maiden?" She sashayed between my legs and walked me back to the house. But I couldn't get the doe out of my mind. The memory of her fleeing tail haunted me until I walked through the back door and flung my soaked headband on the counter.

For the rest of the day, I attended to last-minute details for the party. But while I swept off the front porch, my mind drifted back to the scared doe. I had tried to communicate with her, assure her I was no threat, but I was unable to convince her I was just another being passing harmlessly through her world. Her reaction had been disconcerting and disappointing, but the revelation that emerged from the encounter—that each creature is part of a larger family of life—would no doubt keep me thinking for months to come.

The next day, soon after the caterer set up and the steel-drum band hit a few practice notes, the guests began arriving. The season's horse shows were over, and our clients had had a full summer of trail riding the woods of Pennsylvania. People whose horses and other animals Edgar had been treating for years gathered in our backyard, more as friends than clients, for wine, a buffet, and Caribbean-style entertainment. Our own family of animals—the cats, the horses in their pasture, and two of our four pot-bellied pigs—joined in the fun, too.

We'd rented an old-fashioned popcorn machine to supplement the luncheon. What Edgar didn't know, however, was that I really wanted it for our pigs. They love popcorn, especially with butter, and this was no dry, air-popped stuff. The kernels exploded from their hot griddle of grease and beckoned all the weak-of-diet to indulge.

When the first guests arrived, Lowell had made a grand entrance from the shadows of the barn. He surveyed the area, sniffing the air for food and the varied scents of our guests. As I squeezed through the crowd, I overheard several folks giggling and joking with each other about their furry, scaly, and feathered friends. Between chatting and directing people toward the food, I kept my eye on Lowell, guessing what my precocious pig was "up to"—and it wasn't 200 pounds either.

It was obvious what was on Lowell's mind. He wanted popcorn. But since he couldn't get it for himself, he had to rely on strangers to get it for him—no easy task for a hefty, intimidating animal whose only perception of the world was eighteen inches from the ground. Being so much shorter than people put him at a socializing disadvantage. And he was well aware that some people didn't take too well to pigs unless they were on a spit or in a sandwich. So, if he was going to be fed anything, he knew he must first instill a level of confidence in some human partygoers. And he wasn't taking a chance on the men falling in love with him. No, as the charmer I knew him to be, he went straight for a group of women. He needed to gain the adoration of the women first to prove he was a kind, affable fellow who deserved a morsel of popped corn.

Within minutes he found a place for himself standing, nose pointed, at the perimeter of a circle of women. Instinctively, they parted their circle, allowing him inside but barely noticing that the low-to-the-ground animal was listening intently and soaking up the human language like desiccant. Ivy Mae, too, was greeting people who just thought there was no other cuter creature on earth. She went from table to table and visited each guest, accepting bits of buns, carrots, and Swedish meatballs. The last time I looked, Ivy lay on her side enjoying a belly rub from Jon Mirkovic.

I turned toward the circle of women in which Lowell stood like a perfect gentleman. He was enamored by them, and the ladies were loving the attention.

Karen Schell, my friend with hair as dark as Lowell's, asked him, "My, you are a big boy, aren't you?" She smiled and crouched down beside him.

"Frump—frump—frump," he said.

"Are you having a nice time at the party?"

"Froom—froom," Lowell sang in a deep, operatic voice. Karen patted his head and stood up to say hello to Carole Polentes, a veterinary technician at Valley Central. Lowell didn't appreciate the dismissal. He reminded Karen of his presence, "Ip—ip—ip."

"What? What's wrong?" Karen asked bending toward him.

The "ip" became longer, more sustained. "Ii—eem, ii—eem, ii—eem," he pleaded, his brow knitted.

"Well, I really shouldn't give you anything to eat." She started to turn away.

"Whree, whree-ee, whree-eee!" Lowell shrieked with insistence.

"Oh, okay, Handsome. Here's some popcorn."

Carole giggled and nodded appreciatively at Karen.

Lowell munched the handful of popped kernels, and as he savored them, he hummed a low-toned, comfortable note. "Vru-u-u-umm," he thrummed. "Vru-u-u-umm." He relished the buttery treat.

Karen smiled. "I know. Popcorn is so-o-o good." She sighed, "Look at you—you have grease on your nose." Lowell whined. "Well, okay—just another handful. But then that's enough. I don't want to be responsible for making you any bigger." And she slipped another fistful into his mouth.

"Vru-u-u-umm," he thrummed. He munched with closed eyes.

Just then another guest, our farrier Jim Kindred, headed toward the cookie table. He was in a hurry and didn't see Lowell standing there. In his rush to the treats, he accidentally sideswiped my pig.

"Whrock, wrock!" Lowell barked, skittering out of the way. Jim came to an abrupt halt, and Lowell faced him with a look of annoyance.

"Whoop! I didn't see you there, fella," he said, looking down. Lowell stepped politely aside, but Jim pushed past in a big hurry, grabbed a handful of cookies, and strode off in another direction.

"Rih, rih, rih, rih," complained Lowell, his head hanging. My pig was not used to being regarded perfunctorily.

But another of our friends, Diane Nicrone, was quick to the rescue. She rushed over and stroked Lowell's head as she would one of her grandchildren's, "It's okay. He didn't hurt you. You're all right. Here's a cookie just for you."

"Vroo—oo-oomm, vroo-oo-oo-oomm," Lowell hummed, a smile on his face. "You're very polite, Lowell," she said and sneaked the rest of her own cookie into his mouth.

"Frup, frup, frup." Lowell said in an appreciative voice. Munching the last crumb, he sashayed into the front yard, where he stood transfixed before the steel-drum players. Savoring the music, he observed the crowd from a distance.

It was fascinating watching my pigs communicating with our clients. Diane knew what he needed, depending on the tone of his voice. She knew when he was really delighted with a piece of food; she knew that Jim had upset him and that Lowell was concerned for his safety; and she understood "frump-frump" as his language of contentment. To me, this discovery was a major breakthrough the likes of which should have been documented in *National Geographic*—breaking language barriers with animals as had been documented already with chimps, gorillas, and whales. Has no one studied the pig for its ability to communicate with people? I wondered.

My own observations of the conversations between my pig and people belong in the annals of scientific discoveries, though mine was by no means very scientific. I'm sure Lowell's myriad vocalizations could be analyzed much as the dancing of bees and the calls of whales have been. My pig may not be as exotic as a bee, whale, or primate, but he may well be smarter than those and even more skillful at conversing with people.

How interesting that Karen, Carole, and Diane invited him into their circle of conversation as though he were just another person. Sensing his intelligence and understanding the nuances of his language, they responded by asking him questions, interpreting his answers—carrying on entire discussions with him. Talking with Lowell wasn't silly; it seemed only natural. And as I watched my friends inter-acting with him, I realized I was witnessing a level of trust building between them. In a short time the women knew he wouldn't threaten or bite them, and in turn he felt their kindness.

Edgar and I communicate with animals in similar fashion during our vet calls. When we connect with a needy animal, we transcend our own species; we commingle with and temporarily become earth ani-mals ourselves. Part of the connection is fostered through nonverbal communication. In contrast, my own animals communicate with me on a vocal level. I understand their needs for food, snacks, freedom to roam the outdoors, freedom from cold or want, all according to their tone of voice. But Edgar's animal patients communicate in other ways than oral; they inquire with their eyes, the stance of their ears, their posture. Communication through body language, however, is no less clear than verbal communication. It seems, though, that the more intelligent the animal, the easier it is for him or her to interpret human language.

That's why the pigs and people could converse so naturally at our party.

Yet the pigs weren't the only ones socializing with the human crew. After observing our pigs "working the crowd," I observed our other animals' interest in the partygoers. The pigs were so obviously gregari-ous and mingled so well with everyone that I hadn't even noticed the cats milling around or the horses craning over the fence. All our ani-mals were curious about the human horde. Mr. and Mrs. Barry and their daughter were petting our horses, Fancy and Fax, while the other three horses picked pockets for treats. Only the fence kept them from formally attending the dinner party. The cats, too, strolled amongst the diners, and, from what I could see, they were getting their share of meatballs, too.

Observing all my animals as they interacted so well with our friends and clients made me happy, and once again I thought about the deer the day before. While the doe was totally unable or unwilling to inter-pret my verbal and body communication, my pigs' ability to interact with humans proved that people and animals could appreciate each other—once a level of trust on both sides had been established. As far as I was concerned, Lowell's conversation represented itself purely as an act of familial bliss. The socialization between different species boiled down to creatures trusting each other and visualizing themselves and behaving as equal beings—as families, for example, or the "family" of the human species, should interact.

I knew then that the difference between my pigs' behavior and the deer's came down to a matter of trust. She lacked trust that I would do her no harm. Yet I didn't understand what had initiated her distrust to begin with.

At the party all us animals were separate souls sharing a universe, communicating in spite of each one's idiosyncratic speech patterns and different body language. The family relationship was further cemented by the food—the most critical kernel of bonding between different but similar beings. It didn't matter that humans and four-legged creatures were eating, per se; what mattered was that all species were interacting in a shared meal. It was a communion of sorts with pigs, cats, horses, probably ants and flies, and people partaking of wine, iced tea and edibles—all a symbolic gesture of camaraderie and acceptance. Mingling in moments of conversation, music, and food, we became like family—each human and animal accepting and acknowledging the presence and importance of the other.

This was the way things were meant to be—not with humans dominating and exploiting creatures of the home, farm, woodlands. rainforest, and oceans. The deer shouldn't have distrusted me any more than she should fear another deer, for I carried no history with me. I had never harmed it or threatened it before, and it was unlikely another person had either, since there were "NO HUNTING" signs posted along our property and the seminary's. Why wouldn't the deer have reacted to me as the seals, iguanas, and sea lions in the Galapagos Islands had—with no reaction, with nonchalance? The Galapagos animals had scant experience upon which to judge humans, so they had no reason to fear us. We were one with them, and they accepted us in that spirit.

Both the deer and Lowell, in their different ways, revealed that animals were somehow meant to join humans, hoof to fin to hand, in a celebration of mutual respect, appreciation, and life. When it came right down to it, all the world's creatures, from humans to the creatures they have domesticated, to the sloths in the rainforest, were in it together, struggling and thriving at this time, in this life, on this planet.

Tomorrow we would be back at work tending our animal patients in Pennsylvania. Then I would begin testing out my new idea during our vet calls. Why? The revelation spawned by a fearful doe and a gregarious pig—the desire that all creatures should regard each other as family and live on Earth without fearing or exploiting each other— begged for validation on a real-life level. The dream, the wish for a global family, couldn't just exist platonically in my mind. The philosopher in me demanded that I put to the test not only the idea but also its existence in the real world.

At that moment I resolved that over the next few months, perhaps years, I would search for solid evidence of hope that some day humans could, indeed, live in peace and with mutual respect alongside creatures so different yet so similar.

Monkeys, Muntjac, and the Milton Machine

THE NEXT DAY, EDGAR went out to the Trexler Lehigh County Game Preserve, where he and the animal crew faced the task of snagging each green guenon monkey in a net and injecting Koch's tuberculin antigen into the eyelid—the test for TB. That yearly routine leaves almost everyone involved draped in monkey excrement.

I donned a ratty pair of jeans, a sweatshirt, and mucker boots, then headed out to the barn where I grabbed the wheelbarrow and pitchfork to clean stalls. By the looks of the leafy canopy above, before long I'd be wielding a rake instead of a pitchfork. The ash trees would be the first to release their small, oblong, yellow leaves. The few maples in our woods would cling to their reddish-orange and pink-hued plumage for quite a while. But the rusty oak trees that made up most of our forest would relinquish their leaves over the entire course of Pennsylvania's fall, dribbling a few every day well into early November.

When Edgar came home, I asked him how the expedition went.

"Well, everything was going smoothly," he recalled. "The monkeys were flying from one perch to another, and the shit was flying admirably. No big deal. But the animal crew looked like they were

15

planning a military coup. With their green coveralls decorated with all that manure and pee, it made them look like guerrillas wearing camouflage. They could've hidden in the local swamp for years. For a change I survived the whole ordeal unscathed—not a speck on me. I was very proud of myself."

"Did you try to reason with the monkeys? Explain that you were testing them for their own good? After all, you never asked them if they wanted the procedure."

"Yeah, right," he said, rolling his eyes. "Next time I'll take a poll before we do the testing. If they refuse, we'll just cave."

"Well, maybe you could do it in such a way that they wouldn't even know it's being done."

"Yeah. Like they wouldn't know I was injecting them in their eyelids. Sure."

I scrunched my face, thinking. How could a vet test, vaccinate, and do all the things that needed doing to wild animals in preserves without causing distrust and fear among the caged residents. Caged . . . God!

"You're getting pretty good at dodging shit, aren't you, Hon?" I laughed. "Mighty good thing you had all that college education. Boy, that's one job I refuse to help you with. Retained placentas are one thing, but monkey doodley-doo is entirely another."

"Yeah, well, I *thought* I had escaped flying monkey missiles. Actually, it wasn't all that clean-cut. Pardon the pun."

"What do you mean?" I said, noticing the pained expression on his face.

"After we finished, the monkeys were still clinging to their wooden ledges at the ceiling. They were suspicious. And that stuffy primate room reeked like a sewage plant."

"A different kind of aromatherapy, wouldn't you say?"

He nodded. "Plus, the animal crew smelled of eau de ammonia. Their caps reeked of monkey piss, and shit smudges decorated their shoulders. Steve got some on the back of his neck and somehow smeared it right under his nose. I laughed like hell. Dan was all dotted up, too. But me, I was as clean as when I had first walked into the pen. So I said to the guys, 'That's it, done for another year,' and with that I turned around, grabbed the doorknob, and . . .'"

Edgar winced, remembering the scene, and I wondered what could have gone so terribly wrong. "And . . . ?" I prodded.

He looked down into his open hand as if visualizing it there for the second time, and then he said, "It was covered."

"Covered?" I gulped.

"Sure was," he said.

"The doorknob?"

"Covered."

"Don't tell me." But I couldn't stand it. "With shit?" I asked, unbelieving.

"You got it."

I stifled myself. "Nope—*you* got it."

He held his hand even wider, and a horrific pumpkin-grimace stretched across his face. "I had a whole fistful of monkey turds."

Laughter shot from me in short bursts. "Seems those monkeys always have the last laughs," I said. "Every year they *reek* vengeance on you guys for that TB testing ordeal you put them through. I think they're trying to tell you something."

"Yeah," Edgar admitted, chuckling to himself. "You should've seen Steve. He had this shit smudge on his upper lip—made him look sort of like Hitler. He was grinning like the crazy bastard, too. He had no idea why I was saluting him, 'cause he didn't know he had a wedge of monkey shit hanging on his lip. Too weird, but funny, too. What do you call it?"

"Black humor?" I said.

"Yep. Boy, when he finally discovered his schmeared-up lip, he was pissed, especially since I had gone unscathed. Of course, then I grabbed the doorknob to leave. I yelled when I felt it, and boy, did he laugh when I opened my hand."

"So, he *really* wore a shit-eating grin, you might say," I laughed.

"Yeah, right," Edgar moaned. "Meanwhile I'm standing there with a fist ful of monkey feces."

Several days later, I accompanied Edgar to the game preserve to check the monkeys' eyelids for any reaction and help with a few other tasks. Our truck wound beneath the lacey canopy of dense oak and maples dripping with broad-leafed grape vines and fiery poison ivy. I always loved the approach to the preserve with its winding narrow road gently lifting us up and down along the hills. We found ourselves draped in shadow beneath the trees but could catch glimpses of deer and buffalo camouflaged amidst the underbrush on the sun-coated range. In autumn the ride was particularly spectacular, curving and rolling along the road in synchrony with the sensual hills and valleys of nature.

To check the monkeys' eyelids for any reaction, we didn't have to get in the pen with them. All we had to do was look them in the eye and see if their lids were swollen. As we walked into the primate center, I warned Edgar to look before he grabbed any door handles.

We stared through the glass doors at the monkeys. Suspicious of being chased again, they jumped onto their ceiling perches. We scrutinized their faces, and they all stared back, blinking and hanging onto each other. Each one struggled to crawl into the next one's lap; no one wanted to be alone and vulnerable. They were scared to death of us. The monkeys were lucky. No lids were puffed, which meant they were all negative for TB.

In the next moment, they must have remembered Edgar as one of the human gang that had chased them three days before, for, when they saw him, they all raced toward the outside pen. The foot-square exit door was hardly large enough for three monkey butts to squeeze through at one time. A trio of ape ends, wiggling and struggling, strained to push through the tiny door. Finally, they burst through to the outside. One peeked back at us through the door but dashed away. After several minutes of coaxing, they came back inside where we could look at them a final time.

For an animal so closely related to the human species, these guys weren't accepting us as friends—let alone family—one bit.

Our next job was to check the baby camel, a baby llama that had only been born a day ago, and one of the muntjac with a swelling on the side of her face.

First, we drove past the camel pen, where the baby was nuzzling its mother. It looked perfectly content and healthy. We watched for a few moments and noted that it was already beginning to fill out its hump. It regarded us without interest, but the mother swiveled her head around in a more suspicious manner. Both looked fine, so we continued quietly on our rounds.

The next stop was at the llama pen. The newborn llama appeared fine, but its legs were still a little crooked and weak from being cramped inside the mother for many months. Edgar assured me they would straighten out in a few days.

Then we drove to the muntjac pen. Muntjac are small deer of southeastern Asia and the East Indies, also known as barking deer for the noise they make when disturbed. We parked the truck by the side of the chain-link fence and observed the herd of muntjac grazing calmly. I didn't see the one with the swollen jaw until Edgar pointed her out. "There she is," he said. I squinted in that direction and saw the protrusion—like an old hillbilly with a chaw of tobacco.

"Gads, what is wrong with it?" I asked.

"Don't know yet. She just developed that lump on her cheek this week. Looks like she's chewing a huge wad of gum, huh? It came up awfully fast, so I think an abscess is a possibility. She probably ran into something—a splinter or something—and her cheek got infected. Anyway, the other day I told Brent we'd hold off doing anything to see if it would recede on its own. It is obviously much larger today. I better take a closer look at it. Let's go back to the service center and get some help to catch her."

"How are you ever going to catch a deer in a pen that large? Surely she's too fast for you guys."

"Oh, it'll be easy to get her with a net. You'll see. You can help, too, by herding them back in our direction when they veer away from us."

"Okay," I said doubtfully. "I'll do what I can."

Within minutes we had summoned help in snagging the deer with the swollen cheek. The captors consisted of Edgar and me, along with Brent, the head caretaker, and Diana, one of the animal crew. Except for me, everyone was armed with huge nylon nets. It looked like a Jurassic movie set. Expressions serious and determined, the three looked ready to capture some prehistoric, people-eating moths. I had my doubts as to whether this was going to work. The lightning-swift deer would give us quite a chase in the large pen, and they would probably run together, as they would in the wild, to better elude capture. That would make it difficult to distinguish the one with the swollen jaw from the other healthy ones.

We entered the pen. Edgar, Brent, and Diana hunched down, holding their nets close to the ground. With that the herd of deer came to
immediate attention, twisting their tiny heads around, their ears alert.
I bit my lip and walked into the pen, too. For a few seconds the muntjac made no attempt to run; they were still assessing the situation. Had
these people come for another feeding, I imagined them wondering, or
were they going to fix the fence? What, exactly, was their purpose for
being here?

But as the four of us spread out on diagonals, thus preventing their
escape, they snorted an alarm and darted, as one, into a corner. I leaped
toward the deer that appeared to be the leader of the pack, and Edgar
and Brent ran off after him. Suddenly the whole pack turned on its col-
lective heels and headed to the opposite corner. Diana sprinted after
them with Edgar and Brent close behind. I moved toward the corner
to head off their next escape attempt, but just as the captors came to
within four feet of the petrified muntjac, the herd spun in place and
turned abruptly—right toward me.

These were not animals to fear. They barely came up to my knees,
and even though there were about fifteen of them, they posed no danger. They were deer—virtually harmless. Of course, I had once been
nearly trampled by farm animals in the petting yard for a piece of leftover McDonald's bun. I was determined to prove that I could get along
with any creature as if I were one of its kind. Unfortunately, there was
no way a wild muntjac was simply going to walk calmly up to us and
present his abscessed face to be sliced open.

With arms at right angles to my sides, I leapfrogged at them. They
did an about-face not three feet from me and flew right towards their
captors. Nets were flailing in every direction. Edgar's net swooped onto
the ground, capturing a nasty-looking weed. Then the entire herd
twisted out of the corner and ran across the field to the opposite side
where I waited. With arms windmilling, I persuaded them right back
into the nets of the three captors.

Again the nets assailed the air, and finally one muntjac became
ensnared.

"Got her!" Diana yelled. The tiny muntjac struggled and plunged
against the net. She shrieked like a small child—an eerie, humanlike
distress call. I cringed. The rest of the herd barked a warning, clearly

upset one of their own had been captured. Edgar and Brent ran to the caught deer just as she hit the ground in one more plunge against the entangling web. Then it happened.

A cartoonlike whoosh of pink fluid the color of a strawberry milkshake squirted into the air. As it rained down to earth, the captors let out a unanimous cry of disgust. The deer's fall to the ground had burst open the contents of the abscess—a veritable fountain of pus. I had seen too many abscesses on our own cats, in horses' hooves, and elsewhere, not to have recognized one here. Sometimes the pus is under so much pressure at the site that just sticking a scalpel into it will blow the gross goo skyward.

"Ar-r-r-rgh!" Brent yelled, backing madly away. Edgar pinned the muntjac to the ground, and then it stopped struggling. "What the hell was that?" Brent said, looking up. Then he examined himself. "It's all over me!" he yelled, his expression horrific. "Christ, it smells awful."

Edgar laughed as he pinned the deer to the ground. "Looks like she

Game preserve keeper Tony LaPorte with muntjac
(How many can you spot?)

broke open the abscess herself. Guess I don't have to do it now. But we'll clean it up with some Betadine scrub and put her on antibiotics right away."

I ran through the gate to the truck and in moments was back with the surgical scrub. An aura of rotting putrefaction surrounded the workers, and as Edgar cleared the debris from the muntjac's face, I could see the pencil eraser-sized hole through which the abscess had burst. Not surprisingly, the cheek was no longer swollen.

Brent turned his face away in disgust, but he managed to hold the animal to the ground, as Edgar wiped the area clean and injected some antibiotic cream into it. He said, "Now we know it's only an abscess. Brent, I need you to express the pus out of the hole every day and fill it with Hetacin K until it stops swelling."

Brent's face was the color of algae. "Oh, no," he said very seriously. "Really, Doc," he said in almost a whisper, "I don't think I can do that. Please, ask me to do anything else around here and I will, but don't ask me to mess around with pus. Not pus. If I have to even look at that stuff, I'll blow my lunch all over the muntjac. It won't be pretty."

Edgar looked at him and laughed, "Okay, then, I'll come back and do it. You know, she may have a foreign body caught in her cheek— maybe a piece of wood or something that has to work its way to the outside. So, if this doesn't clear up in a few days, we'll have to go in and take another look; otherwise, she'll just keep on abscessing." They released the female muntjac, who trotted back to the herd cowering in the opposite corner of the pen.

Diana looked fine, but Brent was not anxious to head for the snack bar. "Okay, Doc. I'll keep an eye on it—from a distance. But I don't mind telling you that was about the grossest thing I've come across here."

"Yeah," Edgar admitted. "Abscesses are never pretty. And you might want to wash off those nets, too, since that gunk's all over them." Then we left the pen.

Diana and Brent climbed back into their truck, waved, and backed down toward the service center. The muntjac herd glowered at us as we headed out, maneuvering past some people in jogging outfits on a trek up to the preserve's summit to benefit Alzheimer's research. We climbed steeper and steeper until we came to the top where the buffalo herd lived. Seeing the holding pens immediately reminded me of last year when we vaccinated the buffalo. With a shudder, I realized that this year we'd have to do it all over again.

Every year the game preserve improves its method of testing the buffalo for brucellosis and tuberculosis. It still has a long way to go so that the animals will not be scared beyond belief. I will rejoice when, in the year 3003, the buffalo line up calmly at the border fence and smile in appreciation when the vet pulls blood from beneath their tails.

Years ago members of the animal crew went out amongst the herd and single-handedly chased the animals into the holding pens. The workers yelled and swung sticks and brooms in the air to scare the buffalo into submission. But on more than one occasion the attempt nearly resulted in disaster—someone pinned against the side of the pen or forced to scale a wall to escape a charging bull. Buffalo disliked bossy people with sticks. If the workers didn't develop a better routine, someone was going to get seriously hurt. So, under Edgar's and Dan's advice, they tried a new method of capture that seemed to work fairly well. Surviving the experience was no longer a worry; tending twisted ankles and sprained wrists was, though. But even the most fearful of the workers could tolerate those working conditions.

Examining a buffalo at the Trexler Game Preserve

As was customary, the ten buffalo to be tested were lured into the first holding pen with an unexpected banquet of rich and tantalizing alfalfa. The bulky beasts walked calmly into the large pen, grabbing delicious mouthfuls of hay. For a while they truly enjoyed the feast. But too quickly the tranquility ended as three workers climbed atop the heavy equipment and started up the diesel engines. First, the feed truck roared to life. Then the stake body truck revved its motor. Finally, the front-end loader sputtered and began its Brobdingnagian purr.

The buffalo stopped chewing immediately. Several, led by Milton the bull, tried to find a way out of the holding pen. But where they had entered, they found themselves trapped by a closed gate, and the wooden pen that moments before had been a lovely dining hall was now an inescapable fortress. A worker guarded the closed gate as the buffalo snorted around it, worried about what was to follow.

The worker began to open the gate slowly inward toward the buffalo as the machine team, one behind the other, plugged up the opening left by the gate. Escape was not an option for the buffalo, at least not against such a team of diesel mentality as this. First at the gate opening, Milton, the bull buffalo, was met immediately by a large pressboard positioned on the front of the front-end loader. As the gate slowly opened, the front-end loader lurched forward with its eight-foot-long, five-foot-high squeeze board. Milton took one look at it, snorted, and turned on his heels. His girls followed him into the far corner. After the front-end loader, the stake body truck entered with another wooden partition attached to its front bumper. It lined up next to the front-end loader so that a squeeze wall of around sixteen feet faced the buffalo.

Positioned so, the buffalo cowered in a far corner of the first and largest holding pen. One buffalo, in particular, stood out from the rest—Milton the bull. He was much heavier and stockier than the rest of his herd, and he was also a good foot higher than the others. Everything about him was massive, imposing. Clearly he wore the pants in the family, all the rest of which were girls. He had first pickin's at the alfalfa hay when feeding time came. He was always the first to check out the feed vehicles when they drove onto the range in the morning. When the workers began to hay everyone, Milton believed it was only with his permission. He protected his girls from the feed truck as if his very life were at stake, and any intruder would find himself faced with a set of curled buffalo horns the size of giant Frisbees. Milton strolled the buffalo range with machismo flowing through his veins.

In this situation, however, Milton wasn't his usual macho self. At first he confidently led his girls into the trap where the alfalfa buffet had been displayed, but his hubris fizzled quickly when the diesel engines fired up behind them. Once set upon by the trucks and pressboards, Milton, the formerly proud, pumped-up husband to all nine of his women, abandoned his role of protector and instantly turned avian. As the girls gathered around their fearsome leader for some sign of assurance, he bellowed for them to get out of his way, for his eminent life was at stake, he believed. As the vehicles approached, he rooted one of his women with a horn, dropping her to her knees and dashed through the other whimpering females in a mad escape attempt.

But he was too late. By then the last vehicle had entered through the gate, which closed immediately behind it. In seconds, like a scene from an Indiana Jones movie, the walls began closing in, slowly and with determination—24 feet of plywood pressing in on the small buffalo herd. Three of the girls managed to escape off to a side and squeezed themselves past the vehicles, but they couldn't escape to the range because the gate was closed. They stood panting, terror-stricken, looking out at the fields and woods where they envisioned safety from the pressing machines. In a second, Milton discovered a few of his girls missing and turned tail after them. He too slid past one of the squeeze boards. Clearly he expected his wives to protect him. Instead, he could only join the three helpless women looking fearfully over the gate.

The gamekeepers weren't concerned that they had lost four of their prospects, for they had actually wanted to divide the herd at this point. It was much easier to take just a few than the entire herd at one time. Five females ran in circles in the holding pen, which by the action of the squeeze-machines was becoming smaller and smaller by the minute. Soon the trucks had formed a new narrow pen, about 24 feet long by six feet wide. Trapped there, the females could no longer run; they also couldn't gather enough speed to butt into anyone or anything.

The gate worker ran to open the next gate, allowing the five girls to escape into the next, much smaller pen, which in turn eventually opened up into a third, much narrower and more confining pen. From there one of the squeeze machines would come up behind a buffalo and push her to an area behind which Edgar and his blood tubes lurked. There, with the buffalo squished into complete submission, Edgar could lift the tail of the animal and take blood from the tail vein. When he was finished, a chute would open, and the buffalo could run out onto the range—free at last.

Since the second holding pen was in the shape of a V, the five girls naturally gravitated to the narrower opening. The front-end loader with the pressboard was behind them to persuade them to move in that direction. The girls trotted to the end where they found the gate miraculously open. Two buffalo went through and were met on the left by another squeeze vehicle. So they turned right down the narrow alleyway. But they obviously hadn't figured out that the squeezer would follow them, pushing and prodding at their backsides until they reached the end of the wooden alley.

Edgar went to work as the first buffalo rump came into sight. He had stationed himself at the end of the alley behind a slatted, wooden wall, which he maneuvered until he could get both arms between the rungs of wood. Then I could hand him the needle and tube as he lifted the tail and focused in on the tail vein. He was quick as usual. There was little danger of his getting hurt in such a position, but he still wanted to shorten the experience to reduce the stress on the buffalo. In seconds he handed me a syringe filled with blood. He shouted out the number of the buffalo's ear tag, and I emptied the syringe into a tube and scribbled the number on the outside. Then he pulled a flap of tail skin to the side and injected the tuberculin.

"Okay!" Edgar yelled. "Let 'er rip!"

With that the gate sprung up and open, and the buffalo ran out. Just as the one behind her realized that escape was possible, the door dropped down like a guillotine. In seconds the second buffalo rump appeared. I handed Edgar the syringe, and in seconds I had it back, filled with blood. Again I squirted the blood out of the syringe and into a tube, numbered it, and put it in my pocket. The other three girls were tested similarly, without incident. We only had to go back and get the bull, Milton, and the rest of his harem.

We watched as the feed truck with its pressboard turned around in the first large holding pen and headed toward the group that leaned over the gate with yearning. Milton and three girls skirted the side of it and ran into the next pen, which a worker had wisely opened in anticipation of their escape. Then he snapped it shut.

But in the larger pen one of the girls named Buffy decided she had clearly had enough of being bullied. As the feed truck closed in behind her, Buffy danced back and forth in front of the gate. The truck squeaked and grunted as it lurched towards her, and in one frantic attempt, Buffy lunged at the gate beyond which she believed freedom lay— out on the range. She used her head as a gigantic battering ram and hit the chain-link gate with the force of a tractor. The chain-link broke from its two-inch pipe supports, and Buffy's horns lodged between the fencing and the center support. In one move the female buffalo had transformed herself into a pressing machine to rival the others.

She jerked her head forward, and the gate became securely locked onto her horns. She plunged forward, and with a great CRACK! the gate ripped from its hinges. Off she went onto the buffalo range. But she didn't run far. Once free among the five girls that had just been tested, she stopped and shook her head, and the gate dropped off her like a wind-blown cap. She rooted the metal partition one last time and stomped right over it.

Milton and the other girls had already been ushered into the bottom-most pen—the one that led to Edgar. A female was first in line to be tested, with the bull right behind. Milton, as I would have predicted for a male of a species, was scared silly. In the turmoil he forgot all his manners. He just wanted to be out of harm's way. Probably, to his mind, the female in front of him was blocking his passage to safety. So, he did what buffalo tend to do. He rooted her in the ass.

"Oh, God!" Edgar yelled as the female horned an alarm. "He got her in the behind! Back him out of there. Hurry!"

A worker scaled the wooden scaffolding around the pen. He stuck a broom down between Milton's face and the female buffalo's hind end. The pressing truck had backed off, allowing Milton to back down the narrow pen and trot back into the previous holding pen.

Meanwhile Edgar ran to the truck for wound dressings. Carting bales of cotton sheeting under his arm, he cursed a blue streak. "Damn, why did the dumb son-of-a-bitch have to root her like that. Look at her bleeding. Got her right in the groin. What a damn mess we've got." The female buffalo was still backed up to Edgar's partition, and, indeed, there was a lemon-sized hole in her hind end. Blood trickled from it.

I was aghast at the sight. He had rooted one of his own kind, his mate, his dearly beloved—right in the butt—to save his own ass. So much for a buffalo's sense of family.

"I'm going to give her antibiotics and a tetanus booster right away." Edgar shouted to Dan. "Then I have to clean it up as best I can. I'll inject some Hetacin K in the hole and pack it with gauze to stop some of the bleeding. Actually, it's not bleeding nearly as bad as I'd expect." He went to work, injecting the antibiotic and scrubbing the wound with Betadine. I was surprised the buffalo didn't object to all the fuss, but she stood, squeezed to the wall, with little complaint. Could I hope that she knew instinctively we were trying to help her?

In a few minutes Edgar was finished. He shoved all the bandaging material into my pockets and arms while he did the brucellosis and TB testing. Then he gave me that syringe as well. Finally, the female was released to the outside, and she ran out almost as if nothing ailed her.

Edgar finished testing the other two girls, but Milton was the elusive buffalo. He was the most trouble, mainly because he was so large and so scared. If he had gotten up the courage to challenge one of the trucks, the machine would have offered him no contest. He was a huge animal, as solid as a cement mixer and almost as big. He could have pushed a truck hundreds of feet—if only he'd had the guts. But he was tons more brawn than bravery. Instead of meeting the vehicle head on, Milton raced in fear around the pen, frantically looking for a way out as the workers tried to maneuver him into the last pen and towards Edgar's station. Meanwhile, I ran all the equipment back to the truck. I put the bandage material back in its case as well as the Betadine scrub. Then I ran back to my position behind Edgar.

Milton's final mistake was to run from the truck, which put him right where all the humans wanted him—in front of Edgar's partition. At last Milton's butt was facing us—his thick male tail a full foot higher than his girls' tails. It was a massive, rock-hard backside—no cellulite on this guy. He was one mighty monster of a buffalo. Edgar lifted his tail, and I could hear Milton snorting. He was indignant and madder than hell, but he was helpless, too. With the truck squeezing him into the corner, he was against the wall tighter than a pig's ass in fly time. He had no room to struggle but could only make a verbal protest.

I handed Edgar the needle and injection tube. In moments I had them back. I felt the hotness in them—part of that heat caused by Milton's anger, I thought with amusement. Then, the worker snapped open the gate, and Milton plunged out.

The only buffalo not done was Buffy, who had torn the gate from its hinges in her mad escape. She would be wise to a second attempt to catch her, so Edgar advised catching her at another time—when she wasn't already suspicious.

Once the herd was together on the range, they grazed calmly as the trucks backed out of the pens. Everyone left. The female with the gored groin moved about as if nothing had happened, but I knew she would be sore tomorrow. Edgar told the animal crew that when he came back in a few days to catch Buffy again, he would pull the packing out of the wound. He said it should be able to drain and heal up nicely on its own.

That afternoon Edgar and I rode back to the clinic and processed the paperwork for the blood work. We carefully packed the blood tubes into their separate cardboard compartments inside specially prepared boxes. Once they were nicely insulated and protected for shipment, I ran them to the post office.

Several days later we received a call from the lab that tested the buffalo blood.

"What's the problem?" I overheard Edgar say into the phone. "A tube broke during shipment? Could you make out the number on the side of the tube?"

There was a moment of silence.

Then a shriek.

"Number seventy? That's Milton. Don't tell me the bull's blood tube broke! I know. I know it's not your fault," he said in a contrite voice. "Yeah, I know there's no hurry. I'll have it to you by next week." He hung up the phone, and Edgar slouched over the table.

"Can you believe Milton's blood tube broke during shipment? Now we have to catch that big sis again!"

I couldn't help being amused at Edgar's frustration. The probability of a blood tube being broken was slim: it had never happened before. But how ironic it was that the only one to be damaged was the bull's, the biggest and the most gritless of them all. The next time we attempted to catch him, he would be even more recalcitrant.

Several days later we did Milton's retest—without mishaps. Milton was quickly segregated from his girls, and the job was completed in minutes.

It would remain to be seen how this year's testing would go. Each year seemed to find the buffalo just a little more accustomed to handling and the workers more skillful in rounding up the great beasts. Our job was still the same. In a few months we would gather up the blood tubes and syringes and head out again onto the buffalo range. And this time we would make sure Milton's blood tube was sent out in a suit of armor.

Henny Penny Deconstructed

THE GAME PRESERVE DISASTERS hadn't offered much to confirm my vision of harmony between humankind and the rest of the animal kingdom. Nor would our next misadventure—a case of "Henny Penny" transmogrified into a modernization of *The Birds*.

We'd first seen Guy Barry's large white rooster when Edgar was called to his farm to vaccinate sixteen lambs for tetanus and overeating disease.

"You might as vell cass-trate dese lambs, to-a, vhile ya're at it. Andt band dere tails right away, to-a, vy doan't cha?" Guy said, pointing to the pens at the far end of the old Dutch bank barn.

Through the twilight of the earth-cradled barn, I could barely make out approximately four small pens, each containing two ewes, each with a pair of lambs. In the dusk of the barn I could discern a vapor-like figure, like a Lilliputian ghost, perched atop one of the pens.

"Sure," Edgar said. "No big deal. I'll just run to the truck for my emasculator and rubber bands."

"What is that white thing down there?" I asked Guy when Edgar left for the truck.

31

"Vy, dat's Henry, my rooster. He's always down there, guardin' the sheep. I doan't need a sheep dog—I godt Henry. He makes a racket if his sheep are disturbed—kinda guards the whole barn here-a, in fact."

Guy was a giant of a man, built like a soft mound of dough. In contrast to his ample, spongy appearance, he wore a tiny, trimmed beard attached to the tip of his chin like a patch of moss on a slippery rock. With each smile his face expanded from cantaloupe size to that of a honeydew, the moss-beard clinging to the chin for dear life.

Raising sheep was a hobby for Guy. His calm, nonplussed personality was good therapy for his company of sheep, whose personalities tended regularly toward hysteria. He was one of those laid-back Dutchy farmers, his general reaction to things nothing short of blasé. Not much could rile him.

To fill the silence I said, "I hope Edgar brought along enough rubber bands to de-tail the lambs."

"No proplem," Guy said. "If we can't get 'em done today, ve'll chust do 'em another time arawnd naw."

Edgar returned, tools in hand. "Okay, Guy. Ya ready?" We began walking toward the dimly lit end of the barn. The sheep, sensing trouble, stirred restlessly in their pens.

Guy shooed Henry from his perch atop the gate, and the feathered dictator complained loudly, cawing, clucking, and strutting, his wings spread in a threatening stance. "Cut it awt, naw," Guy scolded the rooster. "You've got no proplem. Chust stay awt off the vay."

With that, Henry, his beak agape, leaped to the top of the neighboring goat pen where he shook himself off. When Guy stepped over the low-walled gate, the mothers with their four babies raced into a corner. Guy crouched down, opened wide his arms, and leaped toward the nearest lamb.

Guy Barry was a plumber by trade. I knew right away that Guy must specialize in leaky pipes and plugged potties simply by the level of his "crack exposure."

At first light, setting out to catch the lambs, Guy began a battle with his denim drawers, which gravitated with each step toward the ground. But his efforts to hitch up his pants were hardly "No proplem" as he regarded most everything in his life. In fact, the slippery jeans were foiling his ability to catch the lambs. Once the jeans let loose,

Guy found himself in a "no-win" situation. While he reached with one arm toward a scared sheep, his other arm was pulling on the waistband of his denims. Consequently he had succeeded at capturing neither. Obviously the crack had the upper hand. After fifteen minutes, we still had no lambs to vaccinate, castrate, or de-tail. Edgar waited patiently as Guy flailed about the pen, one hand gripping his pants, the other weakly grasping the air around the elusive sheep. "Need some help, Guy ?" Edgar finally offered.

I had respectfully avoided staring at Guy's butt fissure as he plummeted amongst the sheep. With each lunge at an animal, his pants crept lower and lower, threatening to slide off and expose him in the "altogether"—dodging naked amongst the animals like a Sumo without his loincloth.

So, instead of focusing on the gluteal cleft, I glanced toward the cobwebbed ceiling. But my curiosity was stronger than my self-discipline. Shortly my attention toward the barn loft faltered, and, despite my attempt at self-control, I peeked.

With complete abandon I turned toward the speeding cranny. In just the short time that I had diverted my attention from it, it had lengthened to twice its original size. A grin erupted on my face, and I stifled myself, for I imagined the three-inch crack to be smiling at me. I burped a giggle, then felt immediately embarrassed for Guy and irritated with myself. But I couldn't turn away. I was fascinated with it.

The chasm continued to grow and widen like a section of the San Andreas fault. Again I suppressed a giggle, concentrated dutifully on a rusty horseshoe hanging on the wall, and then caved in, turning back to the sneering slit. The crack had magne-

Guy Barry

tized me; I was obsessed with it. After one desperate lurch after a wily lamb, Guy stood straight up and with a look of frustration yanked his waistband skyward. Again I turned away so as not to add to his shame. Yet, much as I empathized with his situation, I still had the sadistic, perverted, but very human urge to enjoy both his gaping butt crack and his embarrassing predicament.

How strange was the obsession in whose grip I lay. Why was I so fascinated with it? Perhaps the cause of my obsession was the lure of the hidden finally exposed, of the disguised finally revealed, of the undercover cleft finally uncovered in all its glory. And perhaps the adage "misery loves company" fit all too well. In my lifetime, I, too, had endured the mockery of others who found my recalcitrant underwear and ill-fitting clothes hilarious.

Finally I decided that helping Guy capture the lambs would divert my attention away from the beguiling crack. It would be good therapy for me, so I jumped into another pen and ran toward the startled sheep in the corner. After an hour, we had succeeded in vaccinating, banding, and castrating all the lambs.

We took the tools back to the truck, and Edgar closed the tailgate. "Your sheep and lambs ought to be good for a while now, Guy. We just have to de-horn your goats some day."

"Yop. Any day vudt be fine naw. I'll be here, but effen if I'm not here-a, you can do it yourself, right? Those baby goats von't giff anyvon a rough time." He pointed out the three baby goats that occupied a pen next to the sheep pens. Henry was sitting calmly atop the goat gate while the baby goats lay sleeping in the straw.

"Sure, I'll just pop in, and we'll do them then," Edgar said.

"No proplem," Guy answered, and with that we said good-bye and drove away.

Three weeks later I overheard Edgar talking with Guy on the phone. "So, then, today is all right for de-horning the goats? You'll be there, then. Good. We'll see you later."

I could imagine Guy's answer: "No proplem, Doc."

Guy's was our last call that morning. After we arrived at the Barrys' farm, Edgar unlocked the back of his truck and handed me the dehorning equipment and antiseptic powder. "Here. There's no electricity in the barn, so I have to plug the dehorning iron into an outlet in the milking parlor. Once it heats up, I'll catch each goat and bring it into the parlor. First, I'll need to anesthetize them, or they'll scream like hell. Then we'll dehorn each goat in the parlor and afterward put it back in its pen. We should be done in a half hour or so."

"Okay," I said, heading toward the milking parlor. Strange—no one was around. The barn and house were silent, devoid of human movement. Perhaps Guy was on an emergency plumbing call. We were on our own, which wasn't all that unusual. Many times Edgar and I will treat a client's animal ourselves when the owner can't be home to help. As long as the animal is tractable, we don't mind.

I went into the sour-smelling milk parlor and found an outlet into which I plugged the de-horner. I placed it carefully on a concrete block so that it wouldn't accidentally start a fire and began to walk toward the barn where the baby goats would be in their pens.

Suddenly I heard a scream—a man's yell. Edgar's yell. I broke into a run. What in the world could have happened?

Dashing from bright sunlight into the barn, I squinted, trying to focus in the dark. As I drew closer, I could see Edgar inside the goats' pen, his arms flailing. He hopped and writhed as if dancing among a sea of scorpions. I raced down the barn aisle. "What's wrong?" I yelled.

Then I saw it. Henry, the ghost rooster turned banshee, was attacking Edgar for all the fowl was worth. Amid Edgar's swinging arms and legs darted Henry, his wings out straight, his body propelling itself forward robotlike in a series of lurches and lunges at Edgar's legs. At each attack Edgar shooed the rooster with a booted foot, but Henry always came back stronger for another round. Who did Henry think he was attacking—Little Bo Peep? Having wrestled hundred-pound pigs, steers, and thousand-pound horses, Edgar was no shrinking worm. He certainly was not about to be intimidated by a silly rooster who forgot his manners.

Finally, before Henry launched his fourth attack, Edgar scooped a baby goat into his arms. Again Henry charged. Again Edgar swiped a leg at the advancing rooster, knocking the bird off balance. Just as Henry advanced for another foray, Edgar leaped over the four-foot-high wooden gate with the goat.

"The little bugger was trying to attack me," Edgar said as he took the struggling goat to the milk parlor and I followed close behind. "Christ, he's better than a watch dog. Didn't like me at all in that pen with his goats. Boy, was he pecking and digging into my legs. Those spurs on his feet are really sharp. Damned nasty rooster, he is."

Edgar set the goat down on the parlor floor. I held it, one arm around its haunches, the other in front of its chest, while Edgar administered the anesthetic. In minutes it slumped in my arms. Edgar made quick business of the de-horning and de-tailing. When we were assured that all the bleeding had stopped, I poured antiseptic powder on the burned stumps. Then Edgar scooped the goat into his arms and headed back to the barn for the next one.

Again I heard Edgar's shriek echoing from the barn. Then came yelling and cussing. After several moments he emerged with the second goat in his arms. His hair was whipped into a storm around his head, and his eyes were wide. "I can't believe that rooster!" Edgar said, shaking his head. I held the goat while he injected the anesthetic into the muscle. "He went at me again! He's a real bully, he is. He just hates the idea of my invading his goat pen. Where the hell is Guy ? He could at least keep the damn chicken off my back."

"He was on your back?" I gasped.

"Yep. When I bent over to grab the other goat, he flew right onto my back and started digging his spurs into my side. I'll have some marks from that. The Son of a B is nasty as hell. Okay, let's get this second goat done."

In ten minutes Edgar was walking back to the barn, the goat asleep in his arms. "This time I'll help fend Henry off while you get the third one," I said. "Maybe I can divert his attention."

We walked down the aisle of the twilit barn. In the distance I could barely make out the phantom-rooster looming on the gate of the goat pen. As we approached, his head swiveled toward us. A chill trickled up my spine. We had rarely met barnyard beasts that proved as menacing as Henry, even though he weighed only a fraction of what a human did and had a brain that could probably fit into his own gizzard. What a formidable opponent he proved to be. Such unyielding courage in such a diminutive beast, I thought. He had grit. He had pluck. He had integrity, for no other being, regardless of size and brainpower, was going to dampen his resolution to protect his goats.

Indeed, he had a sense of family with those goats, though he certainly didn't consider us any kind of kindred spirit.

"Damn bird," Edgar muttered as we approached the formidable chicken once more. "He's all ready for me. Look at him. Can't wait to get me. Why? I never did anything to him." Leaning over the wall of the goat pen, Edgar placed the sleeping baby goat carefully in the straw.

Henry didn't budge from the gate. Edgar looked around the barn. "Do you see any pitchforks or shovels or anything I can use against the little bastard?"

"Yeah," I said running to a corner by the water hydrant. "How about a big grain shovel?"

"It'll do. I don't want you going into the pen, so don't even try to help me. Just give me the shovel, and I'll scoop him up in it when he comes at me."

I picked up the shovel but hesitated. I didn't really want Edgar to use it. It wasn't a nice thing for a person hoping to change the way animals and people regard each other. But after all, my own immediate family was more important to me than cosmic ideology.

I handed him the weapon.

Henry eyed us suspiciously. He sat up straight, his wings held stiffly to the side—a prelude to an attack. "I think he's ready for you, Edgar," I said. My fingers flew to my mouth. All this hassle from an overprotective chicken. It was ridiculous. Who did he think he was?

Edgar stepped into the goat pen from the opposite corner.

Henry swooped into the pen with a flurry. His flaming comb stood erect; his feathers bristled.

Edgar turned toward the chicken, the shovel poised.

Henry let out one sharp cluck and flew at Edgar.

I gasped as Edgar caught Henry in the bowl of the shovel. He rotated the shovel head and lobbed the rooster over the pen wall with as much grace as a professional cricket player. Edgar was quite gentle with the shovel. For that I was glad.

Henry unfurled himself out the corner and gathered his senses as Edgar stooped to pick up the last goat. The other two kids lay fast asleep in the straw, unaware a battle was being waged in their pen. Just as Edgar lifted up the last patient, Henry hurled himself again upon his leg.

This time Edgar was defenseless. He'd laid down his weapon in order to retrieve the goat. Before he could even leap over the wall of the pen, Henry had wrapped his demonic white wings around Edgar's left leg. Clucking and cawing, his mouth opening and closing like a possessed toy, Henry proceeded to dig his spurs pistonlike into Edgar's leg.

"A-aa-aah! Get off me, you bastard!" Edgar yelled. He didn't want to drop the goat, because then he'd only have to retrieve him again from the maniac's lair. Quickly I leaped into the pen and grabbed the shovel. I took one swipe at the crazed rooster and whipped him out of the pen and onto the concrete barn floor. He landed with a plop, feathers squirting in all directions. With that Edgar and I cleared the pen and dashed out of the barn into the milking parlor, goat in hand.

"Whew!" Edgar said, setting the goat on its feet. "That's one mean chicken. He could do some real damage with those spurs. Now let's get this de-horning over with, once and for all."

In minutes we had put the last antiseptic powder on the seared horn buds. We took the last goat back into the barn and lay him next to the other two.

Henry sat atop the goat pen gate. He glared at us, and his wings stood away from his side. He clucked a warning. "Don't get any ideas," Edgar scolded. "Those goats are all yours, Henry. We're leaving."

We gathered the dehorning equipment from the milking parlor, made out a slip for Guy telling him what we did to the goats and what care should be given in the next few days. Then we walked back into the barn, past Henry glaring from his stoop, and down the barn aisle. The goats were beginning to stir, and no blood was leaking from the stumps. We broke out into the blazing sunlight just in time to see Guy stepping out of the family's Chevy truck. He stooped to retrieve a paper bag from the back seat, and when he turned toward us, I saw that his shirt was all bloodied. And that wasn't all. A trail of white gauze hung out of each nostril.

"What happened to you?" Edgar said.

Guy stood, looking rather dejected with fluff, the color of Henry, protruding from each nostril. He looked pathetic.

"I hadt a little problem dis mornin', Doc. I was awt in the fields plowin' vhen my nose started to bleedt." He looked as sheepish and embarrassed as the time he almost lost his pants.

"Yeah?" Edgar coaxed.

Guy looked uncomfortable, almost as though he didn't want me to hear the story. So, I turned around and pretended to study the tire rims of our truck. He said, "At first I sniffed it back real gudt, but that didn't work. I didn't haf any hanky nor nothing, and it vas starting to come pretty badt. The only ting I had on me vas my oldt shirt, so I pulled out a corner and used it to sop it up. Then it really started to bleedt, so I used the other corner.

"Pretty soon I hadt them both soaked. I didn't know vhat to do-a. Finally, I chust tore off the pocket and stuffed it up my nose."

I choked back the laughter and continued to regard our truck tires. I could only imagine what Guy must've looked like with a green-plaid shirt pocket hanging from his nostril.

Guy was obviously embarrassed by his nose-bleed story and the white cotton dangling from his nose. When he spoke, the edges of it moved up and down inside the nostrils, making for a very disconcerting conversation. Luckily I didn't have to watch the cotton vibrate in his nose. How did Edgar keep from laughing? Once more the cotton protrusions came alive as Guy said, "Vhy, I came in and called my chiropractor. I quick drove myself there, but he couldn't get it to stop bleedting either. So, he sent me to a ear, eyes, nose, and throat doctor."

"What did he do?" Edgar said.

"Vhy, he took a gizmo as thick as my little finger," he said, demonstrating with his pinky in the air, "and stuck strip after strip off cotton up my nose." Guy looked sideways at me to see if I was listening, and I quickly diverted my attention back to the truck wheels. He continued, "It hurt so badt, I broke awt in a sweat." He hesitated then whispered, "I thought I vas gonna cry."

"Yes, getting your nose packed with gauze can be quite painful," Edgar commiserated.

I continued to stare at the truck tires and mustered the self-control to maintain a serious face. How perverted was I to find humor in the most pathetic situations? Probably no more perverted than the average person, I decided. A bloody nose wasn't inherently funny, but in this case I found it hysterical, imagining a man Guy's size jamming his colorful shirttails and then his flannel shirt pocket into his nose. The vibrating cotton-gauzed nostrils certainly didn't help, nor did the picture of a farmer sobbing from getting his nose packed.

"I take it your nose stopped bleeding then," Edgar said.

"Yop. It's done. No proplem," Guy said. "Sorry I couldn't help vit da goats, but I've been drivin' all over trying to get my nose fixed. I gotta get awt of dis shirt," he said, pointing to the bloody tails. Wait'll Clara sees me." He looked toward the house. "She was at the grocery store vhen dis all happened. Looks like she's not home still. Gudt thing. If she'd see me, she'd think I was knifed by a awtlaw or something."

"Yeah," Edgar laughed. "Or she may think you were attacked by a homicidal rooster. You better go into the house and lie down."

"No proplem," Guy said.

"Here's a slip detailing what I did to the goats and the charges. Everyone's fine and dandy. Apply antiseptic powder for a few days and observe the goats for any kind of infection. Those stumps should heal in a few days. Now go inside and take care of that bloody shirt. Give me a call if you have any other problems, Guy."

"Thanks, Doc. Sorry I couldn't help awt."

I turned away from the truck tires and wished Guy well, pretending not to notice his nose. We both climbed into the truck and drove away.

The Allentown Fair

THE GREAT ALLENTOWN FAIR was historically a summer-end celebration and display of Pennsylvania Dutch crafts, garden harvests, and award-winning, prized, hand-raised livestock. Edgar had been tending to the health of the livestock there for the past ten years, and this year he again received the phone call asking him to be in daily attendance. The director of the animal and agricultural division, Sterling Ritter, requested Edgar to come early Tuesday morning for his first inspection of the sheep flocks.

We drove under the giant distelfink hex sign that read, WILKOM in Pennsylvania Dutch. The distelfink, unique to Pennsylvania Dutch country, is a colorful Dutch emblem, often depicting birds or animals, a symbol of prosperity and familial bliss. Many folks in our area adorn their doorways with distelfinks as a sign of good luck.

As we continued toward the livestock exhibition area, we took in the midway at a glance: pony rides, amusement park rides, freak shows, and games of chance (or rather, no chance). After venturing out for vinegar fries, deep-fried veggies, and funnel cakes, we found the animals—the fair's real entertainment, as far as we were concerned—tucked far off in a corner of the ten-acre fairgrounds.

Edgar's job that morning was to check incoming animals for signs of contagious diseases and to see that health papers from exhibitors were in order. He would also make daily herd checks of the dairy cows, cattle, sheep, goats, and pigs. As human doctors do in a hospital, Edgar made his rounds of the livestock pens. With my help he inspected each animal for diseases prevalent in that species. For example, in cattle he looked for signs of respiratory and mucosal disease, BVD or bovine viral diarrhea, IBR or infectious bovine rhinotracheitis, and pinkeye.

In the sheep and goat pens Edgar inspected for the contagious disease ORF, or sore mouth, the telltale sign of which was a cracking at the corners of the animal's mouth. Goats and sheep could also contract pinkeye, and they were susceptible to hoof rot, a sludging away of the skin and tissue between the digits. One of the nastiest diseases he was on the lookout for was caseous lymphadenitis, a condition in which nodules of pus raise up on the animal's skin, the sides of the face, the throatlatch, and behind the front legs. Should the pus burst from the skin, the disease can spread to any other sheep and goat species.

Swine have diseases all their own, too. One, erysipelas, raises welts that mimic a red diamond pattern along the pig's back. Hogs also contract the respiratory diseases pasturella and bordatella. Swine who are carriers of atrophic rhinitis are easily recognized by their deformed noses.

"I didn't realize there were so many species of goats in the world," I said, as Edgar bent down to inspect the toes of one award-winning animal.

"Yeah, sure are," he agreed as he stood up and looked in the goat's large, questioning eyes for traces of pinkeye. "Hey, girl, are you a woman of La Mancha?" he said with a smile.

I looked up at the large sign spanning the barn's ceiling above the goat pens. I was in for a history lesson. Lamancha, I learned, was the name of the short-eared Spanish breed of goat crossed with a purebred. They had funny-looking faces like ET's. Edgar's tan-and-black friend had no ears, only ear holes known as "gopher" or "elf" ears—a characteristic of the breed. Historically, Lamanchas were raised as dairy animals. Our healthy friend propped her front feet on the wire fence and sniffed us inquisitively. Her inspection of us was as thorough as ours of her.

Across from the Lamancha goats were the Alpines and Nubians. Nubian goats, of oriental origin, had roman noses and large, pendulous ears. They sported any color coat from tan to white to black. Their notability lay in the milk they produced—very rich and high in butterfat. The Nubian dairy queens who so daintily craned their necks over the fence at us competed with the Toggenburg breed, Swiss dairy goats from the Toggenburg Valley. Toggenburgs had erect ears and straight faces and ranged in color from solid light brown to dark chocolate brown. Each goat sought the fair's award for most-prized milk.

Other goats on display and for show were the Oberhasli, another Swiss dairy goat, and the Saanen dairy goat from Switzerland, two breeds I had never heard of before.

The sheep, scheduled to be judged the next morning, were in every stage of being prettied for the big event. Some had already been completely clipped and wore white jumpsuits so that they would remain free of stains until the morning; some were in the stanchions waiting to be coiffed and perfumed; still others hadn't even been brushed. They still lay in the clean straw and chewed their cud, occasionally dozing off while enjoying their view of the human parade.

In the sheep pens a young 4-H girl was busy with her flock of Shropshires, accessorizing their ovine ensembles and the droopy hoods that had twisted around their faces. Beneath those body suits was wool that had been painstakingly washed, picked through, and contoured with body clippers. I reached beneath one Rambouillet ewe's hood and felt her wool: dense, thick, lanolin-rich, with not a speck of dirt to be felt anywhere—truly groomed to show perfection.

Then there were the 200-pound, white-faced Dorset sheep from Southern England, first brought to the United States in 1885, the only sheep with wool on their legs. The tiny, all-white Cheviot sheep was the smallest breed. The Suffolk was white except for its contrasting black head and legs. Mixed together in one pen, they would make quite an odd Rorschach design.

Next Edgar walked over to the almost endless rows of cattle. I had never heard of many of the breeds. Of course, there were the familiar red-bodied, white-faced Hereford from the southwest of England as well as the Shorthorn, raised in northeast England in the 1580s. The chestnut or pure white shorthorns came to America in 1783. First identified in 878 AD, the Charolais hailed from southeastern France. These white cattle were used as draft animals and for their milk and meat. We in the United States didn't meet them until 1936. The fawn-colored Simmental, I learned, still comprised fifty percent of the cattle in Switzerland. The Angus originated from a prehistoric, solid black breed from Scotland and were introduced into the U.S. in 1873.

An intriguing breed was the Chianina of Central Italy with its short, white to steel-gray hair. Only in 1971 had the Chianina come to the U.S. Another unusual breed, the Limousin wore a red or black coat and was famous for weathering extremes of hot and cold temperatures in South Central France.

The breeds of cattle were many, especially those raised primarily for meat. I saw them as the quiet, unsung heroes of the bovines—those courageous enough to endure man's domination over the centuries. Their milking counterparts were almost as delightful a study—the Ayrshire, the Guernsey, the pretty-faced, smaller Jersey, the Milking Shorthorn, the Holstein, and the Brown Swiss. For their service to man and womankind, the cattle won a soft spot in my heart—right next to the pigs.

Edgar scrutinized the cattle for pinkeye and snotty noses. He listened for coughs and made sure all were chewing their cud, which sick or malcontent cows were reluctant to do. He checked their mouths for sore mouth and their toes for foot rot. I rubbed every other one on the forehead, and they didn't seem to mind. They, too, had been bathed and groomed spotless. Even the inside of their ears sparkled.

Finally, we came to the highlight of the livestock: the pigs. Boxes and boxes of muscular, tubular animals—Berkshire, Chester White, Landrace, Poland China, Spotted China, Yorkshire, and other breeds—filled a long barn. Lively swine of all ages and sizes were conversing heatedly. The pigs obviously considered this an occasion for socializing.

The pig section was more energetic and animated than the goat, sheep, and cattle yards. I felt qualified to evaluate the dramatic activity since I was the owner of four pigs myself. The Allentown Fair livestock exhibition was a swiners' social event. They reveled in the camaraderie, the conversation, and the one-swineliness that consumed them. Yet some didn't tolerate the strangeness of other pigs very well at all—another human trait.

I propped my elbows on the first row of pens and stared down into a ten-by-ten box filled with pigs who, I thought, weighed approximately 500 pounds each. I was amazed at how nicely they shared their space. They lay against each other, one a pillow or headrest for another. One made himself a bunk bed atop another two. The ones on the bottom didn't seem to mind his weight. Such closeness was not only tolerated but reciprocal. When the ones on the bottom grunted, the pig on top jerked and swayed to the quaking vibrations below. One reaction triggered another reaction on the pig pile.

A hopeful chill wriggled up my neck. Was I actually witnessing family closeness among these pigs? I stepped near for a better glimpse.

Most of the pigs were asleep, contented in the typical pig position, lying on a parallel plane with nose to butt and butt to nose. Seldom did my own pigs lie side-by-side with their heads together and their butts together. Any set of pigs lies like two shoes in a shoebox—heel to toe, so to speak. From time to time a pig stood up, yawned, and changed position, stepping groggily over the other five in the pen. Complaining in shrill voices, the steppees scolded the steppers as they marched over their hocks and trampled their tails. Typical sibling behavior.

It seemed as though the swine had certain rules already established for life in a crowded pen. The number-one rule was to step lightly and carry no big sticks. Life was easier lived with as little fuss as possible. Considering that, a pig brother or sister should take up as little space and move as infrequently as possible, keeping teeth to oneself, not defecating or peeing on another's back for fear of reprisal.

To be sure, most of the swine, confined six to ten in a pen, generally observed the rules, but in all social climes, there are detractors. Although pigs are social animals, living in ghetto conditions taxes even the kindliest of them. If a pig accidentally trod on another sleeping partner, the sleeper nipped his heels and squealed a warning to others to step lighter. Interaction among pigs is a give-and-take kind of thing.

I continued to watch the barn full of hogs and listen to their conversations and complaints. Pigs, like humans, cats, or primates, foster radicalism and anti-establishmentism. One pig rebel grabbed a rubber water bucket by the teeth, emptied it out on his neighbor, sending him into a pig-squealing fit. The drenched pig danced to his feet, then punished the other with a swipe at his retreating butt. He managed to extract a few hairs and a high-pitched complaint from the dish thrower, but discipline had been duly meted. The other would not toss a rubber dish any time soon.

I sighed, a vision of hog loveliness before my eyes—such a substantially-bodied and variegated crowd. The Yorkshire pigs were completely white with upright ears and long snouts. Originally from England, they matured to between 700 and 1000 pounds. Their cousin, the Landrace, was white as well, with a long nose and floppy ears. Another white pig, the Chester White, sported a shorter nose like that of the Landrace. The Poland China was black with floppy ears, and the Hampshire, which came from Hampshire County, England around 1830, was black with a wide white band running vertically through the center of its body. The Duroc, a redhead with floppy ears, was said to have the most cantankerous personality. The Berkshire was mostly black with upright ears and a white face.

Most of the pigs weighed between 200 and 400 pounds. The boars, on the other hand, spanned five to six feet and tipped the scales at between 700 and 1000 pounds.

Altogether 900 to 1,000 pigs filled the rows upon rows of fair swine. With so much socializing and entertaining, I was surprised that the barn was as quiet as it was. There were comparatively few complaints or fights, considering the tight quarters.

As I made my way through the hog barn, I marveled at the firm, muscular bodies of the pigs and their uncanny ability to govern themselves so wisely. Suddenly a pig squealed behind me. I turned and laughed as two Landrace pigs played tug of war with an empty grain bag like two brothers pulling on the same blanket. Finally, one lost his grip on the plastic, and the other, triumphant, began flipping it into the air.

"Hey," I said, squatting down beside the pig clown. The bag flew again into the air, and the pig leaped after it, his lips spread apart in a wide, mischievous grin.

"Where did you get that?" I laughed. "Did you steal that from this pen beside you? It's okay. I won't tell anyone," I confided in a low, stealthy voice. Then I saw the pile of empty oat bags alongside some feed and water dishes in the next pen.

Never content to sleep away an afternoon when more exciting activities beckoned, a clever pig can figure out how to pilfer a farm

"toy." Just like humans, pigs dread boredom, seeking entertainment in unlikely places. Clearly, the differences between pigs and humans are negligible compared to the similarities. Just like humans, if entertainment isn't provided by an outside source, pigs are capable of making it for themselves. For a pig, planning a heist is surely more the entertainment than the bounty itself: how to best position oneself on the floor and maneuver toward the object without the human barn tender realizing, how to worm one's snout through the narrowly spaced bars enough to grab the end of a broom handle, how to manipulate the handle so that its big end could snag a grain bag, and how to coax the bag, via the broom, close enough to the bars so the victorious swine can drag the toy into the pen without attracting human attention and without creating a jealous ruckus among his roommates. Obviously this happy Landrace pig had thieved his bag toy in such a way.

Again the playful swiner whipped the bag into the air as his roomie watched with quiet awe, his mouth wide with delight as it landed on his friend's back. In a flash the Landrace twirled around and caught the bag by an edge, shaking it like a dog does a dishtowel. I laughed, squatted beside the pen, and watched for several minutes until the Landrace, using his snout and feet, folded the grain bag into a curious lump. Then with a final grunt he lay down, his head upon the bag pillow. He sighed, then closed his eyes. Such entertainers are hogs, such inquisitive, humanlike creatures.

Again the chills crawled along my back as I reveled in the likeness between these animals and humans.

I called Edgar, who had been making his rounds of the hogs checking for snotty noses and diarrhea. He joined me beside a pen with five Berkshires. Immediately three of the white-faced pigs ran toward us, scrambling over each other to get our attention. They were like a bunch of curious kids at a zoo, only these guys were on the wrong side of the bars. I reached into the pen, and a black pig with a big white face and a wide-mouthed grin jammed his nose into my hand—a pig's "Hello." We crouched down as he inspected us with a friendly, open-mouthed huffing and snuffling, as our own pot-bellied pigs do. Edgar patted him on the forehead, and I huffed back, saying, "Oh-oh-oh-oh, yes-yes-yes, you're such a handsome pig, you are—oh,-oh-oh-you are, indeed." He talked back in his own pig language, grinning from ear to ear.

"You're such a beautiful pig. And you have such a big white face. It's a pleasure to meet you, Whitey," I cooed through the bars, honoring him with a name. He worked his rubbery nose against my hand with a gentleness not often afforded the swine species. In return I tweaked his nose and scratched him behind the ear, where the skin felt like human skin—thin, resilient, and incredibly soft. He closed his eyes and smiled, his head jammed into the corner, all the better to rub him. Between strokes we managed to converse with and pet the others, too. Edgar smiled, and while I stroked the secret, sensitive place behind Whitey's ear, Edgar ran his hand along his broad back, as clean and sleek as a polished floor. Typical of a pig, whose inborn cleanliness hails from swine ancestry, he had managed to keep himself immaculate despite living with four others in the crowded ten-foot square pen. Not one smear of manure stained him.

Suddenly one of the Chester White pigs who had been asleep in another pen began to squeal. It made me wince, and I stopped petting Whitey to hold my ears. What was wrong? I looked around, but there didn't seem to be any trouble. No other pig was harassing it; the others in the pen were asleep. Perhaps the pig had just had a nightmare.

Then something very strange happened. I watched as another pig, a red-bodied Duroc in the pen next to the screaming pig, got to its feet and walked over to the Chester White. He stuck his nose through the iron bars and huffed, his mouth open, his cheeks puffed. The whining white pig stepped toward the Duroc, and when the two touched noses, the Chester White became suddenly quiet. I was amazed. It was a situation I've only witnessed between humans and between animal mothers and their offspring. The Duroc had offered comfort to the white pig. Within seconds, by only the effort of the Duroc's presence, the Chester White had calmed to quiet. It was obviously familial.

I turned back to Edgar, who was still rubbing Whitey's big forehead. Whitey was leaning his entire weight into the bars of the pen so that Edgar would have an easier time stroking him. "He's a real character," Edgar said. Whitey squinted his eyes in ecstasy, and I agreed that he was, indeed, a special, very happy pig. Then, as if on cue, Whitey slid his whole body to the ground in a langorous abandon to Edgar's touch.

"Typical relaxed pig, huh Eggie? Whitey really likes you," I said. It was then that I noticed the pink dot on his back. "What's that?" I said, pointing.

"You don't want to know," he said as he stopped rubbing Whitey, who lay in a relaxed lump against the side of his pen.

I looked at Edgar anxiously, and then he pointed to the sign hanging above Whitey's pen, a sign that was meant to include all the pigs we had met and petted for the past hour. I stared blindly, in denial, at the sign that read, MARKET PIGS. "Market" I muttered under my breath, not wanting to admit my worst fears. It wasn't a nice word.

But what did I think these animals were brought to a country fair for? It certainly wasn't merely to entertain families and trot safely back home afterward. "Tell me it doesn't mean what I think it does," I said.

Sleepily, Whitey sat upright on his haunches, suddenly aware that he wasn't being rubbed behind his ear.

"It's sad. I know," Edgar said, putting his arm around me. "But that's why these pigs were raised in the first place. They're kids' 4-H projects. Today or tomorrow they'll be judged on the hoof. Right after the judging they'll be butchered. Then their carcasses will be judged."

My feet felt unsteady beneath me, and a coppery taste came to my mouth. I hesitated, looked down at Whitey, who had stood up and put his snout through the bars to win my attention.

"So, these pigs in these stalls here," I said, pointing all down the side of the barn, "are going to be dead in probably two to three days."

"Unfortunately, yeah."

"Whitey, too? But he's so young," I said, fighting back the tears. Whitey was half asleep propped up against the bars of the pen.

I hadn't raised the pig I'd just named Whitey. I had only met him moments ago, yet I couldn't accept his dying at such a young age. The others, too—the Landrace, the Chester White, and the comforting Duroc. At six months of age, they had only begun to enjoy some of the simpler pleasures of swine life—swinging grain bags in the air, appreciating a human's touch behind the ear.

Shocked still as moss beside Whitey's pen, I envisioned what his death would be like. I recalled William Hedgepeth's description in *The Hog Book*. Whitey would be herded into a chute where, only moments before, another of his kind had met his demise. Whitey, his keen snout detecting the scent of another swine brother's sweat-fear and the acrid smell of blood would experience terror unimaginable to any human. . . .

A stick pokes Whitey in the back—a gruff voice to "move up" where he belongs, where his "kind" belongs—next in line on the Green Mile. But Whitey didn't do anything wrong. He didn't kill anybody or commit a crime. Whitey stumbles up the ramp, the smell of blood more pungent the closer he gets. Bars on either side of him allow no escape, another swine brother behind, being poked too. Then the pig before him drops, and he balks as the stick pokes him again. Consumed by a desperate urge to run, to get away from the horror he knows awaits, he gasps, terror-filled, huffing now, not in greeting, but in indescribable and incapacitating fear.

The stick pushes him forward on legs weaker than twigs, and he sees two human legs and feet before him. Without a kind word or a scratch behind the ear, a metal object contacts his big white forehead. The trigger is pulled. As the electric current charges through his skull, Whitey's world turns black. On fire and unconscious, but still clinging to life, Whitey drops to his knees, his snout in the blood pool of hundreds of other pigs before him. From now on, he won't ever know the touch of a kind human nor the comfort of a swine friend. Nor does he feel the slice into his throat that drains his blood. At six months of age and with enthusiasm for life a mere bud, he is dying. . . .

I looked back over the animals, fighting back the tears that my imagination had caused. But it wasn't just my imagination; that's how pigs really died at the slaughter. It wasn't a myth; it was a farm pig's reality. Most humans who eat pork have never had to witness, let alone experience, that kind of torture. They only have to face the victim in pieces on their dinner plates, and that's not so hard to take on an empty stomach. Torture it surely was for the pigs, intelligent animals that can conjure a toy from an iron-barred pen; one that can comfort another the way only humans comfort each other.

I had long ago given up eating pork or pork products, but millions of my own kind in the U.S. were still indulging in hog flesh to the tune of 15 billion pounds of it a year. Yet, the terror of the slaughter is still lost on pork diners. History has predisposed them into thinking that pigs deserve and have inherited their lot: they are dirty, gluttonous, dumb and insensitive creatures that can do little good other than fill human bellies. What they don't realize is that a pig is intelligent enough to serve human communities in other ways. For example, he can assume many canine duties: as guide pigs for the blind, search and rescue pigs, land mine detectors, and guard pigs. Pigs can be avid hunters, and they can replace horses by pulling carts. In addition, they are perceptive enough and easily trained as sources of entertainment. They are natural-born comedians. And, most importantly, they can be the finest companion animal or pet that a person would ever want.

The cruelty of the slaughter lay in the knowing. The terror lies in the awareness—in the fear-sweat and blood-smell of those "gone" before. It's not the same for other barnyard animals destined for human palates. Steers, sheep, and chickens don't have the keen intelligence of swine, so they probably have no foreknowledge of their doom, no prescience that drives the fear to the very center of their bones.

I bent down and stroked Whitey's snout, which wriggled and worked itself against my hand, looking for a treat or just wanting to share my world. The others in his pen lay asleep, so contented with their stall friends, so agreeable, oblivious of their fate. Some lay in REM sleep, their noses bending and twisting, their jaws working—probably dreaming of a pig feast complete with apples, corn-on-the-cob and pints of Irish ale. Little did they know life would cease within hours. They would never again have fine conversation with barnyard buddies. They would have no chance to reproduce themselves. They would never see the light of a summer's afternoon or feel a fly's self-realizing bite. And they would never dream again.

Quickly I wiped my eyes. Many emotions surged through me. At once I felt weak, grief-stricken, helpless, and angry. Butchering pigs, the fifth most intelligent animals on earth, enlightened enough to realize their own impending death, was nothing short of animal cruelty. The Pig, accused of no crime except that of being a pig, rests in no grave. His body is hacked into pieces, delivered, devoured, digested, and at last spewed into the sewers. There is no peace for the pig. He suffers as a wraith upon the earth, without a grave he can call his own.

With the impending death of these pigs came the death of the hopeful seed within me—the one that united all people with all animals. Obviously familial ties existed between pigs that had been strangers to each other until they had been penned as neighbors at the fair. In the few minutes we sat with Whitey, he had shown me and Edgar that he also enjoyed our company. He'd accepted us as fellow beings, unaware that others of our kind were bent on hurting him.

Familial affection had been radiating from the pigs—in the side-by-side sleeping, in the playing, in the comforting of one for the other. *They* were the ones accepting each other, and they accepted the human element as they did themselves. The breakdown of my idyllic, unified world, however, came with the people—those who exploited pigs for food or for research, and those who reputed the animals to be among the dirtiest beings on Earth.

How could I envision a world in which all beings cooperate and respect each other when the one was making dinner of the other. My world vision didn't seem able to accommodate that idea, and as for an answer, I had no clue.

I said a glassy-eyed good-bye to Whitey and leaned, weak-kneed, against a box stall containing six sleeping Duroc "market" pigs. One snorted and coughed in his sleep; another snored regularly through an open mouth. I reached down through the wire pen and stroked the back of one. His hair was coarse, the skin underneath spotless. I ran my hand delicately along his back—my apology. Though he knew I was there, he didn't stir, comfortable with my presence. The touch of his skin made me shiver. I dreaded the fear that he would feel once he stepped off the truck and smelled the blood of the other market pigs who had marched bravely before him. Most of all I dreaded his realization of his own demise, the epiphany of the snatching away of his self.

I swallowed hard, blinked frantically, and stumbled out of the dark barn.

Our Family

THE FATE OF THE PIGS AT THE ALLENTOWN FAIR put a damper on my cosmic family vision for quite a while. As I saw it, humans spoiled the whole stew. It seemed, as far as I could tell, that the animals were doing their part, but I didn't think people were. With the shocking thought of Whitey's death and those of the other happy, vibrant six-month-old pigs, I was depressed. But I didn't isolate myself, even though I felt resentment toward the human condition for quite some time. About the only thing that helped me deal with it was my own family at home.

Most animals thrive in the summertime. Our own pets love the verdant season, as the agreeable temperatures offer them and me more time outside. The only drawback is the overwhelming number of insects that feast on our sweat and stick to our hides. If one can fend off the annoying bugs, then summertime in Pennsylvania proves as inviting as any tropical clime.

The house cats love being let out every morning in anticipation of a whole day playing in the woods. The rexes, in particular, are anxious to dart outside after they have breakfasted on tunafish and trout. When I open the front door at 7 AM, I know that is the last I'll see of them before suppertime, except for maybe a brief glimpse amongst the grape vines and azalea bushes. The outdoors offers something special for the rexes, who were born and raised in a skyrise in Manhattan. They act just a little bit schizoid, for cats. Their natural feline instincts lure them to the outdoors with its wild smells and exotic plants, while their urban upbringing makes them fear anything else with four legs: shrews, moles, deer mice.

There's no mistaking the rexes for the other cats on our property. The greyhound of the cat set, the long, thin-bodied rexes look like feline aliens with their pointy, oriental-like faces, and Furbee-sized ears. But they don't consider themselves superior to the barn cats. They can barf up a hairball with the best of them.

Ricky, my brown-and-white tuxedoed Cornish rex, hunts alongside his companion cousin, Rudy, a red-tiger rex. Both strut amongst the mayflowers on tiptoe, looking, because of their willowy legs, as though they are wearing high heels. Rexes are fairly frail cats, and, likewise, their prey is fragile. I have yet to see Ricky or Rudy catch anything substantial. Their quarry consists mostly of butterflies, gypsy moths, and scaly grasshoppers presented proudly on our front doorstep. Even though I giggle with a twinge of embarrassment for them, they still march proudly with their quarry held high, for surely they believe they have taken down an eagle. Whatever their prey, be it a single feather or a caterpillar, I always make a fuss as would any proud mom. In the rexes' case, the phrase "Everything is relative" applies.

Ricky plays adventure games in our woods, an overgrown patch of oak and ash trees dripping with poison ivy vines and wild grape. I imagine a fantasy in which he envisions himself a foot soldier in the wilds of Bhutan. His outpost lies atop a fallen tree stump where he lies in wait—a sentry of the woods, a protector of humankind and that of his kin. At attention, he guards against winged beasts of the forest and other scaly creatures. He is master of his domain, or so he thinks.

I feel strangely at ease with Ricky guarding the woods from his stump-tower. I feel as though none of the dangers of human civilization can penetrate the borders of his patrolled haven. His watchfulness and lion-heartedness, his courage in a sphere so fraught with strange creatures around every twig and leaf, give me the confidence I sometimes lack in claustrophobic, frenzied malls or traffic backups. My

Ricky, so slight of bone and sinew, standing alone and stalwart in the wild and dangerous woods, makes me feel somehow more brave occupying my own, more tenuous human world.

Though courageous beyond his size, Ricky has never brought me anything the likes of Kenny's catch. Kenny is our large, copper-eyed, beige domestic shorthair, a true Braveheart, wise to the wiles of the woods. Often while I am doing chores inside, I glimpse Kenny outside stalking prey. He is a master of the hunt—no butterflies or crickets for him. The catch he brings onto the porch as a gift—a starling, chipmunk, squirrel, blind shrew, or a whole nest of baby mice—is usually alive. After I thank him for his generosity, I scoop it up and set it free.

One time I saw him stalking a pheasant, but after several minutes of sizing up the animal's girth, he abandoned the project. While the great cock bird strutted unconcerned through the field, Kenny headed toward the barn for less formidable prey. It is one smart cat who knows his limitations.

Though he weighs perhaps fifteen pounds and is somewhat flabby between the legs—feline middle-age spread—he moves swiftly and tenaciously on his prey. I have gone running to the rescue of a poor wild thing—a mouse or chipmunk—Kenny has challenged to a duel. Like a true knight-errant, he has a self-satisfying joust with the creature first, treating the frightened mouse to a battle of fisticuffs. It tries to get away during the melee, but Kenny is lightning fast, despite his size, and wrestles it back into his grip lest it escape. If I arrive too late to discover the *duel accompli* and just in time to see Kenny preparing to dine on his dead prey, I allow him the spoils, but I refuse to stick around to witness the joyful munching and crunching of the bones.

Purrl, too, is an afficionado of our woods and the secrets it sustains. Our exotic shorthair is a pastel calico who was born with stubby hair but sports the typically round Persian face. Probably the most woods-wise of all our inside cats, she dashes outside first thing in the morning and doesn't come back until early evening—a ghost of the wilderness. And some pleasant evenings she doesn't even return home at all. Unlike Kenny, who is a backyard hunter, she roams far for her quarry, scouring the fields and seminary property behind us and killing out of human eye or earshot. I have yet to witness Purrl snuff her game. To her, it is an almost religious rite, a private, singular, serious, primal ritual that calls for no braggadocio or special recognition. For her the importance of the hunt is in the method, the doing rather than the bloody goal. Her hunt in itself defines her as feline.

Then there are Timmy, our flame-point Siamese, and Wendy, our snow-white angel rex kitten, two feline "humans." They prefer the comfort of indoors during the summer. Timmy, if he deigns to go outside—just for a change of pace—lounges on the deck so he can be close to the safety of the house. He's not crazy about wilderness or anything that smacks of nature. He will usually bed down right before the front door in a ray of sun, basking in the heat to the point of suffocation. When he's had enough, he begs at the door to be let into the air-conditioning. Wendy, too, sticks fairly close to the house. When she has strayed too far pursuing a noisy wood bee or moth, she runs for her haven under the deck. In her braver moments she walks between the

Wendy

rhododendron and azalea bushes, pawing at the spider webs and tasting the flowers. Timmy and Wendy are content to enjoy just a "taste" of the outdoors; they prefer indoor life.

We have had a host of outside cats. At one time I believe I counted a total of 27. I fed them all cans of cat food twice a day and left a good supply of dry food in the barn loft. These days the count of outside cats is meager—only about fourteen in all. Many have already lived out their brief lives, and others seem to have just wandered off, never to return. Our outside cats are as friendly as the house cats. They sidle next to me in the yard and wrap themselves in and around my legs in their love dance.

We have saved numerous loving cats from "nuisance euthanasia"— the abhorrent practice of putting an animal to sleep because it has become bothersome or the human owner is going on vacation. We've adopted many others whose owners needed to find them new homes for any number of reasons: a pregnant wife couldn't handle both a cat and a baby, the cat didn't get along with the dog; the family was moving. Though I cannot welcome any more animals into my house, I can always find room in the barn and at the barn cats' supper table for one or two more discarded animals.

Many cats have been dropped off in the countryside near our home and instinctively gravitate to us. They see other happy cats here and join them for a piece of the rock. Some cats we've acquired have simply been kicked out of their homes and find themselves on our doorstep by accident and by luck. The homeless ones are always thin to the point of emaciation. They have desperate, weary faces, glazed eyes. In weeks they begin to look hopeful again.

One of my more memorable cats, Sticky Bun, was used as a blood donor at the clinic where Edgar first started working. The cat went nameless at the clinic, known only as "the donor cat," and lived in a small animal cage in the kennel area full of yapping dogs. Only a few times a month was he allowed to walk around the office; the rest of the year he lived in his low-ceilinged cage. When Edgar began taking small animal appointments, I went along to help him and soon became attached to the blood donor cat. Finally, I begged the office manager to let him come home with me. After all, the animal had given half its life saving the lives of other cats. Hadn't he earned the right to live out his remaining years in freedom and happiness?

Several days later Edgar and I brought the blood donor cat home. I named him Sticky Bun because I was as fond of him as I was of my breakfast delights. When I opened the door to the cat carrier, he slinked out, all hunched over—a cat who should've towered eight inches reduced to four. He could only crawl on bent, weak knees.

At first we didn't know what was wrong with him. Later it occurred to us that Sticky had been molded into a perennially crouched position from living in a squashy little cage all his life. When he walked, he stooped low to the ground, his shoulders rounded, afraid he was going to scrape his head on the imaginary ceiling above him. For weeks he skulked through the fields and woods, as bent as an old dowager. Throughout the day we'd catch glimpses of Sticky Bun prowling the woods in his "low-rider" stance. Finally, after two months, his body began to relax and stretch, and he began experiencing life for the first time. Sticky lived with us for many years, always a little hunched over, always half-squat-walking across the ground in fear of a falling sky. He lived out the rest of his life satisfying his curiosity for life that all cats relish and deserve.

When we had first moved to our farm, we had adopted two kittens that one of my high school students begged me to take. Her grandmother had found them in her outhouse and grown tired of feeding them. Edgar and I rescued the red and black kittens, and they became our "flower group": Violet and Hyacinth. We had lots of room then—all the more to fill up with animals. I wanted kittens, so Violet and Hyacinth supplied us with babies. Thereafter I began giving them human names: Bruce, Allen, Gadney, Kermit, Milton, Mindy, Sophie, etc. Only twice besides the flower group did I stray from using human names for our litters. One was the "volcano group"—Irazu, Poas, and Arenal, named after three volcanoes in Costa Rica. The other was a "vegetable group"—Spinach, Broccoli, Eggplant, and Turnip. These days any new arrival on our patch gets a human name, for, indeed, our animal friends are as worthy of human names as persons are.

Over the years several people asked to adopt our kittens because the "flower" mothers had passed on very desirable genes: long hair and fancy, kaleidoscopic colors, so puffy with long fur that they were irresistible. Folks loved them at first sight and wanted to own one. I was reluctant to part with them, however, because I couldn't guarantee their safety. Once I gave them away, I had no control over how they would be treated. Edgar persuaded me to part with a few, assuring me that "they're going to very good friends."

The next time I saw the "friends," I asked about the kittens. "Oh," they said with little concern, "They're dead long ago—got hit in the street. The traffic in front is horrendous these days, but they really wanted to go out. So we let them." I was furious and sad for placing my kittens into a situation in which they would most likely be killed by vehicles. Thereafter I warned Edgar never to ask me to adopt out any kittens. I wouldn't allow it. Only I could assure our animals' health and happiness.

Another memorable cat that showed up on our doorstep one day was Marvin. Early one morning I had gone out to the barn to feed the horses and cats. Suddenly a creature ran up to the cat dishes and began gobbling up the food as fast as I plopped it onto the dishes. I stood back, mouth open. The thing was emaciated and scruffy-coated, its fur hanging in patches. He was as thin as Ichabod Crane, so skinny his ribs and pelvis stuck out like those of a desiccated mummy, and he had no whiskers. Much of his hair was missing; the tail was nearly bald. At first I thought a sick possum had joined the ranks of my domestic cats. I was shocked that a wild animal was dining with my cats.

Then I looked closer. It wasn't a possum; it was something else. A possum wouldn't dare to eat in the midst of a hoard of cats. What was it? "Kitty? Are you a kitty?" I said in a soft voice as he ate frantically.

The animal looked up, wraithlike.

"Oh, my! You are a cat!" I exclaimed. "You poor thing!"

For a moment it just looked at me with dazed, uncomprehending eyes and then lowered its head and continued to plow its way through the tasty canned cat food. I bent over and stroked its back, so sparsely-haired, dry, and dirty to the touch. It obviously had not had a good home for a long time. Then it looked at me again with a drawn, strained expression. Surely it thought I was going to hurt it or chase it away.

"You don't have to worry," I said, bending down. I petted his scaley back. Surprisingly he didn't flinch from my touch. "I will feed you, and you can stay here forever—if you like. Once you're settled in, I'll give you a flea bath and get rid of any worms you have. You'll like it here. You'll have lots of company."

We named him Starvin' Marvin after his physique and voracious manner of eating. He was the most pitiful creature I had ever seen. He was barely-living proof that domestic cats have a hard time taking care of themselves in the wild. And the way the other cats treated him and he regarded them was so strange. At first, they kept their distance from him, as though he were a leper. Whenever he approached, they moved slowly, cautiously away, staring after him as though he carried a pox. He, on the other hand, didn't mind the others at all; he never hissed at or fought with any other cat. He was simply grateful to be a part of their feline community. Likewise, he was appreciative of the food in his belly and the company of fellow felines. From the time he came onto our property, Marvin kept a constant vigil on our back doorsill, guarding our house. We always had to step over him to get into the house. Marvin lived with us for six years before dying in my arms of kidney failure.

Our pigs—all four of them—also love the call of the wild, even though they are also notorious couch potatoes and relish lounging before the woodstove during a winter blizzard. In summer they adore the intense warmth of the sun. Lowell and Lucille relax on my beach towels for hours. If I lay in the sun that long, I would be parboiled, but the pigs don't seem to mind—they soak up the rays like ripening figs. Only when the flies start biting do they dash to the comfort of the shaded barn.

After my morning run and chores, the pigs and I gather poolside. First, I set up Lowell and Lucille on their pig beds under the garden umbrella. I gather my essentials for the afternoon: a book, a phone, a sun hat, some SPF cream, and a frosty Diet Snapple. I hunker into a wrought-iron chair, and the three of us sit for hours.

The other two pigs, Ivy Mae and Annie Louise, are already on their second breakfast of the morning by the time I have Lowell, Lucille, and myself set up. They are cleaning up any ripened cherries or plums that have fallen. I have long since given up the idea of harvesting a garden with pot-bellied pigs around. They guard the garden gates more diligently than Cerberus does the entrance to Hades. At day's dawn they have already absconded with the crops before I am even out of my nightie. What produce they can't simply snatch from the plants and vines, they dig up with their snouts, leaving us with little more than a sniff at the vegetables. I have found that all my weeding during the spring and mid-summer only benefits the pigs by making it easier for them to navigate and inspect the carrots, red beets, beans, tomatoes, and potatoes. At least they leave us the onions. Last year, frustrated, I turned the vegetable garden into a flower garden. The pigs don't have a fancy for flowers.

Each summer day Ivy and Annie make systematic rounds for edibles. First, they check out the barn for spilled oats. Then they peruse the orchard area for apples and peaches. Knowing the birdfeeders have been empty of any tantalizing morsels since spring, they pass them by for a foray into the woods, where already the first acorns are beginning to fall. Once they have devoured them, they head into the neighboring farmer's fields of plenty: sweet corn, pumpkins, alfalfa, gourds, and other truck patch goodies. Ivy Mae and Annie are "pigs on a mission."

Nick Cihylick, our neighboring farmer, never seems to mind that Ivy and Annie rob his fields. He has a pot-bellied pig of his own—Arnold—and appreciates hog appetite. Besides, a couple of pot-bellies can hardly do much damage to hundreds of acres of crops. When Nick sees the girls hiding in his pumpkin patch, I can hear him laughing above the chugging of his tractor. Pigs are not known for their stealth. Once discovered, they race from the pumpkin field, their snouts yellow with pumpkin juice.

We also have another family of animals across the street on our other property, which we call the "old farm." They are an odd group—gifts, adopted animals and those whose owners had threatened to put them to sleep. At the old farm resides Scotty, the Scotch Highland steer that Edgar gave me for Christmas many years ago. He was only a little tyke at the time, and we've had him for about twelve years. He has a set of horns that Hemingway would have coveted, but Scotty wouldn't think of threatening others with them. He only does his "toro" routine—brandishing his two-foot-long horns as though before a matador, when he wants first dibs on a meal or when one of his roommates is blocking the barn entrance.

The beefy Scottish Highland has a good bit of poultry mentality in him: like Milton the buffalo, he's basically a chicken. At 2,000 pounds he may look as if he could pulverize most anything in his path, but just a stamp of the foot and a warning finger sends him fleeing and shaking his horns in trepidation. A big, hairy red-headed guy, he smells rancid, like sour grain—not a companion to share close quarters with. He has a disgusting habit of constantly cleaning his nostrils with his tongue. I don't know how he ever expects to win over a female doing that.

During the summer Scotty finds solace hanging out in the center of the pond—keeping cool and bug-free. In this way he provides entertainment for passers-by. So many times friends and acquaintances have made the pond-bound Scotty the butt of their jokes, especially when they see the tongue-in-the-nose routine. Just as Lowell has endured jibes about his ability to fill yards of sausage casings and numerous cans of Spam, so does our roughly-hewn, ungainly steer abide peoples' mockery when they suggest we form him into hamburgers or fit him for a spit. Irritated with their remarks, I vow to skewer them in return. Edgar continues to smile at their remarks, though, and says, "Oh, no. He's just a big pet. He'll die here but only from natural causes."

Scotty's bedside, or barnside, companions are Sophie, a Mammoth jenny or large donkey, Benjy, a miniature Sicilian donkey, and their offspring, Thumbelina. Sophie and Benjy were given to us a few years ago as payment for veterinary bills. They share a barnyard with Larry the llama, another Christmas present, and Al the alpaca. This motley

Lowell and Lucille

crew squeezes into two tight rooms in the old barn. Despite the different breeds, they all seem to get along. The donkeys, particularly Sophie, dominate the domicile. If Scotty tosses his horns like a bad boy, Sophie will give him a good humbling kick. Benjy and Thumbelina are much less aggressive, content to occupy their days feasting in the pasture.

The llama and alpaca are docile creatures who "go with the flow" because they are at the bottom of the pecking order. Al was given us by one of Edgar's clients who threatened to euthanize him because of his perennially snotty nose. Initially Edgar told him the runny nose was caused by an infected tooth and that no course of antibiotics would help. The owner has a large alpaca herd, and it irritated him to no end that one of the crowd had a pusy nose all the time. Finally, the owner had enough. When the client called Edgar to put the animal to sleep, Edgar offered to take the alpaca off his hands. Gladly the man delivered Al (we had him named before we got him) to our doorstep. Edgar tried numerous remedies, but so far nothing has worked. Al still has a river of green cascading from his nostrils, but he has no trouble breathing or eating and seems to have no other problems. What he does have, however, is life, thanks to Edgar and his soft heart, and he is happy at the farm. Al grazes the pastures as if he had not a care in the world, except for a good case of post-nasal drip.

Of course, Al became good buddies with Larry, who walks with a limp to this day—all because of me. Larry was so adorable as a baby that when Edgar presented him to me that Christmas, I decided to move him up to our farm to live with us and the horses. I thought friends would get a kick out of seeing one llama grazing amongst a herd of horses. Edgar agreed, so we went into action.

Before introducing him to the horses, we first needed to familiarize Larry with our place, so we built a small pen for him in the riding arena. Then we loaded him into the horse trailer and introduced him to our farm across the road.

When we released him into the indoor riding arena, he went berserk, running first to one end and then to the other. For the entire day he seldom slowed to a walk, and we didn't know how to calm him. We watched him carefully through the day, but he was a Nervous Norman. When we came back into the barn that evening at feeding time, Larry became startled and bolted into the wall. When he got up, his hind leg dangled behind him, broken. We felt terrible and responsible.

Clearly he hadn't liked our moving him from the old farm, so with regrets we carefully urged him back into the horse trailer and drove him back there. Edgar gave him some anesthetic, and we cast his leg. Larry had to be confined to a back stall in the old barn for several months. Now his leg supports him well, but it is crooked and hangs eerily out to the side when he stands. Nevertheless, he and Al share good lazy days in the pasture.

Our horses, Fancy, Julie, Lucy, Fax, and Timmy, love the outdoors, especially in spring and summer when the pastures are lush with fescue and Kentucky bluegrass. For them it is worth braving the insects to dine daily on clover. In between courses I may ask one of them for a ride, which I do in a much more relaxed manner these days. There's no working the horses as I did many years ago to ready them and myself for a horse show. I've outgrown the horse-showing stage; I decided years ago I had accomplished what I set out to do. Now my riding forays are sporadic and for pleasure only—just a few minutes around the woods—enough to feel the breeze in my hair and the oneness with my horse. My horses are older now, less fit, and content in their fields of green, like oldsters at a banquet. For all the rehearsing and practicing I subjected them to in the past, they deserve to spend the rest of their days in semi-retirement, accommodating me for a fifteen-minute ride once a week or so.

Our menagerie is as much family to us as a human family would be. As busy as Edgar is with clients and their pets' problems, he often comes home to someone who needs his care. It's the law of probability. With that many animals around, problems are bound to happen. Considering the sheer number we have and all their different personalities and idiosyncrasies, a dull moment is rare, and we wouldn't have it any other way. I wouldn't give away any of them. In fact, sometimes I wish I could help more animals than I already have.

All our outside and inside cats are spayed and castrated, so we won't have any new kittens to play with. The only things reproducing around our place these days are the wildlife. Our animal population is static; but when one dies of old age, a stall or place at the dining table awaits for another poor soul who needs a home. Having so many animals takes a lot of work and time and money for food, but the veterinary care is free.

While we provide our animal companions with food and shelter, they, in turn, provide us with friendship and fodder for self-contentment. The significance is all around us: Annie and Ivy in Nick's field, Lowell and Lucille at my feet, the cats in a lawn chair, behind the spirea bush, in the sawdust bin, under the blue spruce, on the deck around the house. It's in the horses snorting in the pasture and the crows complaining in the canopy of the woods. It resides in the deer peering at us through the windows. Without our animals, I would not have half the energy or inspiration for life that I do. Without our animals, I would not be the person Edgar loves and respects. Without our animals, I would not be myself, the person I have come to know and like. Our animals have given me the peace, the love and contentment of self that one needs in order to thrive in a postmodern world.

Jim's Saga

BESIDES OUR ANIMALS, A FEW SPECIAL PEOPLE have become part of our extended family: Tom, the grain delivery man, who provides us with horse feed, bird seed, and cat litter every two weeks; Debbie, a friend who works at Alpo and buys and delivers cat food for us regularly; Kathy, my housekeeper, who treats the cats and pigs as if they are her own; Jessie, a friend who has been mucking stalls and babysitting our animals since she was thirteen—she's 22 now; Nick, our friend and neighboring farmer, who would help us with any problem; Dr. Arlen Wilbers, our pig doctor, and Dr. Randy Bimes, our colic surgeon when we need him. All these people make our life easier. Without them we both would be far less efficient at managing time and caring for our animals.

And, of course, there's Jim Kindred, our family farrier or horse-shoer.

Jim was—and still is—a great storyteller. Each time he came to shoe our horses, we relished the treat—tales of incredible events that have happened to him while shoeing horses and to other people in their daily dealings with the beasts. Often he recounted shoeing rank young horses, like the time a mare sat on his back as he was trimming her back hoof. It took three men to pry her off his spine, and as a result he required weekly treatments at the local chiropractor.

One day Edgar and I were waiting for Jim. He was uncharacteristically late by an hour, and we were a little concerned: Had he been kicked by a horse he was shoeing at another barn? Had he been in a car accident? Maybe something was wrong at home.

I finally sat down with a magazine I had been promising myself to read when an old vehicle crawled up the driveway.

It wasn't our horseshoer's truck.

The ancient, rust-complected jalopy lurched once, heaved a second time and finally sputtered to a stop in our driveway. It was missing a chrome fitting over one wheel well, and the front bumper was hanging precariously toward the ground. Surely it couldn't belong to our rather fastidious farrier, whose vehicles were always in immaculate condition. Who was that parked in our roadway? What forlorn traveler had lost his way, finally shipwrecking on this isle of woods, our doorstep? Who owned a truck in that degree of disrepair and apparent "dementia vehiculis"? No one that we knew.

The pockmarked truck sat expectantly, eerily, in the driveway. It stared for several moments—no movement, no intention of movement. Surely, I thought with a chill, if one of us dared venture outside, its headlights would flick on, casting us in a glaring, ghostly spotlight. The engine would roar to life, and it would charge us in a tire-squealing, demonic delirium. No way was I going out there.

Edgar was chicken, too. "That's not Jim, is it?" he asked, squinting at the idling truck. "I can't see. The sun's too bright to see who's inside."

"No, I don't think it's Jim," I said with some assurance. "And don't think you're getting me to check it out, either. For all I care, that beat-up heap and its most likely alien owner can sit in our driveway and rot. I'm not setting foot outside. I'm glad our pigs are safe in the house. Besides, remember Jim just bought a new silver truck with a matching horse trailer. He'd never drive a dump like that thing. And where would he keep all his farrier tools in that truck? It's way too small."

Edgar shrugged his shoulders. "Beats me. I guess I better find out who it is, though," he said.

"I wouldn't go out there if I were you," I warned in a throaty voice, like Rod Serling's on *The Twilight Zone*.

"Don't be silly," Edgar said as though someone as innocuous as Little Bo Peep was sitting behind the wheel of the abominable vehicle. "It's probably just someone who's lost."

"Yeah, right—lost in *our* driveway—and just sitting there, not asking for directions or anything—sitting there like an ol' graveyard ghost," I said in my best *Grapes of Wrath* accent. "It gives me the creeps."

Edgar walked out the door, and I watched him disappear into the barn. The derelict truck continued to mope in the driveway. Whose could it be? The thought pestered me until several minutes later, with no sign from Edgar, I mustered enough courage to venture outside. I couldn't just stand by and let my mate become the victim of a lunatic—at least not without a halfhearted attempt to save him.

As I tiptoed out of the house, I stopped short, gripping the door handle as a high-pitched scream filled the air. I cringed, and my stomach twisted sickeningly. Again it sounded. I recognized the familiar shriek—howl, actually—of Jim, our horseshoer. The truck, I thought, must be his.

"Hey, Jim," I yelled, walking over to him and Edgar, who had propped his leg on the truck's tailgate. "What in the world are you driving? What a piece of junk! We were almost afraid to see who it was."

"Ha, ha-ah, ha-ah, ha-ah," Jim machine-gunned a laugh. "She does look pretty bad, huh?" Jim opened the rusted tailgate, and it crashed with a cloud of dust onto its hinges. Then he threw open the scratched lid of the cap.

I gasped at the sight before us. The inside of the truck was

Jim

stuffed like a roaster turkey to the very brim with tools of the farrier's trade. I giggled, and Jim hoisted himself onto the tailgate, pulling at a piece of iron that stuck from the bottom of the twisted mass of metal and wood.

He jerked on the metal leg, but it wouldn't budge, entangled in a jungle of grinders, vices, steel shoe punches and pritchells, storage boxes, and other horseshoeing paraphernalia. "Had a little accident with my other rig the other day," he began as he pulled again on the stubborn iron appendage.

I peered inside and could make out only a few of the familiar tools that had always been so neatly organized inside his silver horse trailer. The former trailer had neatly stored the anvil and forge, each in its proper place on opposite walls. Then, along the walls on three racks hung row upon row of silvery horseshoes and aluminum and steel bar shoes. In storage drawers were the pads, lead, borium, and numerous files. Along the back side had rested the belt sander alongside the bench grinder and electric drills. At the other corner sat the threader for drilling and tapping shoes for screw-in studs and caulks.

With a flick of a switch, Jim had always had a fire glowing in the forge fueled by the acetylene and oxygen gas tanks. From the forge, smoke and fumes exited safely and neatly through the pipe he had retro-fitted through the roof of the trailer. There in the forge he roasted the shoes like weiners, flipping them periodically and stirring the hot coals with the metal tongs until the shoes were hot enough to be shaped to the horse's foot. So, too, had the anvil easily rolled out on a tiny buggy so as to make hammering the shoes an easy task. The process flowed smoothly, quickly, as he flipped the malleable shoes onto the anvil and back into the fire again. It was all so handy, so organized, so ordered.

This truck, on the other hand, spelled complete chaos.

I snickered as Jim battled the recalcitrant piece of iron. He pulled and pulled, bracing his leg against the tailgate, his cheeks puffed out, but it wouldn't budge from the menagerie of metal.

"What happened to your new truck and trailer?" Edgar prodded.

"Well," Jim began. He tugged harder on the iron leg sticking from the twisted pile of iron rubbish that had once been an organized, working farrier shop. "Can't seem to get the tripod out," he grunted, pulling with both hands. "Damn. One of the legs is caught on the support beam of the truck cap." He tugged harder. All the horseshoeing equipment was knotted together, tangled like a bunch of pick-up-sticks. He pulled on the leg again, then rocked it back and forth to dislodge it from its trap.

"You're going to hurt yourself," I said in a fleeting instant of motherly concern.

"Oh, this damn truck," he moaned. "It's a total nightmare. Nothing fits in here right, and I always have a hard time unpacking it and packing it after each barn call. I can't wait until I get my new set-up next week. I can't take much more of this." With that he slammed his foot into the pile of tangled metal, yanked, and wrenched the tripod free. A pile of tools and supplies flew out onto the floor along with it. Then he set it on the barn floor and dove back into the twisted mass of metal for another piece of equipment.

"This certainly isn't your style, Jim. Where did you get this rusty jalopy, anyway?" I said, looking at the olive-green and red-primered vehicle whose rear was hanging low with the tonnage of horseshoes, nails, anvil, and other heavy metal.

"It's my old farm truck," Jim said as he arranged the anvil on its table. Then he reached into the metal mélange for the forge and its gas tank. In a few minutes he had connected them. He rolled up his flannel sleeves, wrapped his leather chaps around his jeans, and put the grinder on its stand. In twenty minutes he had everything arranged outside the truck, and I could barely see racks and rows of horseshoes lining the back of the truck and the cab. Various drawers filled with glues, horseshoe nails, and shoe punches lined the side of the truck bed, too.

"So, tell us what happened to your silver truck and trailer," Edgar asked.

"I guess you'd say I had a bit of a mishap," he said, his lips firm. Strangely I could sense a grin behind them.

I bit my thumbnail anxiously.

Jim hitched his chaps and wiped his hands along its edges. Licking his upper lip, he began to snicker, remembering the event. While he contemplated, I brought Fancy to the crossties so that Jim could begin shoeing.

"Yeah?" Edgar said, fishing for more information. "Tell us more, Jimbo."

Jim stood up straight, the stance of a stand-up comedian. "Ya know Route 100—where it connects to Route 309—where that curve is?" We nodded.

"That's where it happened," he said, shaking his head in disbelief. He licked his lips, and his eyes closed for a couple of seconds. Slowly he shook his head as if trying to forget the images he was conjuring. The corners of his lips drooped. I had anticipated a funny story, but this just might end up being a serious account. By his pained expression, it must have been terrible.

"I'd just finished shoeing at Klein's," he began with an ache in his voice, "and I was headed down the road with the truck and trailer." There was a long pause while he contemplated a crack in the concrete floor. Then he regained his composure.

"Everything was going along as normal," he continued. "But when I started around that bend, I heard a loud CRACK." Suddenly Jim struck the anvil with a hammer; it sounded like a pistol shot. The horses started at the sound but quieted immediately. "Little did I know," he said, raising a finger, "that the chain attaching the trailer to the truck had busted." He rolled his eyes and clenched his teeth.

"Oh, God."

"And then—you wouldn't have believed it . . ." He turned, his back toward us—a gesture of pained remembrance.

"What? What?" I shouted

When he turned around again, his face wore a strained expression. Then, in a few minutes he became animated. "I just happened to look out my driver's window, and what do I see?"

"WHAT DID YOU SEE?" I yelled, unable to control myself for the suspense.

"I see my *trailer*—the one that should've been *following* me—going past me, racing me down the road."

"No *way!*" I cried, poking him in the chest.

"Yes, *way!*" he yelled. Then he cupped his head as if the pain of reliving the tale was too much to bear. "I couldn't believe my eyes! It was unreal! The thing I was pulling behind me was passing me, speeding alongside me down the highway!"

Jim wasn't amused, but with that vision in my mind, I had to stifle a laugh. "Get *awt!*" I blurted, accidentally slipping into a Dutchy accent. "What did you say when you saw your trailer passing you?"

Jim thought for a moment, and then his horrific expression turned comic. He laughed with a hiccup. "I said, very quietly, in fact, 'Oh, shit.'"

I bit my lip.

"Then what happened?" Edgar said.

"I quick pulled the truck over to the side of the road. But I couldn't do anything about the trailer. All I could do was watch it go by with all my horseshoeing tools inside. And, boy, *did it go!* It was headed straight for this little white house."

Suddenly a large crack parted his lips, and Jim let out a single roar of laughter. "The trailer was rolling on its back wheels, of course, and on that one tiny front wheel that ya crank up after ya've hitched the trailer to the truck. Well, that little wheel was down, and that's what the front of the trailer was riding on. There it was speeding straight for this little, white, gingerbread-type house."

Jim blanched again, and his lips drooped. "It made me absolutely sick to my stomach because all I could do was watch helplessly as it roared past me. It was *flying* down the road—all three tons of it." He rubbed his stomach painfully and groaned. "Can you imagine being the owner of that house, looking out the window, and seeing this silver behemoth coming right for you and your favorite Barcalounger?" His eyes were big as pasta bowls as he relived the scene. He stared past us into the cobwebs of the barn as if watching the trailer plummet down the road again.

He went on, pointing at an imaginary road in the air. "Then it crossed the highway and started right through the grass toward that house. Thank God that little front wheel collapsed before it hit the house. When the wheel collapsed, the front end of the trailer ditched into the ground." Jim clapped his hands: the trailer hitting the earth. "Then the trailer tongue bit into the grass!"

He let out one short laugh. "That sent the whole shebang careening head over tincup and onto its side. What a hell of a racket it made, too, with all that iron upsetting inside. But I was so glad the thing had stopped, even though it lay in the middle of that little house's yard. At least it didn't crash right through the house."

"Then what happened?" I shrieked, unable to contain my amusement.

"Well, luckily I have a cellular phone, so I called Curley's service station for a wrecker. He said he'd be right there to help me out.

"Then I thought I ought to tell the people in the house why a horse trailer was on its side in their yard, along with about twenty feet of tire ruts. So, I walked to the house and knocked on the door, and this tiny Oriental woman answered. I explained that I had had an accident and that part of my vehicle was in her front yard. I said I would be happy to pay for any damages to the yard, but she didn't seem to want to hear any of it.

"In the background I noticed a man sitting with his back to me typing away on a computer. He was jabbering to himself the whole time he was typing and didn't even notice me at the door. He also was probably oblivious to my trailer crashing onto his lawn. I pointed at the trailer in the yard and smiled kind of sheepish-like. The woman nodded as if she understood my predicament. Then she promptly closed the door in my face. I later found out the little house was actually a computer repair shop.

"I didn't know what to do, exactly, so I went back to the trailer and stood beside it waiting for Curley and his wrecker. And would you believe that as I was standing there, this tractor trailer pulled up alongside me."

Jim paused, and a sly smile crawled across his face. "Would you believe the driver leans out his window, shakes his head, and says to me, 'Ya know, there's an easier way of unhooking a trailer from a rig.' Then he drove off, just like that!" Jim made an incredulous face. "Wise ass!"

Edgar and I were bent double with laughter, and Jim was snorting pretty well, too.

"So did anything fall out of the trailer?" Edgar asked.

"Did anything fall out of the trailer, the man asks! I guess I'd have to say so. Specifically . . ." and then Jim paused, "specifically . . . *horseshoe nails*—THOUSANDS of them—all over the guy's yard."

I stifled another laugh.

Jim became pensive, and he cupped his chin like Rodin's *The Thinker*. "Do you suppose I should stop by that place sometime and tell them about those nails in their yard? On account of, in spring when they mow the grass, . . . you can imagine it. Somebody could get hurt!"

"Yeah, I think telling them would be a good idea, Jim," I said.

"Get in there with a commercial magnet or something," Edgar offered.

"Yeah, that's an idea!" he said. "I guess I better do something."

Jim walked over to Fancy, lifted her leg, and began hacking at the hoof wall with a hoof knife. After a time he grabbed the hoof nipper, picked up her front leg, propped it between his knees, and started clipping off the overgrown nail. After he had rounded the hoof, big chunks of nail falling onto the concrete, he threw the nippers to the floor in exchange for the rasp, a sort of industrial-strength emery board, which he used to file the foot down so there were no rough edges. Then he made a visual check of the hoof to see that the planes were straight and set her foot back down on the concrete floor.

He started to laugh. "That wasn't all that happened, either," he said.

"Something else happened?" Edgar said.

"Goodie," I yelled. Jim chuckled.

"After the accident I took my farm truck—this one right here—and loaded it up. I had no other vehicle. I have another rig on order now, and I should only have to be inconvenienced with this thing for about another week. But for the meantime, I put all my horseshoeing stuff in my farm truck and scarcely have lost a day of business through it all. I just picked up where I left off and kept doin' the barn calls.

"Then one day I was driving into Palmerton on Main Street, and right up from the traffic light going into Palmerton—right at that little hill—I heard a loud *BANG!* from the back of the truck. I grabbed the wheel (he demonstrated with wild arm gestures) to steady 'er because I thought for sure the axles had broke or something else let loose. After all, I was forcing my old quarter-ton farm truck to do a job it wasn't cut out to do—hauling around a ton of metal. But after the bang . . . nothing. The truck didn't cut out, swerve, stop, or do anything. We just kept driving up Main Street as if nothing happened, which, I assumed by then, it hadn't."

Suddenly Jim's eyes rounded to walnuts, and his mouth opened like a startled clown's. "Then I looked in my rearview mirror. God! I couldn't believe my eyes! There behind me about a quarter of a mile back down the street stood my toolbox—you know—this here one that sits up about two feet on rolling legs. It was standing in the middle of Main Street! My tool box!"

I held my breath for fear of exploding with laughter. I could easily picture Jim's homemade, top-heavy metal shoeing box stopping traffic with the authority of a crossing guard.

"Yeah, right in the middle of the damn street—my most valuable possession, helpless and waiting like a groundhog to be run over by hundreds of cars. So, I quick pulled over, jumped out of the truck, and ran like hell back down the road to save it. After all, I made that toolbox by hand. We've gone through many years of horseshoeing together."

He gasped for air. "In fact, would you believe, I damned near got killed dashing between the cars! You should've seen me whizzing in and out of traffic. People were blowing their horns, but I wasn't going to lose my toolbox. No, sirree. It's my buddy; without it I'm finished.

"Finally, I got to it. I darted in front of this red compact car, grabbed the box by the handle, and pushed the thing on its wheels across the street and onto the curb. But guess what?" he said with wild eyes. "The lid had flipped open, and . . . "

"No, don't tell us," I said incredulously. "Nails?"

"Nails," he offered in a dead-pan voice." Then he began to howl with laughter. "Horseshoe nails *all* over the street. But I didn't give a damn. I had my box back, and it wasn't injured. So I wheeled it onto the sidewalk and walked it back down the street by its handle back to the truck."

"How did the toolbox get out of the truck?" Edgar said.

"That bang I heard had been the tailgate dropping open."

"Oh," Edgar snickered.

"It just let loose." Then Jim picked up Fancy's other hoof and began hacking away at it with a knife. "Yeah," Jim shook his head, "it's been a couple of pretty hairy weeks. Luckily I'm getting my new setup next week. I can say so long to this old heap then."

Jim finished trimming and shoeing our horses. He slurped down the last of his iced tea and patted Fancy fondly on the hind end. He led her to her stall and closed the door. Before leaving, he sharpened Edgar's own hoof knife as he always does. Finally he jammed all his tools and equipment back into his farm truck. He slammed the tailgate shut, long and pointy pieces of iron and wood poking from the back of the cab, then he waved, climbed into the cab, and yelled, "Hasta Lumbago, folks. See you in seven weeks!"

Several weeks later Edgar came home from his calls and told me he had passed Jim on the road.

"Oh, yeah? Did he get his new rig, or is he still driving that junk-yard dog?" I asked.

"All I can say is, it's different," he snickered.

"Why, what do you mean?"

"You know those silver, quilted-looking food concession stands that caterers take to carnivals, car shows, fairs, and other outdoor events? Those metal boxes where the side folds up like a kind of awning, and a shelf pops out for the customer to eat from? Well, that's what he's pulling behind him now. It's a riot! Jim looks like Mr. Snow Cone coming down the street. All he needs is the tinkly little bell, and he could sell sausage sandwiches and curly fries from that getup. Next time he shoes our horses, I'm going to queue up and offer him fifty cents for some funnel cake. It'll crack him up! But, that's Jim for ya—ya never know what's going to happen with him next," Edgar laughed.

"Yeah," I added, "maybe Fancy can buy a candy apple from him after he's done fitting her shoes. She'd really like that."

"Good ol' Jim," Edgar said.

"Yep, he's some guy."

Andy

THE BIBLICAL LOCUST PLAGUE had nothing on us.

That fall was the season of the gnats—"gnaticus ubiquitous vampiricus." After the worst drought in one hundred years, the first rains brought gnats back by the billions in squadrons that tainted the air thick with clouds of gray. Every living thing was prey to the blood-draining, eye-diving, microscopic succubi. Our horses hid in their stalls rather than graze, and our four pot-bellied pigs withstood the pesky outdoors, stealing hasty mouthfuls of alfalfa while the gnats dined mercilessly on their ears and eyes.

The gnats sought out humans, as well. Edgar and I were particularly vulnerable because of his outdoor job amongst the animals. Given the choice, however, the gnats always preferred my sweet-smelling juiciness over Edgar's comparatively dry bone and sinew. My husband didn't need bug spray to ward them off. He had me for protection.

Each day before going outside, I armed myself against the winged bastards with citronella spray and a wide-brimmed straw hat. For whatever reason, they were always attracted to my hairline where they fought their way through the forest of hair and began boring into my scalp. The scene repeated itself throughout the day. First, I'd feel a nasty prick to the forehead; then I'd smack my head and rake a bloodied gnat out of my hair with a fingernail. Unfortunately, if the pests didn't have the ambition to fight the jungle of hair, they simply made a kamikaze run into an eye from which I madly plucked the invader and crushed him on my shirt.

Our animals that summer, though, didn't have hands and fingernails with which to defend themselves. Their only defense against the irritating pests was to flick their ears and shake their heads each second and every minute of every day. For them the torment must have rivaled the second level of Dante's Hades. I did what I could to help, but it didn't seem to be enough. To the horses I applied insect repellent. On really buggy days I brought them into the gnat-free barn. The pigs wore bug repellent thick enough to resemble suits of armor. I also coated them with citronella spray, put Vaseline in their ears, and finally,

Bob, Andy, and Edgar

when all else failed, I covered them with blankets or brought them into the house. Yet determined insects still plagued them. I was constantly checking their ears, plucking out and mashing gnats that had been feeding there.

I believe it was because of the relentless daily attacks of the gnats that I had unconsciously plucked my hooded red fleece-lined sweat-shirt from my dresser one summer day when Edgar was called out to attend a deer. I rushed upstairs for the article of clothing, even though it was a sweltering, humid September day. Why? I had only worn that sweatshirt during the winter. So what possessed me to drag it from the bottom of my drawer? What strange prescience led me to it?

"What are you wearing that for?" Edgar said incredulously. "It must be ninety degrees out."

I looked down at my sweatshirt and said, "Uh—I don't know. There's a chill in the air, I guess."

He just gave me a strange looked and started the truck.

Just a bit north of the town of Lehighton, we drove down a narrow, winding driveway toward a clump of woods. Surrounding it was an eight-foot-high fence in which lived a family of deer, one of whose members was having a problem with a strange growth on an antler. We passed the owner's industrial-sized warehouse—a 5,000-square-foot, aluminum-sided building—out of which he conducted a home business, B&C Bait, for breeding and selling bait fish. "This is a unique place," Edgar explained. "It's a drive-through for fishermen, believe it or not."

"Drive-through bait?" I asked in disbelief. "No hot dogs or fries or soda or anything? Just snacks for fish?"

"That's right—bait is all." He pulled the truck around the side of the gray building and parked at the end of the parking lot. I could see many low concrete tanks inside.

"Are the fish alive when someone goes to pick them up?"

"Oh, yeah. That's the only way a fisherman's going to catch a fish, you know."

"Silly me," I said, rolling my eyes. I stuck my head out the truck window to take in the view. Immediately I noticed the quiet. Fish don't make much noise. "I've got to see this operation," I said, turning back toward Edgar. Then I looked in front of us past the box fencing that ran down a hillside and into the woods. "Is that where the deer live?"

"Yeah. Andy's down there somewhere—he's the one with the antler to check. A real tame deer. He'll come right up to anyone. Bob really likes his deer. They're like kids to him and his wife."

We climbed from the truck and headed toward the bait building to find Bob. As we approached, a very tall, sturdy man in his fifties appeared from the shadows of the warehouse.

"Hi, Doc," he called, hoisting his jeans to his waist. Edgar waved, and I followed, anxious to see this phenomenon that easily could be named Bob's Drive-Through Bait Bar and Grill. Beside the warehouse, a truck sat with a beckoning logo. It resembled an ice cream truck—low and boxy—but I was fairly certain we couldn't milk any ice cream out of it. Against a white background a red-lettered advertisement read: The Minnow Express. B & C Bait Shop. We bait 'em—you hook 'em!

We met Bob at the large garage-door opening, and Edgar introduced me. Bob was a towering, burly guy with a mere netting of hair over his scalp. He smiled and nodded to me and then followed us as I walked into the warehouse, curious as George, toward his fish tanks. All along both sides of the building stood concrete tanks perhaps six feet wide by twenty feet long and four feet deep. Some were empty, but most were filled with circulating water and millions upon millions of small fish.

I peered into one tank, and Bob proudly stepped alongside me, eager to give me a quick tour of his enterprise. Surprisingly there wasn't much of a fishy odor; it was a clean, well-lighted place. Bob grabbed a net and swept it through the tank I had been inspecting.

"Wow!" I said, as he tipped the net writhing with hundreds of fish the size of my little finger.

"Dese are shiners," he said. With his Dutchy accent he pronounced the word with a prolonged long "i" sound—"shy-y-y-y-ners."

"They're like shards of mercury come alive," I marveled. "Look at them moving! What can you catch with them?"

"Ya can catch bass, pickerel, and walleye with shi-i-i-i-ners. Naw, dese here ones over here-a," he said, striding over to a tank on the other side of the warehouse, "are fatheads. They're good for trout, perch, and crappies."

"Crappies?" I asked. Perhaps I misunderstood. Did he mean some fish called a crabbie that he pronounced "crappie" in his accent or were they, indeed, fish called "crappies"?

"Yeah, crappies," he said again. Then he walked over to another tank, raised a metal lid, and pointed to a few foot-long fish. "I only haf a few of dese ones right naw. Dese are bass carp; they're gudt for keepin' the algae (pronounced "alchee") dawn in your pond."

"This is some operation," I congratulated Bob. "But where are the minnows," I said, remembering the truck in the other building with the minnow logo.

"Oh, dose I get from Arkansas," he said. "I don't ship 'em in until springtime."

"Okay, Gay," Edgar interrupted, anxious to get going on the deer. "Bob, where's Andy?"

"He'ss ova dere in hiss pen," Bob pointed outside.

We left the warehouse, heading toward the deer pen when suddenly, as if by magic, all of Bob's family appeared at the deer fence. Evidently they wanted to watch the action, if there was going to be any. Whenever Edgar worked on deer or elk, it seemed something notable occurred. One deer might take several darts from the blowgun to finally feel the effects of the tranquilizer, but another might only need one injection to make it sleepy and safe to work on. It all depended on the temperament of the animal—high-strung or calm. Depending on how the anesthesia worked or did not work, any situation could arise: the patient could escape, or, if he had antlers, try to attack and gore.

Edgar stopped first at the truck to draw up an injection of xylazine to tranquilize the deer while he examined the antlers. Then we all gathered outside the fence, and Bob threw pieces of apples into the pen to summon his deer family.

"Andee-ee-ee, Barnee-ee-ee, Nickee-ee-ee, Sunshi-i-i-ine, Cookie-ee-ee, Candy-ee-ee. Come on, naw, Andee-ee-ee! Vy, here comes Barney naw. Vhere's Andy?" Bob called to his wife, who was standing with their grown daughter and granddaughter farther down the fence towards the woods.

His wife yelled back, "I see Andy naw. He's comin'! He's chust slow, that's all. He's alvays slow. Yup—here he comes, naw." Then she coaxed Andy to hurry. "Come on, Andy. Hurry on, naw. Daddy hass some apples for ya."

By then all the other deer had assembled: Barney, Nicky, and Sunshine (the mother of Cookie and Candy). Only the father, Andy, was lagging behind, though he was slowly making his way along the fence toward Bob and Edgar and me. As he got closer, I could see the abnormal growth that had attached itself like an alien thing to the base of one of Andy's antlers. The right side of Andy's antler looked normal, with several normal-looking spikes, but a secondary mass of antler had erupted at its base, right where it attached to the head. It was eerie-looking: a four-inch high, three-inch thickly rounded growth. It looked like a tumor, smooth and round, but, from what Bob said, the lumpish segment felt hard, like bone or antler.

"Holy cow! It looks like it's pushing right into his temple! How in the world am I going to remove that thing!" Edgar said miserably.

"Yep," Bob said. "I knew I hadt to call ya yesterday because vhen I gave Andy his snack, I looked real close at that thing, and I thought I cudt see somethin' movin' right arawnd the base, vhere it's pressing inta his headt. I didn't know vhat it culdt be, though. I chust hope it ain't maggots." (He pronounced it "makkets.")

Edgar peered again through the binoculars. "It's *right* against his head. One thing's for sure: I've got to remove it—absolutely." Then he said in a somber voice, "If we don't get it off, it could put enough pressure against his head to kill him in only a matter of a few days."

I shuddered.

"I think the best approach is to knock him out first so that I can examine the thing better. Maybe I can get underneath it with a gigli wire and saw it off. Or, depending on how it looks and how it's attached, I could use a hacksaw to cut it partially off and then snap the rest of it off with a screwdriver or pliers. But we've got to remove it—no matter how we do it."

"Yop. I agree," Bob said. His wife was nodding.

"Andy's pretty tame, right?" Edgar said. He took the syringe of xylazine out of his vest pocket. "Will he walk up to us if we walk into the pen?"

"No proplem, Doc," Bob said. "He'll walk right up to ya—thinks he's a person. Then, if ya can be real quick abawt it, stick it to him. He propaply voan't even know the difference."

"Gay, get some Betadine scrub and cotton in a stainless steel bowl and the screw worm spray, just in case." I turned toward the truck while Bob and Edgar entered the deer enclosure.

Yuck, I thought. Screw worm spray was for killing maggots. I hated maggots worse than anything. I considered the situation and determined that the likelihood of finding maggots on Andy's head was probably slim. I was hoping so, anyway.

Grabbing the materials, I unlatched the gate, closed it behind me, and crossed the pasture, following to where the men had disappeared into the woods. I couldn't see them in the dense foliage, but in the distance I heard a loud complaining and moaning. It was Bob, and I wondered what the problem was. As far as I knew, Edgar had slipped Andy the injection of anesthesia so easily that Andy hadn't even known it. So what could be wrong?

I didn't have long to wait.

The first one plunged into my left eye. "A-a-a-a gh!" I yelled, plucking the object from my eyeball with my coat sleeve. Then another one landed on my forehead. I shook my head to dissuade the attackers.

Within seconds I was surrounded, completely enveloped, by gnats—hoards of them. They thrived in the woods. When we had first seen Andy in the close-cropped pasture, the bugs were barely noticeable. Here, in the woods, they flourished. I was completely at their mercy, for my one hand carried the bowl of Betadine and cotton, and the other carried the screw worm spray can. I had nothing to swish them away with. Already they had begun to dive-bomb into my hairline, and I squinted so that they had a harder time attacking my eyes. The only other thing I could do was run, so I did—down the hill, over fallen branches and large stones—toward where Andy had gone down in an anesthetized stupor. But for only a few moments had I managed to outrun the swarm of gnats. Perched over the deer were Edgar and Bob, busily at work. Bob's wife stood to the side; her brow knitted both in worry for Andy and irritation at the gnats surrounding her own head.

Then the second battalion of insects flew overhead. "Ach, these damned gnats!" Bob roared again. A huge cloud was swarming around his bald pate like hungry pigs atop a corn pile. I had already jammed the screw worm spray into my sweatshirt pocket so that I had a free hand with which to swing at the bugs. But Edgar had asked Bob to hold each antler to prevent Andy from getting up unexpectedly, so his hands were tied—useless for batting gnats

Despite the insect attack, Edgar went to work, poking and probing the area beneath the lumpy tumorous growth.

"Ach, *no!*" Bob yelled suddenly. I thought perhaps it was the bugs that were finally getting the better of him, but then I found it was something worse.

Then I saw them.

Maggots! Hundreds of them—swirling and wriggling in a celebratory feast around the base and underneath that horrendous growth on Andy's head.

"Christ! Look at them all!" Edgar yelled, nearly as grossed out as Bob and I. "Quick! Give me the screw worm spray!" With that I yanked the can from my sweatshirt pocket and tore the cap off. Edgar grabbed it and sprayed its blue fluid all over the base of the offending growth. On contact the maggots began to die, their bacchanalian dance slowing to a fox trot as they swam in the sea of blue poison.

Meanwhile Bob and I battled bugs of our own. I only had a brief moment to note that very few gnats were bothering Edgar. How could that be? They were all over Bob, his wife, and me like buzzards on shit wagons. But there were none around Edgar.

"Oh, these gnats!" I cried. "Doesn't anyone have any bug spray?" I begged.

"Yeah, back at the haws," Bob moaned.

A few more maggots crawled from underneath the bony growth, and Edgar dispatched them with the blue poison. "Argh-gh-gh!" I yelled like a cartoon character in a bad situation. "Look at all the maggots! They're all over his head! And another couple are oozing out from this side of the antler," I said, pointing them out for Edgar to kill. Then in anger and frustration I swung my arm around my head to rid another swarm of gnats. What with all the gnats and maggots, I was squirming uncomfortably.

Edgar sprayed the area again, poking a finger up and under the horny growth, and said "I believe I can get the gigli wire between Andy's head and the mass. Then I'll see if I can saw it off."

"That sawnds gudt. Chust do it fast, Doc. These gnats are real badt, naw. They're biting me all over my hedt."

"You ought to have a cap on, Bob," Edgar offered.

"Too late naw," Bob said. "I chust haf to put up vit 'em."

Such a reaction was typical of a Pennsylvania Dutchman. One born of such ancestry must have had Elixir of Hardship coursing through the veins. Dutch farmers characteristically tolerated and endured a tough life on their farms, eeking a harsh existence from the soil under conditions that would have rendered the average person incoherent.

Edgar had set up the gigli wire. He attached the wooden handles to each end and, using the wire like a piece of dental floss, began to saw back and forth very quickly along the bottom edge of the tumorous growth. Faster and faster flew his hands, sawing, cutting through the horn so fast that a white cloud appeared—bony dust in the air. In minutes he began making significant headway. In another few seconds it would be off, and then we would be able to see what lay underneath the growth that had been pressing against the deer's head. Would there be a gigantic hole beneath where those hundreds of maggots had been feasting their way toward Andy's brain? Would there be more maggots—thousands, katrillions of milky-white pustule-like creatures—from where the first ones had originated? Had Andy's brain already been devoured, its neural sac now a writhing, throbbing home to some gigantic mother of all maggots? Would it be too late to save Andy? I tried to calm my overactive imagination.

"There!" Edgar yelled, and the lumpy growth popped into the air with the last saw. Immediately Edgar looked into the space in Andy's head that the tumor had been occupying for the last few months. The hole was soaked in blue fluid and dead maggots. Bob and I peered with dread into the cranial abyss. Edgar probed the hole with his fingers, but he still couldn't see properly, so I handed him the Betadine scrub and gauze to clean the site.

In moments Edgar smiled.

"I think we're in luck, Bob," Edgar said. "I can see pretty good. I don't think those maggots were really eating into his head. I think they were just feeding on the velvet on the underside of that tumor thing."

"Gudt! I'm so gladt naw," Bob hollared, shrugging his shoulders in a vain effort to drive off another swarm of gnats. He still held onto both ends of Andy's antlers. "I was so worried abawt vhat you'd findt dere, Doc. I vondered vhat vudt ve do if dere vas a bik hole there. How vudt ve keep da buks awt of it for the rest of the summer. You're sure there's no opening dere naw?"

"Yes, I'm fairly sure," Edgar said, poking the area. "There's actually fur there, under where the mass was."

Bob's wife had retrieved the tumorous growth, which had rolled away down the hill, and was examining it between swatting bugs. "Phew, it stinks! It must be from the rotting velvet (she pronounced it "welwet") on it. Ve're gonna save dis, Bob. After all, it's kind of a souvenir from Andy." She swung her arm around her head and said to me, "He vas our first born deer here."

By that time I had had all I could take of the blood-sapping gnats. I wondered how the animals tolerated them all day. Our gnats were bad at home, but they were nothing compared to the voracious bastards in Bob's woods. Then I thought about the squirming maggots that had been feasting on Andy's head. I shivered, and goose bumps paraded up and down my neck. I wondered about the deer ticks that were probably busily boring into our ankles and pants legs. I began to feel nauseous.

Suddenly I had an idea. Why hadn't I thought of it before? I had a hood on my jacket. Quickly I threw it over my head. Setting the Betadine bowl on the ground, I drew tight the drawstrings so that it gathered like a second skin around my face. My hairline and scalp were protected from the sucking incubi. Only my cheeks and eyes bulged out of the hood. I smiled, free at last from the biting devils.

Edgar had already gone back up the hillside toward the truck to get the long-acting penicillin and the reversal drug to bring Andy back out of the anesthesia, abandoning Bob and me to the unconscious deer and the gnats.

Andy was snoring obliviously on the ground. Amazingly no gnats were around him. In his stuporous sleep he was making strange sounds like those of a Geiger counter. "Rup-rup-rup-rup," he snorted in his sleep. "Rup-rup-rup-rup."

"Iss he all right?" Bob's wife worried. "He's not suffocatin' iss he?"

"No—he's just snoring," I said. "He'll be fine."

"Gudt. Yep, Andy vas our first baby," Bob's wife said with a maternal glow. "He'ss six andt a half years naw. He'ss the father of all our little vons. He andt Sunshine, his mate."

Finally, Bob could stand no more of the gnats sucking on his head. He let go of Andy's antlers and stood up, flailing his arms. Such a big guy, I thought—a *really* big guy. How nice it was to see such a large man completely enamored by an animal, particularly a deer. Most of the men I had ever met would rather have shot a deer than befriended one.

Bob remembered Andy from the time he was small. He batted the gnats from his scalp and said with a sweet grin, "Yeah, Mrs. Balliet, Andy was our first one. We raised him from a titty bottle." Bob pronounced "titty bottle" with a lilting voice—a truly motherly, doting tone.

Titty bottle? I giggled to myself. Titty bottle? The phrase was at once so delightfully sweet coming from a guy so big and masculine, and it was so unexpected from a man of Dutch descent. It wouldn't have been half as amusing spoken by Bob's wife.

"Titty bottle," I repeated to myself as my cheeks began to swell under the pressure of my hood's drawstrings. I hadn't heard those words since I used one of them on my Tiny Tears doll way back in the fifties. My grandmother would always tell me to give Tiny Tears the "titty bottle" whenever she started to cry. Then I stuffed the bottle's nipple into the doll's mouth, turned her upside down, and she would stop crying.

"Yep, we raised him from a titty bottle," he repeated with a dreamy smile.

Edgar came back down the hill. "Okay," he said, "I'm going to give him the reversal drug and a long-acting penicillin." After he darted the injections into Andy's hide, we waited alongside Andy to steady him as he came out of the anesthesia. It was then that I became aware of the tremendous heat building up inside me.

"Boy, it's hot!" I said.

"Well, no wonder you're hot. You're wearing a sweatshirt, and it's ninety degrees outside," Edgar said. "And you have your hood up besides. You're nuts!" He reached out to tweak one of my cheeks protruding from the edge of the hood.

"But it's a good thing I did wear it, considering all these gnats. All I had to do was flip up my lid and close it tight."

"Yeah, I wish I hadt a hoodt, too-a," Bob said. "These bugs drew bludt off my scalp, I svear."

Within a few minutes Andy was awake. He staggered to his feet and then carefully made his way down the hillside. Together, Edgar and I and Bob and his wife climbed the embankment out of the woods to the pasture and to the parking lot. Edgar began putting away the gigli wire, the stainless steel bowl, the spray, screwdriver, and wrench while I climbed inside the truck cab.

The temperature in the cab rivalled a sauna's, and hordes of gnats had found their way into the partially opened windows. As hot as I was, though, I sat there with my fleece hood tightened around my face. I would've rather been oven-roasted than eaten alive by the gnats. Finally Edgar sat down alongside me and started the truck.

He offered me little condolence. "Boy, do you look ridiculous," he laughed. Then he started the air-conditioning, and I batted the gnats out the windows. Seeing the coast was clear, I untied my hood and took off the sweatshirt.

"What happened to your eye?" Edgar said.

I turned around with a questioning look, then flipped down the mirror. I had survived the gnats, but one of the bastards had bitten me in the eyelid. It was swollen to twice its size, and I had a welt on my neck the size of a quarter. But if I had sustained that much injury from the gnats, what could poor Bob have suffered? His bald head was a veritable smorgasbord for the bugs. His scalp was probably as lumpy as a bowl of bread pudding.

"Okay," Edgar said, "let's get outta here. I could use something to drink. What do you want—iced tea or a soda?"

I was thinking of something else just then. I was thinking that the essence to decent existence is an individual's concept of himself as part of the global family of beings. I couldn't imagine myself a relative to gnats, especially ones so hungry for my flesh, but the relationship between Andy and Bob renewed my hope. Andy and his human family constituted real, hard evidence that the cosmic family ideology was working here. It may have been only microscopic evidence, but it was there.

Smiling, I thought about what Edgar had just asked. "Just my titty bottle."

"Huh?" Edgar said.

"Iced tea would be fine," I smiled.

Kenny

OUR CAT KENNY IS QUITE AN INDIVIDUAL. He is usually outside hunting mice or shrews, and when he's not, he's parked in one of our overstuffed chairs, basking in a ray of brilliant sun. He is a rather stout, beige-colored domestic shorthair with a charming, affectionate personality and an overwhelming *joie de vivre*.

"Oh, my goodness. What a beautiful cat!" my friend Karen exclaimed upon first meeting him. She scooped Kenny into the air, and he stared at her, nonplussed, flowing over her arms like a huge sack of cooked oatmeal. He was a big softy—of heart and of body because his flab made him doughy to the touch. Kenny appreciated the company of humans, begging to be held and carried around despite his size. Karen made little kissy noises in his face, and Kenny dangled, smiling at his captor. "He has the most beautiful eyes I've seen on a cat. And their beige color matches his fur so nicely."

"Yes," I agreed proudly. "I've always said Kenny had bedroom eyes." And, to be sure, his eyes did have that come-hither look incurable romantics have cultivated so well. That is, they were not totally round, as in the look of a Persian, but the top edge of each eyelid was drawn straight across, making his eyes look half-closed and flirty.

"Absolutely captivating eyes," she repeated touching her nose to his.

Little did we know that those eyes would soon be in danger of never seeing again. In fact, his entire life was at risk as well.

Kenny and I had a special relationship to which many cat owners aren't privileged. Considering that we were two different species, we were almost surreally in sync with one another, able to convey our deepest wishes and fears to each other, assured that one understood the other "purr-fectly."

People who are incapable of appreciating our relationship might ask, "How can you be sure your cat feels a certain way? How can you be sure he understands what you're thinking? I tell the doubting folks that I have no real proof, that some things will always continue to be a mystery, like magnetism or electricity. I attribute my knowledge of my animals to intuition rather than hard evidence. It evokes what a famous writer, William Hedgepeth, once said, "Some people feel the rain, others just get wet." I intuited what Kenny was thinking and feeling according to his body language and his feline language, and likewise he.

At bath time, in particular, the two of us rekindled our mutual adoration with a special, if not odd, bonding ritual. The minute Kenny heard the water splashing in the tub he sauntered into the bathroom where I was preparing for my warm immersion. I readied the sunken tub—chandelier glowing, steamy water pouring in, vanilla-scented bath oil dripping from a vial into the stream of water, music (New Age or Soft Rock depending on my mood)—piping through the speakers, vanilla aromatherapy candles lit, and travel magazines handy. Until the bath was filled, I sat perched on the edge of the sunken tub, my legs over the chasm of hot rising water, my feet propped on the opposite edge. My legs formed a bridge over the tub-canyon.

When Kenny recognized the "bathing position," he climbed the two stairs to join me. He loved the vanilla scent borne upon the mist of the steaming water. The crevasse formed between my torso and bent legs always attracted Kenny as a nice place to relax. He loved to sit upright in my lap above the steaming water as it rushed into the canyon below.

Before each bath ritual, I could be assured Kenny would magically appear at the entrance to the bathroom, curious as a child. He had no

ulterior motives other than to spend "soft" time with me. He sidled up
to me, perched over the bathtub, and then I scooped the big fellow up
into my arms and settled him comfortably in my "crevasse" while I
arranged his tail neatly beneath him. Then I serenaded him *a cappello,*
stroking him the while. He lifted his face, his large handsome cream-
colored eyes closing to slits, and smiled luxuriously like a little old lady
tasting a butter cream. I rocked him like a baby in my lap and sang and
hummed and talked to him while the tub below us filled. In minutes
he was mesmerized, totally relaxed, curling and uncurling his fisty-
paws in ecstasy. When the tub was filled, I gently lifted him onto the
carpet-covered step below the tub where he fell asleep.

But one day while I was singing and rocking my buddy over the
watery gorge of our tub, I noticed something strange. In his relaxed
stupor he leaned his head against my chest and gazed upward at me.

I stopped singing. Something was wrong. I took his head between
my hands and scrutinized his face. One eye appeared larger than the
other. He looked a little bit off-kilter—just a tiny bit.

I wondered if the aberration was real or a figment of my imagination.

My bath that afternoon wasn't nearly as relaxing as usual, considering my sleeping cat with the crooked face. It worried me. So when
Edgar came home, I asked him to examine Kenny. He agreed that the
left eye did seem *ever* so slightly bigger than the other. Edgar said,
"Give it a week or so to come around. If the eyes still look unbalanced,
take him to see Doc D. I have no idea why the two eyes are different
sizes."

I waited a week. But at the end the eyes were still out of whack, one
obviously more bugged than the other. Nothing was wrong with the
eyeball itself or Kenny's demeanor: he was still an incurable flirt with
those very luscious, smokey eyes of his. By the end of the week, the one
eyeball had begun to look even more popped than the first day I
noticed it. I began to dread that it could be a brain tumor or something. I called Doc D in Reading, and he saw Kenny that day.

Doctor D took one look at Kenny and definitely agreed that the eye
appeared more popped from its socket than the other. I cringed,
thoughts of the "Big C" clouding my head. It couldn't, shouldn't happen—not to my Big Buddy, my Kenny Man, my Kenny Mayonnaise.

"So, what do you think it is?" I said, wringing my hands.

"Well, it could be a hematoma—a blood blister behind the eye."

I sighed with relief. A blood blister wasn't deadly.

Doc D continued with a serious face, "Or, it could be a retrobulbar mass—a tumor behind the eye."

My guts felt liquid when he said the word "tumor." I tried to keep my voice steady as I pressed Doctor D for more information. "What do you think the probability is for it being a mass?" I asked, almost not wanting to hear the answer.

"Unfortunately the probability of its being such a tumor is about seventy-five percent. And, if it is a tumor, it would be inoperable, considering the placement within the skull."

"How much time would he have until . . ." I stammered, ". . . he died."

"I'm sorry to say that probably Kenny would not have very much time because of increased pressure on the brain."

I was absolutely devastated—struck stiff and dumb as a tree. There sat my Kenny Mayonnaise on the examining table looking as calm as if Doc D had just said he had a mild case of worms. Like an automaton, I scooped Kenny in my arms, thanked Doctor D, put the steroids and antibiotics he had prescribed in my pocket, and hurried to the car.

Kenny enjoyed the ride home, but I cried the whole way. I knew the eye wasn't going to get any better with the medication he gave me, which would do as much good for a tumor as would Vitamin C. The sound of Doctor D's voice was evidence enough, I knew, of Kenny's future.

Edgar was almost as upset as I by the news. He had been afraid it would be a tumor, too, he confessed, but unlike Doc D, he had another course of action.

"Well, what are we going to do?" I said. "We have to do something. We can't just let that pressure keep building up inside him."

He said, "Well, the only thing I know to do is to take him to the Hodges brothers for a second opinion. They're probably the only ones, short of the university, who can possibly help Kenny. I'll give them a call and set up an appointment."

The next day Edgar and I planned to take Kenny to Valley Central Veterinary Referral Service in Whitehall. Carlos and Ron Hodges are two veterinary brothers specializing in surgery and internal medicine respectively. Ron would be the one to diagnose Kenny's problem for certain, and if anybody could help Kenny—maybe operate on a hard-to-reach tumor—it would be Carlos.

Carlos was one terrific surgeon. Edgar and I had heard numerous stories of near miracle surgeries he had performed on needy animals. Our own case was just one of many, including back surgeries on dachshunds, every type of tumor removal, bowel resections, and orthopedic work that the local vets preferred not to get involved with.

I was so afraid Dr. Ron would look at Kenny and offer no hope, confirming Doctor D's diagnosis, that I didn't even know if I could take Kenny into the clinic myself. Edgar went with us.

When I introduced my loveable cat to Dr. Ron, the first thing he did was shake Kenny's paw and give him a kiss on the nose. A kiss—from a male veterinarian! Now Edgar's a compassionate vet, too, but I have yet to see him *kiss* one of his horse patients.

Dr. Ron (as he insisted I call him) handled Kenny gently, looking this way and that at his eye, inspecting his head on the right and then on the left, pressing his head, and talking in a soft voice the whole time. Kenny was pure putty in his hands; he loved the attention, and his paws kneaded in and out, in and out, in and out.

"I have to see another client now, but I'll be right back," he said, and he disappeared into another room.

The referral center was buzzing with activity, but Kenny wasn't upset as long as I or another person was with him; he trusted people completely. He was taking in all the sights and smells of the place: a Pomeranian with a bandaged hind leg who hobbled into the waiting room on a leash, a Siamese whining in a small box, and a Saint Bernard with a large blue bandage around his waist.

The veterinary hospital wasn't fancy—no impressive waiting room—but when we stepped behind the front desk, we could see the dedication and the medical expertise behind the operation that was Valley Central Referral Clinic. Dogs of various breeds were lying around the halls wrapped in blankets as they awakened from surgery done earlier that morning. Regaining consciousness in the hallway guaranteed that the animals were under constant supervision as the vets and techs traveled back and forth from the exam rooms to the operating room to the X-ray room. Never did an animal wake from anesthesia unattended.

The veterinary technicians' chores were to administer medication and rehabilitate the week's surgical patients. Each dog was taken outside for a short walk on a leash and a little fresh air; each cat was stroked and played with for a few minutes. Techs were hustling to administer medications and feed those in the hospital, and Carlos and Ron were busy counseling clients about their animals in-house and over the phone. Though the place seemed fast-paced, the vets did not hurry their clients or their time with their patients. They showed genuine concern.

It didn't take a whole lot more for me to realize that, in keeping with my cosmic familial idea, this was the epitome of a working familial relationship between humans and animals: each patient and his

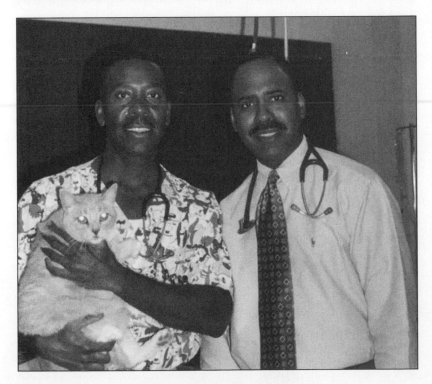

Carlos and Ron Hodges with Kenny
at Valley Central Veterinary Hospital

client were as important to the staff at Valley Central as their own family members were to them.

Since it was a referral clinic, all the animals presented there had already been through treatments with their family vet. When those treatments didn't work, when the animal's condition became too serious, or when the family vet was stymied for a diagnosis and treatment, then the Hodges brothers went to work. Valley Central was like the Last Chance Hotel. If the animals couldn't get the expertise and help they needed here, they weren't going to get it anywhere. The Hodges brothers were specialists in cardiology, gastroenterology, oncology, and orthopedics.

Since they had squeezed Kenny's appointment in, we had to wait while they consulted with other animals already on the daily schedule, so we were privy to all the goings-on in the vet clinic. I overheard Ron's phone conversation with a woman, one he didn't have very good news for. Her animal didn't have long to live.

"It's a real shame for Muffy," he said behind the closed door. "Had it been a different kind of cancer we might have stood a chance with the chemo, but this type is very bad and not very amenable to chemo. You'd only be wasting your money in a futile effort."

There was a pause. Then he said, "You'll know when the right time is. Muffy will let you know. These animals tell us when they can't hack it anymore. Believe me—you won't be wondering when to do it. She'll tell you. Let me know how she's doing next week. Give me a call. If you have any questions or concerns, let me know." There was another pause. "No, Mrs. Everett, we won't let Muffy suffer. I won't let that happen. And you'll call me when Muffy lets you know, do you hear?" He hung up the phone.

Down the hall Ron disappeared into an examining room. The consultation was muffled; I couldn't make out any words other than a thank you from the client and a promise to bring the animal in for surgery in a week. A few minutes later he reappeared. He took us to a back room, and after Ron examined Kenny again, he called Carlos over.

Carlos took one look at Kenny, and said, without a doubt, "No problem, Gay and Ed. Kenny Man here probably has an abscess behind his eye."

Before my mind had digested the good news, my guts had gone liquid again in anticipation of something bad. I felt like I had Lake Superior in my belly. Then as the realization of a silly, innocuous abscess took hold, the liquidy feeling dried up, and I could breathe again. A surgeon of that caliber was unlikely to be wrong. All of a sudden I felt stronger, taller, more able to deal with the situation, and I wanted to learn more.

"Terrific!" I yelled. He could see how relieved I was, and I hugged Kenny with his huge eye staring at me. "I'm ecstatic!"

Carlos said, "I would say ninety percent of these popped eyes are abscesses. Was he in a fight a couple of weeks ago? Did you see any scars over his eye—on the temple, maybe?" I shook my head, unable to remember any traumatic incident, any scar. Carlos said, "I've seen probably a hundred of these cases—most likely an abscess, but we'll do all the tests to see, first."

"What about a tumor?" I asked with less fear than usual.

"Unlikely, especially in a cat as young as Kenny Man," Carlos said. "The possibility is rare. Excuse me, I'll be right back."

Carlos disappeared into an examining room to see another animal. Ecstatic, I was shamelessly hugging Kenny and kissing his nose too. But Edgar reminded me not to get my hopes up too high until we ran more tests. Little did I know that I was about to experience an emotional roller coaster ride. Kenny and I were not out of the woods—not by any means.

When Carlos finished with his client in the examining room, he ordered a leukemia test run on Kenny. The series of tests Kenny had to undergo seemed to me like hurdles in a foot race. In 15 minutes the leukemia test had shown negative. Okay, one hurdle behind us, and we hadn't stumbled. Then the doctors ordered a white count on his blood.

"What's this business with the white-cell count?" I asked Edgar.

"If the white count is high, then there's probably an infection, which means an abscess, which can be drained and treated with antibiotics. A high white count would be good news."

I began praying for a big, juicy abscess.

Finally, after what seemed like hours, Kenny's blood readout popped out of the computer. Edgar gave me a big smile and a thumbs-up to affirm the high white count. I hopped around some more, so glad I would have Kenny for the rest of his life.

"Oh, no," Edgar said staring at the paper in his hands.

"What?" I shouted. I looked over his shoulder.

"Something's not right here," he said. "There's an overabundance of lymphocytes, not neutrophils, as I would expect to see with an abscess."

"Well, what does that mean?" I said, becoming agitated. Edgar's jaw had dropped.

"I'm sorry—this isn't as good as I initially thought," Edgar said. "All these lymphocytes—tons of them—in fact."

"What does that mean? I worried, clutching Kenny.

He looked at me with such a pained expression that I thought I would burst from the strain. "What does it mean!" I insisted.

"It's usually an indication of cancer."

"NO! Carlos said it was an abscess!"

"He said it was ninety percent an abscess. That leaves ten percent of something else. I was afraid you'd get your hopes up too high."

"Ask the doctors to take a look at the white count results. See what Carlos and Ron think. Hurry!" Edgar went back to the offices to show Ron and Carlos the results of the white count. I followed weakly behind, but my heart sank to my feet when I saw Ron's expression as he studied the paper. "Lymphocytes? Lymphocytes?" he said, frowning. "How can that be? Could be lymphosarcoma. What do you think, Carlos?'"

Carlos looked at it, and the same expression clouded his face. Doesn't look good with all those lymphocytes, unless the abscess has been in there for a very, very long time. Only that could cause the lymphocytes to be so high. Well, let's hope it's that, Gay. The next order of business here is to take a radiograph of Kenny's head. We might be able to tell a mass from an abscess on an X-ray."

Kenny, being the good boy he always was, allowed the technicians to position him just so underneath the X-ray machine to take a clear picture of his head. In five minutes a picture of his skull was illuminated on the light board. Carlos and Ron scratched their heads at the results. I was biting my nails. Carlos said, "It could be a retrobulbar tumor, or it could be an abscess. Can't tell from the radiograph. All it looks like is a soft tissue mass."

I cringed at the sound of the word "mass."

"Kris," Carlos shouted into another room. "I'd like you to prepare Kenny Man for an exploratory of the head—in about a half-hour." Then he looked at me, and I hurriedly wiped my tears, "Our only choice is to go in behind the eye and see if there's pus there. If when I lance it, pus flows out, we're in good shape. If there's no pus, then we'll decide what to do from there—possibly a biopsy of the material."

Carlos let Edgar and Kenny and me wait in his office until they were ready for Kenny. Kris, a vet tech, was readying the surgical area and wouldn't need Kenny for several minutes. Edgar tried calming me, but all I could do was project myself into the dreaded, single, solitary second when Carlos would stick the scalpel into the offending bubble in Kenny's head. In that second I would have an answer that would foretell either a long life or a shortened one for Kenny. If no pus flowed out, I would be devastated.

It's so difficult to be strong when the news could sound the death-knell for a best friend. Life is a gamble of the riskiest kind. I only wanted to ride the up side of the roller coaster, the one where a person seemed to be more in control, not at the mercy of chance, safety devices, and unfailing brakes. I dreaded the ride down, the one that transformed the guts to one of the Great Lakes. I sensed the selfishness welling up in me: I only wanted good news—refused the bad and all it forebode. In fact, I wanted off the roller coaster altogether. Just give me a nice, boring life—all on an even keel—and I could be happy.

Kris knocked on the office door, smiled, and took Kenny away.

Carlos invited Edgar to watch the procedure, so after Kenny was masked down and breathing the fumes of virtual sleep, Edgar donned scrubs and a mask. I waited just outside the surgical bay, out of everyone's way but close enough to see and hear the action going on inside.

After Kris had readied Kenny, shaving his head and applying Betadine solution to the skin, she situated him under surgical drapes beneath a large overhead light. Then she called Carlos. In a few minutes Carlos appeared from his office, the strings from the surgical gown flapping behind him as he strode toward the surgery. Like a concert piano player, he flipped his green tails from under him and sat down on what resembled a bar stool. With his back to me, I could see him pick out a scalpel from amongst the bed of surgical instruments. He spoke in low tones to the techs, warning them to be ready with gauze and towels in case he struck a pocket of pus in Kenny's head.

My poor Kenny Mayonnaise.

I bit my fingers and leaned into the doorway.

I couldn't see very much because Carlos' back was towards me, and he blocked my view of Kenny's body on the surgical table. But I could hear the conversations.

"Okay, just lift his head in a more vertical position. I need to open his mouth and get in alongside the soft palate."

Why is he going into his mouth? I thought. The problem was behind the eye.

"I'm going to make a small incision in the roof of his mouth. That should lead me to the mass behind the eye," Carlos said to Edgar and his technician. "Then we'll know what we're dealing with."

I held my breath. My innards felt like concrete and water at the same time. I strained to hear. Several minutes went by and seemed like hours.

Suddenly Carlos yelped.

I went rigid.

"OO—oo-oo-ooh!" Carlos yelled. I knew immediately what that meant. Carlos was seeing pus pouring out of the incision and all over the surgical table. I stood on tiptoe, trying to see and hear, and biting my lower lip. "It's an abscess!" Carlos said, looking up at Edgar and turning to me. "Okay, crew, let's clean it out, and then I'll sew in a drain."

"*YES!*" I chirped, hopping in place. "Yes . . . yes . . . yes!" I made quite a scene where I stood at the outside of the surgery—hugging myself and grinning like a mad thing. I couldn't help it; I was deliriously happy.

A suction machine began to purr, and with it the technicians used it to clean the river of pus pouring from its source in Kenny's head. "Okay, Ed," Carlos said to Edgar beside him in the surgery, "I'm going to create a path from behind the eye to this hole in Kenny's palate, and I'm going to put a drain in there so that until we get the infection under control with antibiotics, it can drain into his mouth. Unfortunately he'll end up swallowing all that stuff, but since we've cleaned it out, it shouldn't be making new pus much longer. In a week I want you to pull the drain out."

"Okay, sounds great," Edgar said through his mask. Then Carlos got up from his stool to reach for some gauze.

In that moment I could see Kenny on the operating table, and it was like a horrific cartoon. Kenny lay asleep, but his head was skewered through on a hemostat, a kind of long, metal surgical tweezers. The metal handle of the scissorslike instrument hung from the top of his mouth while its tip stuck up through his skull. Kenny's head resembled a furry shish-kabob.

Next Carlos reached for a rubber drain. With the hemostat he grabbed the end of the drain and then pulled the rubber tubing down through the head, first through the temple to behind the eye, and then down where the hole ended in his mouth. Deftly Carlos sewed the rubber into Kenny's temple area just anterior to his left ear. I heard the scissors *snip!* and Carlos leaped from the surgical stool.

"Okay, he's all yours!" he roared. "Looks great!" he said, giving me a big smile and a kiss on the cheek. I hugged him tightly, and he hurried out of surgery to his next patient. The techs cleaned the surgical site with Betadine, removed Kenny from the operating table, and placed him in a blanket in a cat recovery area. In a few hours he would wake up with his drain intact and his eye relieved of pressure.

Carlos had run off to attend another animal, so I asked Angie, one of the technicians, to tell Dr. Hodges how grateful I was that he fixed Kenny. "And I am sure Kenny will be just as appreciative," I said.

After fifteen minutes I scooped my drowsy cat into my arms, and Edgar draped our blanket around him. He was sleeping soundly and had no idea how he had gotten home when he woke up. But I was right there by his side when he did.

"How are you Kenny Man?" I cooed in a nursey voice. "Would you like something to drink perhaps? Some chicken soup?"

His eyes were still slits, but when I picked him up, he looked wonderingly about him. He couldn't feel the white rubber drain protruding from his left temple. The popped eye was miraculously back in place, inside its socket where it belonged, none the worse for the wear. Kenny looked curiously at me as if he had just had a dream, and I assured him that the worst was over. His eyes questioned me, and I smiled so that he knew all was right with the world. He blinked, looked, blinked again, then rested his head peacefully on my arm, closed his eyes, and fell back to sleep.

Kenny's eye problem disappeared completely after a week's course of antibiotics. A veterinarian can cure so many conditions with a simple treatment of antibiotics or steroids. Kill the bacteria—kill the disease. Reduce the inflammation—take away the pain. Surgery is another easy fix. Remove the blockage, and the function returns. Secure the bone, and the animal can walk again. Not all cases are that easy, but I sure am glad Kenny's was. I'll be able to gaze into those flirty eyes for quite a while.

Little did we know that another member of our immediate family would be facing a life-threatening problem.

Lowell

LOWELL WAS HALFWAY ACROSS THE DRIVEWAY to the house when we pulled in after a day's veterinary work. Edgar parked in the garage, but he had barely stopped the engine before I was out and running.

"Sweet cakes!" I yelled, squatting to his level and throwing my arms around my 200-pound pig. He squeaked a few notes of alarm, probably embarrassed by such an overt public display of affection.

Lowell put his snout in my armpit, his signature of trust. I stroked the coarse hairs on his back.

"Rep—rep—rep—rep—reep," Lowell muttered appreciatively, then started toward the house to escape the day's flies and gnats.

"Want to help me make some brownies?" I asked him, opening the door.

He grunted and stepped into the garage and up into the kitchen. Then he waited patiently for his cedar bed to be placed before the stove. He always enjoyed my cooking—especially brownies—so that he could lick out the bowl.

"You want to cook, too, don't you?" I asked him.

"Eeh–eeh!" he said, melting comfortably into the cedar sack. I watched him sink down and turn over on his side, his belly exposed. He grunted and rubbed the side of his face into the soft pillow.

Then I saw it.

I bent down and ran my hand over a nasty sore on the side of his belly. It was a large welt resembling a bull's-eye, the size of a Dunkin' donut, with a fifty-cent-piece-sized blood blister dead center. From the crimson center flared an aureole of red inflamed tissue. It looked angry and felt hot to the touch.

"Lowell, what happened?" I said.

He looked at me and stretched out, a front foot tucked up so that I could rub his chest better.

I rubbed my hand gently over the sore.

He flinched.

I reached for some antibacterial ointment and carefully smeared some on the spot. Funny I hadn't noticed it a day or two ago; it looked fairly old. Where did he get it? Maybe he and one of the other pigs had a fight. The sore was nasty, but like anything else, he'd get over it. In a week it'd be gone.

I didn't even bother to tell Edgar about it, especially since Lowell was in such a hurry for me to start the brownies. So I washed my hands, took the mix out of the cabinet, and grabbed a measuring cup. Lowell grunted and sat up, waiting to clean the bowl.

The next few days offered little excitement for me or the pigs. We sat out by the pool. I read; they slept. Ivy Mae and Annie Louise made their usual rounds checking out the crops in Nick's fields. Lowell's sore disappeared so uneventfully that I didn't even notice it go. Everything was business as usual.

A week later I was out at the pool when I noticed that Lowell had not yet appeared from the barn. I called and called, but he was slow to rouse that morning; he probably was up all night watching a late-late movie. Lucille, who usually was more lethargic in the morning than Lowell, was already making her way poolside. Where was Lowell?

I called again.

No Lowell.

Then I resorted to a dirty trick. I yelled, *"Pignic! Lowell, you're missing the pignic!"* The threat of my eating without him was something he just couldn't stand. As far as a pig is concerned—Lowell not the exception—stomach deprivation is a condition to be avoided at all costs. Finally, out he came, yawning, and . . .

. . . limping.

He was lame on the right front. With each step his head nodded when the lame foot hit the ground. Now what! I thought. Maybe he overtrod his ankle. Perhaps he had tripped somewhere and twisted his foot, or maybe he'd bruised the pads of his feet stepping out of the kitchen and into the garage.

Slowly Lowell made his way poolside, hesitating and chirping with discomfort with each step. Then he plopped down on his bed beside me and turned his belly into the sun. I kneeled down beside him, stroked his belly so that he could relax, and then took his right foot in my hands. He was nearly asleep, so he didn't mind when I pressed the pads of his feet to check for pain.

Lowell

No response. He breathed heavily, a prelude to sleep.

Gradually I worked my way up his right leg, pressing and prodding the bones and tendons all the way. He continued to lie flat out like a flounder: no discomfort.

But why was he so lame?

I continued up toward his elbow—no swelling, no pain response. Very strange. Well, I figured, maybe a stone had been caught between his claws, and it fell out on his way to the pool. Remove the obstruction; remove the pain. So I settled back, unconcerned, to my lesson planning.

That afternoon I called the pigs into the barn for their suppers. Edgar was busy feeding the horses their alfalfa, and I was already on KP duty heaping mounds of cat food to the barn cats. Annie and Ivy rushed to their houses for supper, and Lucille sauntered in from the pool.

Where was Lowell?

There *behind* Lucille was Lowell slowly making his way toward the barn. Whenever his right foot touched the ground, his head jerked like an old codger's noggin. "Hey, Edgar. Will you take a look a Lowell?" I called. "He's lame. See how he's gimping on that right front? He was doing that this morning, but when I felt all along his leg and foot, he showed no pain response. What do you think is the matter?"

Edgar squinted into the sun as Lowell measured each painful step into the barn. "Huh, he does seem to have a hitch in his git-along. I don't know. He probably just twisted it or something. If it doesn't come around in a few days, I'll give him Banamine for the inflammation."

Lowell carefully and deliberately stepped up into the barn. With each right-footed step his head bobbed. It was definitely the right foot.

"Yep, lame on the right front," Edgar affirmed. "It'll probably be all right in a few days."

Not even a hurting leg could dampen Lowell's appetite, however, as he stepped into his stall, went over to his feed dish, and plowed his nose right into his supper. I smiled. Edgar and I could hear the contented slurping from outside the barn as we walked back to the house.

The next day as Edgar pulled from the driveway to begin his rounds, I made my way to the pool, books in hand. Again I called the pigs to my side, and again Lucille emerged fresh and rested after her night's sleep.

Again, no Lowell.

"Lowell, pignic!" I lied.

In minutes my stout black fellow appeared at the barn door.

"Come on, Bud. We have a lot of work to do today. And I can't do it all without you."

He grunted and surveyed the ground in front of him. Then he stepped forward carefully, hitching and bobbing.

My heart flew into my throat, and I swallowed hard to get it down. Lowell was still lame, limping and jerking like Grampappy Amos McCoy. But there was something wrong with this picture.

Then I knew what it was: today he was lame on the left front leg, not the right front.

"What the hell!" I yelled. Finally Lowell managed to reach his cedar pig bed. "You poor thing!" I said, bending down and grasping his left front foot. I felt and prodded the foot and his leg, and he dutifully allowed me the examination. Not once did he twitch, even though I squeezed all the way up to his elbow. "Wait until Daddy gets home, Lowell. He'll fix you up. But why in the world are you lame on the other leg today? You don't seem a bit painful on the right one, at least not the way you were yesterday."

"I'll give him some Banamine," Edgar said, as he observed Lowell making his way painfully back to the barn that evening. "I can't believe he's lame on the opposite leg. He must have fallen on his knees or something, but then we should be able to get a pain response there. And, to tell you the truth, it really doesn't act like knee or foot lameness."

"Well, this is pretty weird," I said. "Why would his lameness be switching legs?"

"I don't know, unless he could be developing a laminitis. Did he get into a lot of feed lately, say about three days ago? It takes pretty much for a pig to founder, but I think it's possible."

"He didn't get into anything that I can recall. In fact, he hasn't even been out in Nick's alfalfa field lately. Yesterday I picked him some fresh alfalfa, but it was only a handful. You don't think that could have foundered him, do you?"

Founder, or laminitis, is a deadly condition for horses in which, because of overeating grain or rich grass, the bones of the horse's foot separate from the hoof wall, causing the foot to drop right through the sole of the hoof. An analgesic can reduce the pain and inflammation of founder, but the situation often demands euthanasia. Horse owners recognize the symptoms by the way the horse moves as if walking on eggs and by the way the animal takes a rocking horse stance with its front and back legs splayed apart.

Neither of us had ever seen founder in a pig, so we weren't sure what to look for. It was pretty obvious Lowell was only lame on his front end, though the lameness was switching feet. Perhaps Lowell was in the preliminary stages of laminitis. Perhaps he would be altogether dead lame on his front end in a few days.

Edgar scrutinized Lowell's gait and then said, "I'm going to call Arlen to see what he thinks. He can also give me the correct dosage of Banamine for pigs. I don't deal that often with pigs. I don't know how susceptible they are to laminitis."

I heard a one-sided conversation when Edgar called Dr. Arlen Wilbers of Quakertown Veterinary Clinic. Dr. Wilbers was the pot-bellied pig expert in the area. Lowell had seen Dr. Wilbers several years ago at Susan Armstrong's pot-bellied pig farm when he had twisted his foot. Since that time Arlen had made biennial visits to our farm to do corrective trimming on Lowell's feet. Like the Hodges brothers, Doc Wilbers was family to us and our pigs. "Yeah, two days ago he was lame on his right front," Edgar said. "Today he's lame on his left. It's the weirdest thing. Looks kind of like laminitis to me, but Gay says he didn't get into any large amounts of grain or anything.

There was a pause.

"Oh—unlikely in pigs? Huh. I didn't know." Edgar gestured, thumbs down, that the problem probably wasn't laminitis.

I sighed in relief.

"Okay, I'll give him two cc's of Banamine. No problems with that causing ulcers? Okay, I'll give it for three days and he should come around.

Another pause.

Edgar looked at me and took the receiver away from his mouth. "Arlen wants to know if Lowell got into any fights recently with any of the other pigs."

"No," I said. "Not that I saw."

"No," he repeated back to Arlen. "A septic arthritis? Very suscepti-
ble, huh? Well, he has no wounds on him that we know of. Okay, then,
I'll just give him three days worth of Banamine and see if that helps.
Thanks, Arlen. I'll keep you posted."

Edgar immediately went to the back of his truck and took a bottle
of the anti-inflammatory and a needle and syringe from the Bowie
unit. "Let's go, Gay," he motioned. "Lowell gets the first dose of
Banamine. I'll be giving him Banamine for two more days. That should
reduce any kind of inflammation. It will certainly reduce the pain, and
if it *is* founder, which Arlen doesn't think it is, then it will help with
that, too. Pigs apparently don't founder often—not like horses. But it's
still a possibility." I followed him to the barn to help him give Lowell
the injection.

Lowell did not appreciate our attempts to medicate him. When
Edgar hoisted him into the air and settled him on his back, like a tur-
tle stuck on his shell, he squealed and complained bitterly. It was summer, but I knew enough to protect my ears with a winter wool cap
from the splitting screeches of my pig. To save my eardrums, I could
brave the heat just as I had the gnats in Andy's woods.

The next day saw no improvement as Lowell hobbled painfully out
of the barn. I waited poolside. At one point he looked as though he was
ready to give up, turn around, and go back into his stall, but he didn't,
faithful to the end. It took him maybe ten minutes, but he finally made
it, heaving himself onto his cedar bed beside me.

That evening he struggled less when we gave him his shot.

I was really beginning to worry, so I called my friend, pet pig res-
cuer and connoisseur Susan Armstrong, hoping she could shed some
brilliance on the subject.

"What could it be, Susan?" I asked, my voice cracking over the
phone.

"I don't know, Gay. Probably it has something to do with his
weight, but I really don't know. Would you like me to come take a look
at Lowell? I'm not a vet, but I've seen enough pots to be able to recognize a few common problems. Maybe I could help."

"Would you mind terribly?" I said.

"Of course not. I'll be there tomorrow morning, say around nine
o'clock."

"That'd be terrific," I said, "and . . ."

"Oh," Susan interrupted. "I have a guest right now staying at the cottage. She's a wonderful woman, who lives with her pig in South Africa. She's here at my bed and breakfast for a week of vacation. Could I bring her along?"

"Sure, Susan. Your friends are always welcome here. Any friends of pigs are."

I slept fitfully that night, wondering what could possibly be the matter with Lowell. Morning came too soon, but I was out in the barn by five anyway. Lowell grunted, pushed himself slowly to a standing position, then hitched himself over to his feed dish. The pain certainly hadn't stifled his appetite.

I was in the kitchen preparing a mid-morning grape snack for the pigs when Susan's car slowed to a stop in the driveway. A petite, slim blond, Susan saw me in the kitchen and waved. She climbed from the car and with her a tall, lean, auburn-haired woman with a pixie haircut. I wiped my hands, grabbed a handful of grapes, and went outside.

"Hi, Susan," I said. "Haven't seen you for a while. Thanks for coming to see Lowell."

"Good to see you, too," she said, returning the hug. We were pals on a mission to make the pet-worthy pig a household concept. With a flourish, she presented her guest. "Gay, meet Ivanhoe Perelson."

"Nice to meet you, Ivanhoe," I said, half expecting her to unsheath a sword.

"Likewise," she said in an accent that sounded sort of British. "You have a lovely place here, Gay. And Susan tells me you have four potbelly pigs." Ivanhoe looked to the bushes, took a peek inside the garage, and glanced to the pool in search of one of the elusive critters. "I just love pigs," she said. "That's why I ended up at Susan's bed and breakfast."

"Yes," I said, "Susan told me over the phone yesterday that you have a pig, too?"

"Lucy—yes, Lucy is wonderful. But she's not a pot-belly as you people have in the States. She is an African pig," she said, whipping a picture from her shirt pocket. "Here's a photo of Lucy Einswine," Ivanhoe said proudly. She showed me a photo portrait of Lucy wearing a pair of granny glasses. She looked, indeed, the scholar.

I laughed. "Why don't we go inside before seeing Lowell? You're probably a little thirsty from the trip, and he's busy napping anyway. Would you guys like a Diet Peach Snapple?"

"Snapple?" Ivanhoe said.

"It's an iced tea." Susan said.

"Why tea would be lovely," Ivanhoe said as we walked into the house. "We Africaners love tea of any kind, you know."

I grabbed three bottles of Snapple, and we gravitated to the living room where Lucille was doing her couch potato routine. She lay on the sofa like a Hogarth hoyden, her body stretched comfortably, her toes pointed, and she grunted luxuriously when Ivanhoe sat down beside her.

"Does Lucy love to lie on the couch the way my Lucy does?" I asked.

Ivanhoe patted Lucille on her rump to which Lucille responded by hoisting herself into a better position for a full body rub. Ivanhoe took the hint and began massaging the soft belly skin. "Oh, Lucy sleeps between my husband and me at night, but she's not very content to just lie around all day. She's a bit of a corker, you know. She seems always to be getting herself into trouble.

"A few months ago she and I were engaged in a battle of the wits. Early on, when we first brought Lucy home, she discovered that more delicious food awaited her in the fridge than in her pig dish. It only took her a few weeks to realize that she could wedge her nose around the edge of the refrigerator door and, with a little leverage, open it. She always made sure no one was around to see, but one time I caught her in the act: she pried open the door from the side, pushed it open wide enough for her body, and then grabbed a pumpkin from the bottom shelf. When she turned around, I was standing there, arms akimbo, hardly able to contain my laughter, but putting on a good act of consternation. Then she took off into the living room with the pumpkin in her mouth, running full tilt, with me yelling and chasing after."

I laughed. "Thank goodness our guys haven't figured the refrigerator out yet. If they'd be in the house more, though, I bet they would. So how did you keep her out of the fridge once she had mastered opening it?"

Ivanhoe wore a knowing smile. "For a time we outsmarted her by

moving the deep freeze right next to the fridge so that she had no edge
to hook onto with her nose. And we thought we had outmaneuvered
her. For months Lucy didn't raid our refrigerated stocks, but little did
we realize that Lucy must have been doing some heavy trigonometri-
cal calculations involving leverage and force."

Susan smiled. "These pigs are pretty smart—too smart for our own
good."

Ivanhoe continued, "One day while I was pottering around in the
kitchen, I noticed Lucy on her knees about three feet from the refrigerator. Slowly I turned around toward her and watched her proceed to
leopard-crawl toward the fridge. She looked just like a wild cat stalking prey. In this case Lucy's prey was our cold box.

"I watched, not saying a word, and then finally Lucy pulled herself
on her belly up to the door and hooked the bottom ledge of the refrigerator with the tip of her snout. Then she put her leopard-crawl in
reverse. Very slowly she wriggled her body away from the refrigerator
with the door still caught on her nose. I continued to watch very quietly, not moving a muscle. I wanted to see where this action was leading. I knew anyway, but it was wild seeing her work, finessing that
refrigerator door so expertly. Lucy was so focused on opening that
fridge that she completely forgot I was there. After she had it open, she
got off her knees, walked up to it, and put her front feet on an upper
shelf.

"I was gobsmacked. Instead of grabbing whatever was tempting her
from the bottom shelf, she decided to look around inside the fridge
and take what was most appealing. Talk about one spoiled, fussy pig!"
Then Ivanhoe stood up, demonstrating in pig fashion what Lucy must
have looked like while perusing the contents of the refrigerator. "There
she stood, her body stretched out from her nose to her tail, with her
little hooves perched on the third shelf. She was sniff-tasting everything: a bowl of hard-boiled eggs, another bowl of pickled beets, and
half a salami sandwich. She could smell them right through the plastic
wrap. Finally, she made her decision—a box of strawberries.

"Very carefully she took the edge of the box into her mouth. Then,
keeping it level so that the strawberries wouldn't spill, she dropped
back to the floor and turned around.

"That's when she saw me."

"Oh," I said with a worried look, "I hope you gave her just a few for all her efforts. I'm a sucker for a hungry pig."

"Well, she took off running with the strawberry box in her mouth and me screaming in hot pursuit. In the melee she dumped the strawberries, then she turned around to face me. She was clearly annoyed and grunted a few pig curses at me.

"I told her, 'I don't care if you are angry, Lucy. You can't keep on raiding our refrigerator whenever you want to.' Oh, she was looking daggers at me as I raked the strawberries back into the box. Then I gave in. I just couldn't stand it. There's nothing worse than a pig's disdain. So I gave her a handful of strawberries."

I said, "But now what? How do you keep her out of the refrigerator?"

"Oh, my husband cut a strip of wood and nailed it right under the door ledge. Lucy's stumped for now, but she'll figure out something soon enough, I'll bet. These pigs are geniuses." Ivanhoe smiled and patted Lucille on the rump.

The closest Lowell or any of the other pigs came to getting into a cabinet or the like was when I had forgotten to let Lowell out of the house in the evening. I had become immersed in yard work, and when I finally popped into the house it was too late. Lowell was standing in the kitchen several feet away beside the opened pantry, his face as white as Casper's. "What happened to you?" I yelled. Then when I got up close, I discovered why the ghostly visage. "You got into the flour!" His entire face was white up to his eyeballs, and he looked as contrite as any ghost possibly could. I couldn't be mad; I could only stand there and laugh. In the opened pantry was a five-pound bag of flour with a snout-sized hole in it. Flour dusted most everything around it.

Musing on another tale, Ivanhoe said, "Now I have a cockatoo named Angel. The bird and Lucy are very jealous of each other. When I cuddle Angel, Lucy will complain and whine, trying to nudge him off my lap. And at other times, when Lucy walks past Angel while he's hanging on his rope, he will reach around and bite Lucy in the butt. That, I must say, hasn't happened since Lucy slap-jawed him once after he bit her. I think Angel learned his lesson."

"Birds are very intelligent animals, too," I said.

"No doubt about it—almost as smart as pigs," Ivanhoe agreed.

"And when a bird and pig get together and gang up on us humans, there's hell to pay."

"They act in league together? A bird and a pig?"

"Oh, yes. The two are like a brother and sister. I'll take Angel outside on a warm sunny day to play on his playgym. It sits up very high, and he can't jump off it to the ground. Yet, every time I go inside the house for something, when I come back, Angel is walking around the yard looking to get into trouble. He can't fly, doesn't jump or anything, so how was he getting off his playgym?

"Then one day I saw the culprit from inside the house. Angel was swinging on his playgym when I saw Lucy walk up and stand stock still under the gym. Don't ask me what kind of signal Angel gave Lucy, but it must've been some kind of sign because then Angel crawled onto his gym rope, clambered down it, and then just stepped gingerly onto Lucy's back."

"The pig let him get onto her back?" I said with amazement.

"Yep. Lucy stood still as this empty Snapple bottle here until Angel was standing in the middle of her back. Then very, very slowly Lucy walked over to the grass and lay down. With that," Ivanhoe said, smacking her hands, "Angel climbed down, walked over to the picnic table, and started pulling on the cloth. In a minute she had snagged the cloth from the table and along with it the salt and pepper shakers and an empty ash tray."

"Incredible," Susan chuckled.

"Yes," Ivanhoe said, "I thought so, too.

"Yet Lucy is jealous of the cockatoo when you pay him more attention."

"Yes, they have a great relationship—just like human siblings. They are jealous of each other; they like and play with each other; they snuggle side by side; and they make trouble together.

"Speaking of attention, you should have seen Lucy one day when I had a girlfriend over visiting. Lucy, just like a kid, expects all kinds of attention. Actually, she craves affection from anyone, even a stranger, but most of all, from me. To her I'm the Boss Pig or Alpha Pig; therefore, my admiration is most desirable.

"That day Lucy wasn't getting her share of the attention because Sarah and I hadn't seen each other for a while, and we needed to catch up on things. Well, this didn't set too well with Lucy who, I noticed out of the corner of my eye, was beginning to stage her very own hissy-fit. First, she came into the kitchen where we were talking and paraded around the table as if to notify me of her presence. I patted her half-heartedly on the rump. But that wasn't enough. Then she left for the living room. In a few minutes she was back. This time, involved in the conversation as I was, I neglected to pat her, even half-heartedly.

"When Sarah and I were finished and she was getting ready to leave, we walked into the living room. There, to my horror, was Lucy—all wrapped up in the telephone wire, wire that only an hour before had been attached to the bottom edge of the house walls."

"No!" I gasped. "She ripped the wires right off the wall?"

Ivanhoe laughed. "I don't know how I can still laugh about some of Lucy's mischief, and I probably wouldn't if it weren't for the fact that she's so ingenious about it all. That day with the telephone wire, she had her own little childish tantrum because mum wasn't paying attention to her. Lucy the rebel."

"How did you fix the wires?" Susan wondered.

"With a glue gun," she said.

"Did she continue to rip the wires after that incident?" I asked.

"What do you think?" Ivanhoe chuckled. "I had to call the telephone repairmen out to the house time and again. Every time Lucy wanted me to spend time with her and I couldn't, she took her vengeance out on the telephone wires.

"What did the repairmen say?"

"Well, at first they thought it all very cute—a pig having a tantrum. The first six times they came were all right. They still had a little trouble understanding how or why a pig would rip the wires off the wall. But they didn't understand Lucy's demand for attention, and there was no way I was going to convince them that a recalcitrant pig is much like a stubborn child. But the seventh time was the end for these guys. When they saw the mangled wires, they asked if it had been Lucy's fault again."

"What did you say?" Susan said.

"I lied. I said the cockatoo did it."

Susan and I sat back laughing. Lucille, too, grunted as if she could appreciate Lucy's stunts.

Ivanhoe pulled another photo from the pocket, the proud mum that she was. It was Lucy on the bed. "Lucy is built a lot differently than your pigs. She's slim, weighs about 50 kilograms, or a hundred ten pounds, and has long legs. What is notable about her is the curly hair in her ears. She's much like a Persian kitten: she has ear tufts."

I smiled. "She's extraordinary—like Rapunzel."

"Oh, I'm sorry," she exclaimed, "I have blabbered on too long. I don't want to keep you and Susan from examining Lowell. Sometimes I get so involved with telling people about Lucy, I don't realize it. And I miss her so much."

"Don't apologize. I want to hear about Lucy. Lowell's condition is stable, for now anyway. He's definitely not going anywhere today, so it's not like we have to hurry or anything. So, what does Lucy do all day in South Africa?" I said, patting Lucille on the rump.

"Well, since I've cut back on my work schedule, Lucy and I go to the beach outside Port Elizabeth, about ten minutes from where we live, for her daily constitutional."

Visions of great white sharks danced horrifically in my head. The species was noted for its man- and woman-eating predilections.

"We always swim in a tidal pool there where there's no threat from sharks." She drew another photo from her shirt pocket. Lucy was swimming, submerged to her neck, in the sea. "As I said, the regulars at the beach know Lucy by name.

"The beachies simply go crazy over her! And Lucy definitely thinks they are all there purely to see and make a stink over her. Crowds gather to watch her swim in the tidal pool, and they talk and play with her like they've never seen such a wonderful creature in their lives. She's the talk of the town."

"That's great PR for pigs, then, right? Folks in South Africa might be more inclined to have a pig as a pet in their life after meeting Lucy."

"You might think so, but I doubt it—not in South Africa. Oh, no, I don't think so," Ivanhoe said with a sly smile. "It's far different from here in the States. In South Africa there are no associations or rescue centers for pet pigs. And people don't educate themselves before they commit to owning one. When they find out what owning an animal this smart takes, they just set them loose in the middle of the city or in the country and let them fend for themselves. Things are not the same for pigs in my country as they are for pot-bellies here. What these animals have to endure is shameful. But Lucy is my girl. She's my best friend.

"Why don't we go out to the barn and see how your pig child is doing," Ivanhoe offered. We said good-bye to Lucille still prostrate on the sofa, and then we walked into the barn where Lowell lay napping in his pen. I hated to wake him and coax him to come outside when I knew he didn't feel well. Susan said, "Gay, Ivanhoe is a pilot. What do you fly again?" Susan asked her.

Ivanhoe looked slightly embarrassed. "Well, I'm rated in fixed wing and helicopter. I used to fly a Helio. Now, in my job flying for the police unit in Port Elizabeth, I fly a STOL aircraft, which is good for short take-offs and landings." Then a slight smile spread across her face. "As of only a few years ago I was the first woman in all of South Africa to be rated in both kinds of aircraft."

"Wow," I exclaimed, "I once took flying lessons on a Cessna 150, but when I knew the instructor was about to solo me, I quit, just like that. Big chicken, that's all. Figured I'd kill myself."

"You probably wouldn't have killed yourself, but some people aren't as nuts as others are to fly a plane. You probably didn't really care for it."

"Who knows," I said, dismissing the subject. "My husband, though, managed to finish his lessons, and he's certified to fly IFR, too. But he flies purely for pleasure and for breakfasts: he's always flying with a buddy in search of a good plateful of shit on a shingle."

"Sounds yummy," she laughed.

"Oh," I giggled, "You might know it as creamed dried beef on toast."

"Gotcha. My husband and I are both pilots. He's still flying full time, but since I got Lucy, I cut back my hours considerably. She's a priority, as is my teenage son. And I also do a little sculpting." She popped another picture from her pocket.

"Wow," I said, "you are really talented."

She handed me the picture. "This is my sculpture of Lucy in bronze. I've been commissioned to do one like it for a man in the United Kingdom. I'm almost finished with it. How do you like it? Do you think it looks like Lucy?"

"To a tee," I cheered. Indeed, the sculpture was beautiful, Lucy's every sinuous line and length of bone detailed with finesse and, I could see, with fondness. Ivanhoe was a true artist. "The detail is meticulous, and the ears are so characteristic."

"Thank you," she said smiling.

"You capture a pig's essence exactly," I continued. "The stolidness, the determined look in the eye, the brave stance."

"Yes, well, pigs are wonderful animals. We're so tickled to have Lucy as a part of our family. I simply sculpt what characteristics I see in the animal. A sculptor can hardly have a more admirable subject."

"You can see in Lucy's eyes the capacity for kindness as well as integrity. There's a hint of affection, wit, and intelligence there, too."

Ivanhoe was blushing. "Thank you so much. Pigs are such deserving animals. It's truly the animal's doing. I only transcribe what I feel about the animal into a statue, all the while hoping that my feelings towards it are truly reflected in the piece. I want people to become enlightened, I guess. My goal is to make them realize that a pig is so much more than a beast to be killed and eaten. It's so unfair the horrible lives we people force these good-natured, loyal animals to bear. And the pig is so undeserving of such inhumane treatment. It's such a shame."

Susan was nodding her head.

I had found one of my global sisters in Ivanhoe, and I already felt I knew her Lucy as family. It was amazing.

"Yes," I asserted, my hackles raised at the world's injustice. "They are every bit as deserving of the rights of a pet, as a dog is—more so, perhaps. They should be so lucky as to attain non-edible status."

"Something I'm afraid most people are ignorant of, unfortunately. Anyway, I was so eager when Susan said we would be visiting you today. I'm trying to visit as many pot-bellied pig farms as I can while I'm here. She said that you have some pretty remarkable animals."

By then Lowell was awake. I coaxed him from his stall with the bunch of grapes I had been carrying since Susan had arrived. He lunged from his house, taking wincing little steps with his front legs. I felt so bad for him in his pain. Even the analgesics Edgar had given him didn't seem to have done much good.

"Oh, my," Susan said, watching Lowell take a few steps. "He really is lame." She watched him for several more steps as I lured him with the grapes to the end of the barn. I hated making him walk when he was in such misery. He even seemed worse than he had been earlier in the morning. "He doesn't seem to have Dippity Pig," Susan said.

"Dippity Pig? What the hell's Dippity Pig?"

"It's a lameness condition where, when they're walking along, they just fall over crying. It's supposed to be a skin condition. I also don't see the telltale signs of Dippity Pig on his back. In the later stages, they can get a big crusty sore down the middle of their backs."

"Kind of reminds me of shingles in people," I added.

"Sort of," Susan said. "Usually the Dippity Pigs come around on their own. They—whoever 'they' are—think it may come from a poisonous weed in a pig's pasture. I don't think Lowell has that."

"Does it look like anything else you've ever seen in pigs?" I prodded.

"So lame on the front end, switching from one side to the other? No. It could just be that he's real sore on his front feet, but then that doesn't account for the switching pain."

"No, it doesn't," I said sadly. I thought Susan might have been able to help me, and I appreciated her effort. But we weren't going to discover Lowell's malady any too soon, I was afraid.

"I'll be honest, Gay. I just don't know. You have been in touch with Arlen. Maybe you should have him check Lowell out, not just talk with him on the phone."

"Yeah—if Lowell's not any better by tomorrow, maybe I'll give Arlen another call. This is really starting to worry me. Pretty soon he won't be able to move at all."

Susan and Ivanhoe stared down at Lowell, who had come to a complete halt in the middle of the barn—uncharacteristic behavior. Pigs always had a goal; they didn't just stop. Finally, I coaxed him with more grapes, and Lowell obediently struggled into his pen. Then Susan, Ivanhoe, and I left the barn. Conversing over a couple more cold Snapples, I showed a few pictures of my own pigs to Ivanhoe. We traded e-mail addresses, and after a while Susan and Ivanhoe crawled back into the car and left.

I let Lowell sleep all day, thinking the rest would do him good. That evening he hobbled from his pen, slurped his dinner, and crawled back inside.

The next morning I poured Lowell's feed into his dish, but he made no attempt to eat. I bent down and crawled inside his little house alongside him, pushing and shoving his butt to get him to stand. But he flatly refused. I ran in tears to the house where Edgar was in the den sorting out his calls for the day.

"Lowell won't get up for his breakfast! I can't get him to stand up at all! Please help me get him up. Maybe he'll stand for you. He's more intimidated by you. You can get him up somehow."

I knew I couldn't possibly lift a two-hundred-pound pig in the air, and it would be a daunting task for Edgar, too. But perhaps Lowell just needed the threat of being hoisted to make the effort to rise on his own. If anyone could do it, Edgar could.

Edgar strode out to the barn, me in tow. He bent down and charged into Lowell's stall, warning Lowell to *"Get up! And get out!"*

Lowell struggled to rise, but only his back end seemed to be doing anything. He thrashed and lurched forward, and the straw flew behind him. Dust filled the air of the small pig house. Again Edgar slapped Lowell's backside, urging him in an authoritative voice to *"MOVE IT!"* But my poor pig simply could not move himself. Frantically he tried, his front legs straining in front but incapable of supporting his weight. Edgar pushed, trying to help, but Lowell cried and whimpered as if to say, "I'm trying! I'm trying, but I can't do it!"

"Oh, my God!" I cried. "He can't move at all now! What in the world is wrong with him?" And then my foremost worry flooded my brain. "He's not going to die, is he?"

Edgar emerged from Lowell's house, his hair sweaty and dirty with straw particles and cobwebs. I bit my fingernails, and tears streamed down my face.

"He can't move," Edgar said the obvious, striding from the barn. "The Banamine isn't working. I'm going to start him on antibiotics, just in case it's some kind of infection or something. And I think we better call Arlen to come up here and take a look at him tomorrow. This is the weirdest thing I've ever seen. Simple lamenesses don't switch legs or ignore powerful drugs like Banamine. I'm going to call Arlen first, then we'll give Lowell some Bactrim."

"How's he going to go to the bathroom?" I shouted. "He hasn't gone since yesterday afternoon before he had his supper. "It will kill him to go in his pen. He'll burst before he soils his house."

Certainly the most imminent problem was "Would Lowell ever be able to walk again?" or "Would Edgar have to put Lowell to sleep if he could never walk again?" Instead of facing those horrors, however, I chose to focus on his elimination problems. Lowell's potty problems were decidedly easier to deal with than any terminal condition.

Lowell didn't budge from his house the entire day or night. At mealtime I tilted his feed dish toward him, and he ate, lying down, with his usual vigor. Then I offered him water. Throughout the day I brought him non-caloric snacks—celery, lettuce, an apple—which he ate with enthusiasm.

Nor did he get up for his breakfast the next morning. That afternoon I waited anxiously for Dr. Wilbers to come. When he'd received Edgar's distress call, he'd said he would fit Lowell into his schedule, a real favor since he was an hour and a half drive away. Edgar, too, rearranged his own calls so that he could be home when Arlen arrived.

When Arlen pulled into the driveway, I rushed out to meet him. His complacent manner helped calm me, helped stave away the euthanasia images that clouded my brain. "How's our fella doin'?" Arlen said matter-of-factly.

"He can't get up at all now," I moaned. I hurried into the barn, and Arlen followed while I updated him on Lowell's condition. "Edgar can't get him up either, which is really bad because he's afraid of Edgar." Then I said, "And I'm so worried because he hasn't gone to the bathroom for almost two days now. He must be almost ready to explode."

Arlen laughed. "Oh, don't worry about that. Pigs can hold their manure and urine for up to three days if they want to. And the reason why Lowell probably wouldn't get up for you is because you are no threat to him. In a pig's scheme of things, everybody has a ranking—from the weakest, least powerful, to the bosses. If anything, he considers you just another pig—a peon pig, in fact, an underling. He won't trouble himself for someone he considers his subordinate, especially if his legs hurt him.

"Now his refusing to budge for Edgar is a little bit different because to Lowell, Edgar is King Pig. Edgar ranks pretty high on the social scale, but Lowell is not intimidated enough, even by the King Pig, to trouble himself to move.

"I, on the other hand," Arlen said, smiling and throwing out his chest importantly, "am the Emperor Pig. You remember how afraid he is of me when I trim his nails and tusks? I am snout and tail above both of you in terms of Lowell's analysis of me. Considering that, I just might get this pig to move. Let's see what he does when he sees me."

By that time Edgar had joined us in the barn. "Emperor Pig, huh?" he repeated, laughing. "You mean to say I'm only the King Pig around here?" he joked. "Okay, Emperor Arlen. Let's see you move that two-hundred-pound beast."

With that Arlen took a deep breath and stepped inside the entry-way to Lowell's house. Immediately I heard Lowell chomp a warning. Though Lowell hadn't seen him yet, he had recognized Arlen's voice and knew he was in trouble. The Emperor had arrived and the peasantry was without any weapons.

"Chomp, chomp, chomp, chomp," went Lowell's jaws. "Clatter, clatter, clatter," went his teeth.

"Here we go," Arlen said, and then he disappeared inside Lowell's house.

An enraged squeal sounded from the little house, and in two seconds Lowell burst through the door of his house.

But he wasn't walking with his front legs.

"My God!" I yelled. "He's using his snout to walk instead of his front legs!"

I couldn't believe my eyes. In his desperate need to get away from Emperor Arlen, Lowell had ingeniously decided to use his snout to propel him away from the human monster.

Lowell lunged toward the door of the stall, and Arlen emerged behind him from the house. First, Lowell jammed his nose into the sawdust floor, and then he moved forward with his back legs. Once the back legs were up as tight against his front end as they could get, he released his snout, stretched his neck forward, and planted it securely in front of him again. And he was doing this all as fast as he could.

It was a strange and altogether pitiful sight.

"He's using his nose to walk like someone would use a cane," I cried. "Oh, Arlen, what could be wrong with him?"

Arlen watched Lowell move frantically out of the stall and into the barn. Lowell was trying to escape the Emperor, but he also had another dire need—the urge to go to the bathroom. Using his cane-nose, Lowell swiftly made his way into the indoor riding arena where he was accustomed to "making his potty." Edgar and Arlen watched carefully, noting the helpless, crippled front legs. Then Lowell stepped with his snout into the arena and promptly steadied himself against the wall to urinate.

Lowell peed, and peed, and peed. He peed with no sense of embarrassment or shame—very uncharacteristic. Then he hobbled, his nose leading the way, a few feet away, and made his manure.

"I think we're dealing with a septic arthritis here," Arlen said, "but I want to examine him closer. We'll just wait until he does his duty and he's feeling a bit more comfortable. Then I'll flip him on his back and feel his joints."

I bit my lower lip. "Septic arthritis? What is that, and how does he get it?" I asked.

"Pigs are very susceptible to it. We call it blood poisoning in humans. The pigs suffer a wound, usually, and the site becomes infected and spreads to the blood. Then the blood infection travels and invades the larger joints. That may have been why you guys couldn't elicit any pain in his feet, ankles, or elbows. It normally attacks the large joints like the shoulder. That's why I want to examine him. I want to stretch out those front shoulders to see if he's painful there.

"It appears to me that he's very reluctant to advance the legs at all. They just dangle there in front of him. He's innovative enough to use his nose to walk, but I'll bet the trouble is in the shoulder. That could also be the reason he's not lame behind. His hind legs haven't been affected yet."

"Yeah, now that you mention it, he wasn't throwing his legs out from the shoulder. Interesting," Edgar said.

As Lowell balanced himself between his snout and his hind legs, Arlen stepped into the arena beside Lowell. Lowell let out one short squawk as Arlen hoisted him into the air and slid him onto his back. Lowell yelled and squealed as though the devil himself was upon him. Then Arlen grabbed a front foot and pulled forward, an action normally performed by the shoulder. Lowell's voice became higher-pitched.

"Yep," Arlen said, demonstrating again. Lowell's voice raised another octave. "Look—it's septic arthritis. It's in his shoulders." Arlen rolled Lowell upright, and Lowell stepped away, balancing again with his nose.

"Can you use Baytril on pigs, Arlen?" Edgar asked. "I had started him on Bactrim, just to cover all the bases when the Banamine failed."

"Bactrim is okay. But do we use Baytril on pigs? Absolutely! Do you have any? We might as well use your stuff, if you have it. At least that'll save you that much on the cost of my visit. Give Lowell a good, healthy dose—say about eleven cc's."

Edgar ran to the truck. He came back with a filled syringe. Again Lowell was hoisted into the air. This time the King Pig did the lifting and the injecting.

"Good job," Arlen said, congratulating Edgar. "That was 22.7 milligrams per milliliter stuff, right?"

"No!" Edgar yelled, his eyes wide. "It was 100 milligrams per milliliter! Will that much Baytril hurt him?"

Arlen laughed. "Wow—that is really a whopping dose, then. That's actually a single-dose therapy for a 200-pound calf for three days! But it won't hurt him. Just skip the Baytril tomorrow, and then give him an injection every other day." Arlen chuckled, "I just assumed your Baytril only came in 22.7 milligram per milliliter. I didn't even know Bayer made it in that strength. He'll be all right. He should be coming around in the next day or two. I wouldn't worry about him if I were you, Gay."

"Thank goodness," I said with a sigh of relief. "Arlen," I said, "What did you say could have given Lowell septic arthritis."

"Usually it's caused by a wound of some kind from a fight with another animal. Did you notice any marks on Lowell's skin? Big welts or anything?"

I tried to remember, and then it hit me: the angry red welt on his belly.

"Yes!" I blurted. "Now I remember! A couple of weeks ago I noticed a bad sore on Lowell's belly. I never saw him fighting with any of the other pigs, but that doesn't mean he didn't get into it with one of them. It was really red and had a kind of halo around it. I put some antibacterial cream on it and forgot about it."

"There you go," Arlen smiled. "That's probably what did it. Just keep him on the Baytril. Once it's treated, septic arthritis clears up rapidly. I suspect he'll be just fine in two or three days."

Lowell stood like a statue in the indoor arena, balancing his front end with his nose.

I smiled, knowing my dear pet would walk again. Then I said to Edgar and Arlen, "Well, if Your Highnesses wouldn't mind—could you please persuade Lowell to walk himself back to his house. I'd prefer he not be stuck out here all night."

With that Arlen stepped behind Lowell. At the Emperor's urgings, Lowell used his nose cane to hurry back to his house.

The past few days had had me convinced that my global perception of family could be meaningful in real life. Only recently I had added onto my family with Susan, Ivanhoe and Dr. Wilbers. They were all animal lovers; they respected and regarded each other and their pets as part of a larger family of beings. And the South African town of Port Elizabeth enjoyed Ivanhoe's pig, Lucy, as one of their own.

I mused. What about gnats and other annoying insects being part of the family? Well . . . in anyone's immediate family, aren't there always detractors—siblings that are endlessly annoying but still have their place and importance in the home? But the biggest part of the puzzle had to do with human appetite. How could I reconcile the interspecies family concept with meat-eating humans and other animals eating each other?

It wasn't even three days before Lowell was walking again. The second morning he literally burst from his house. He had proudly stopped using his nose cane and was maneuvering just fine on all four legs. I thanked Edgar for all his help, then called Arlen to tell him the good news.

"I would like to speak to Emperor Arlen," I said to the receptionist at Quakertown Vet Clinic.

"Emperor Arlen?" the questioning voice said.

"Yes," I said. "The Emperor of the Pigs—Dr. Wilbers."

"Just a minute," the woman said in a tentative voice.

I heard laughing in the background and Arlen answered the phone, "Hi, Gay. How's Lowell?"

"Good as new!" I said. "He's back to normal: walking on his front legs and eating, instead of walking, with his snout. I wanted to give you a progress report and thank you for coming up here the other day."

Then I laughed, "I know I, a mere peon of pigs, shouldn't expect such special treatment from you—Thou ruler of the swine empire—but I do appreciate it, just the same. And Lowell, I'm sure, is equally happy."

A Foal

WHAT A SHAME THAT NOT ALL ANIMALS are fortunate enough to have as caring and concerned owners as Lowell had. Part of it may be in the luck of the draw, but the other part lies in the irresponsibility of people themselves.

We just left one of the area's most immaculately kept riding academies where the driveway was paved and landscaped with rhododendrons, and the horses, wearing the equivalent of equine exercise suits, were bedded down in clean, billowy sawdust. In contrast, when we made our way to the Dreck property, we slithered along the mud-pudding lane toward a run-down barn. The four-wheel-drive kicked into gear as we careened dangerously toward the broken-down horse fence. Seconds before we would have hit, Edgar spun the wheel, and we plunged into and back out of the ditch beside the drive.

"This place is always a friggin' mess," Edgar growled, wrenching the steering wheel back onto the mud lane. "This place is a disaster waiting to happen. Just look at the dilapidated fence and beat-up pastures. Poor animals that have to live here."

As the wheels dug for purchase, the truck slipped in and out of the gouges carved by previous vehicles. Edgar was right: the fence was a flimsy concoction of mere two by four rails with at least every fifth section of fencing missing boards or hanging askew. Such a fence was notorious for entangling and wounding the horses they were meant to contain safely. A two-board widely-spaced fence was not de rigeur for containing horses. If one board fell down, an animal bent on escape could step over the lower board or crouch under the upper board.

Besides the lousy fencing, the pastures were in similar disrepair—mere mud holes. Not a patch of green was visible, just the muddy-deep hoof-holes that pock-marked the lava-like flow that should have been a lush field of fescue and bluegrass. Horses armored in muck stood at the farthest corner of the "pasture," straining their necks after sparse grass blades on the other side of the fence. But even that little bit of grass had already been nibbled down to a nubbin.

In contrast to the horses' poor accommodations, I noticed, the Drecks certainly didn't lack for luxuries. A two-story brick colonial stood massive and muscle-bound against the weakling of a barn. Parked in front of the doorway on the circular drive stood a silver Lincoln sedan, and behind the house I could see a large greenhouse-type structure that surely sheltered an indoor swimming pool.

Our truck slewed up the lane and came to a stop at the ramshackled barn that listed like a sinking tug boat. A pile of garbage burned sluggishly next to the open barn door, and its noxious fumes curlicued down the aisle. The stable was heavy with the stench, and I grimaced, covering my nose and mouth as I entered the smoke-fog.

I peeked into the stalls, surprised to find each one empty of manure and, oddly enough, horses. At least by being outside they didn't have to breathe the acrid pollution sifting slowly from the garbage pile. I side-stepped a manure wagon bursting at the seams with urine-soaked sawdust and horse droppings. By the smell of it, it must've been sitting there with its ripe load for several days. Edgar followed as I searched for our patients: a mare and her newborn foal.

For routine births Edgar likes to do a general exam on the foal and take a blood test for colostral antibody levels. Of course, if the owner reports anything abnormal with the foal or mare, then he goes straight off to check them. But as a matter of routine, he checks after 12 hours to see if the foal received the proper amount of colostrum—its lifeline, the part of the mother's milk that gives the foal immunity against diseases that can strike in the first few weeks of life. A foal that doesn't get the sticky yellow colostrum that precedes the regular mare's milk is in danger of contracting a life-threatening illness. Many times foals that fail to nurse right away and are deprived of colostrum need plasma transfusions in order to live.

Another part of the routine foal check is giving the baby an enema to remove the meconium—fetal feces—and to "get things going." Edgar also checks the heart and lungs and drenches the umbilical cord with iodine to prevent a disease called "joint-ill." He checks the eyes and head for possible trauma sustained during birth, and he checks the legs for deformities and for a condition called "windswept legs," a problem in which the legs lean in one direction and resemble the branches of a tree molded by a constant one-directional wind.

After stumbling over a pitchfork, I found our patients at the far end of the barn in a stall too small for both a mare and foal and with too little straw for bedding. The chestnut filly was probably one of the biggest foals I'd ever seen. Unfortunately, she was a victim of her own size as she struggled on gangly legs to nurse from her mother's udder. When she stood alongside the mare, the foal's head was nearly even with the mare's back. She was on stilts that kept her body way above the udder so that to nurse she had to bend her front legs back and dip her neck and head down and then up into the milk-filled bag. It was hard enough for the filly to remain upright, let alone get milk.

Edgar was already visually checking the foal as the owner, Mrs. Dreck, walked into the barn. He took the stethoscope from around his neck and headed into the stall. The owner, oddly enough, did not follow him into the stall. The small-statured, thick-ribbed woman with a peroxide hairdo answered all his questions from outside the stall where she stood alongside me.

"When was she born?" Edgar asked, sidling quietly up to the foal.

"Sometime this morning, I guess," Mrs. Dreck said with nonchalance. "I checked the mare at three this morning, and she looked like she was going to foal any minute. When I woke up at nine-thirty this morning, I had breakfast and then came right out here. And there the foal was."

"So you don't really know when she was born? Did you notice if the baby was dry or wet when you saw it?" he said, trying to pinpoint a more exact time of birth.

"Dry."

"Then it was probably born very early in the morning—more toward three. You said when you called the office that the foal was suckling, correct?"

"Oh, yes. She's been nursing."

"Are you sure?" Edgar said watching the milk streaming freely from the mare's teats. Again the baby stumbled over to her mother's side and reached for the udder. Edgar crouched down and shined a tiny light up at the mare's bag as the foal attempted to nurse. He suspected that she had not nursed at all. He was suspicious because when he felt the mare's udder, it was still dirty and crusty—unlike a rubbed-clean one that had been nursed from. This mare's udder had a year's worth of dirt and debris build-up.

"Yes, I'm sure she's nursed," she said adamantly. She looked annoyed.

"I don't think she has," Edgar replied. "She's probably just a little slow to figure out how to manage her legs so that she can get in there. Then again, she could be a dummy foal—especially if the birth was long or hard. You don't know if it was a difficult birth, right? If it was, she could have suffered brain damage." The foal circled its mother on stick-like, trembling legs, and with each step her big knees threatened to buckle.

"We've got another problem here I should have known about hours ago. She's also windswept in her legs, and she's beginning to knuckle over in the knees. See, here?" He rubbed his hands over the protuding kneecaps. "You'll have to massage her knees like this every few hours to keep the knuckling-over from getting any worse." He demonstrated on the baby the proper way to massage the legs. As he rubbed the knobby knees, the foal sniffed Edgar's head. She made no attempt to escape and wasn't at all afraid.

"I want you to do this every few hours for at least a week," Edgar repeated. "Then I think her legs will come around nicely."

Silence.

The woman clung to the gate from the outside. Her red-lacquered fingernails dug into the wood, and she frowned. Finally, she said, "Oh, no—I'm afraid of horses. I was hurt once by one of them—actually put in the hospital because of one—so I won't do anything with them. No—I can't get in the stall with a horse."

I gaped at her, amazed and horrified that someone afraid of horses not only kept them but also had the audacity to breed them. Breeding horses was not for novices or equine-phobes.

Edgar didn't reply but put the stethoscope in his ears, corralled the foal into a corner, and listened to her heart. I eyed the woman beside me in disbelief. Her crimson fingernails didn't have a bit of dirt on them nor did her shoes. In comparison I looked as though I had been digging ditches. I wiped a dust smudge from my shirt.

All the indications of neglect were there: the unnavigable mud lane, the broken fencing, the barren pastures, a reluctance to help with the examination. She didn't know when the foal was born, preferring to finish her night's sleep when she knew that the birth was imminent. She couldn't tell that the foal hadn't nursed, and she didn't have the mare set up in a proper foaling stall, which was bigger and more comfortable for giving birth in. She should've called the vet earlier, too, seeing the deformed legs, and she was polluting the air the mare and baby had to breathe with fuming garbage.

I was dumbfounded by the human apparition beside me. Most horse breeders would have been delighted to assist the vet with their newborn foal. But not Mrs. Dreck. She watched from behind the stall wall, a passive spectator, hopelessly detached from the whole situation, as Edgar examined the baby himself. Good thing the mare didn't mind Edgar messing with her foal.

The foal's mother was an angel. I opened the stall door and stepped inside. Putting a halter on the mare, I talked quietly to her so that Edgar could examine the foal better. While I assured the mare that she and her baby were safe, Edgar listened to the foal's lungs, checked out her eyes, administered the enema, and rubbed the little bent knees. All the while the blanche-haired woman clung silently to the stall wall.

Finally, standing up, Edgar said to Mrs. Dreck, "Get me a pot with a handle on it. I'm going to have to milk out the mare and give the foal some colostrum—if there's any left." He squirted a few streams of the mare's milk into his palm and examined it. "There's some yellow color to it yet," he said. "Maybe we'll be lucky and have enough colostrum so that the foal can get the mare's antibodies. I'm fairly certain the foal has had nothing to drink yet, and it's been twelve hours since it was born. The way this mare is streaming milk on her own, we'll be lucky if there's any colostrum left in her. But let's try anyway."

The woman repeated, "A pot? You want a pot?"

"Yes," Edgar nodded, "with a handle. I need to hold the pot with one hand and strip the milk from the mare's udder with the other. And I don't want to spill any of it. The foal needs all we can get."

"Okay," she said and trudged out the door.

Meanwhile Edgar watched the foal as it hobbled weakly around to the other side of its mother. Again she reached for the udder with no success, gave up, and stood dumbly, dejectedly, beside her mother. Had there been a caring person around in the first few hours, she could have helped the baby find the teats and steadied her beneath her mother.

"That woman knows absolutely nothing about these animals!" Edgar fumed. "She has no right to be breeding them when she doesn't know what she's doing! Afraid of them? Did you ever hear of anything so ridiculous? If she's afraid of horses, why does she own them? The mare's passive, and so is the foal; they wouldn't hurt anybody! And do you believe she has two more mares out in the pasture that are due to foal in a month or two!" He slapped his hand on the top of the stall. "Money— that's the whole thing in a nutshell. She obviously doesn't show them or ride them or have them for pets because she's scared to death of them. So why else would she breed more horses? The only answer is money. I'll bet she's going to sell the foals thinking she can make a quick buck. Shit like this really burns me up! The animals are the ones that suffer."

Rarely did I ever see Edgar as angry as he was. He usually gave his clients the benefit of the doubt, especially when they meant well. After all, not everyone has the experience with horses that he had. But Mrs. Dreck didn't even seem to care about the foal, which didn't really make sense either if she was in it for the money. A dead or crippled foal was worth nothing.

Presently Mrs. Dreck came into the barn with a metal pot. Edgar took it from her, positioned it beneath the mare's udder, and began stripping the milk into it. The good thick streams hit the pot with a ringing sound, and in a few minutes Edgar had milked out about a cup's worth. He stood up and handed me the pot. Very carefully I moved, pot in hand, away from the mare and foal to a far corner of the stall so as not to risk spilling one precious drop.

Once again Mrs. Dreck propped her elbows on the outside of the stall. Edgar opened the door and left to get the small stomach tube he used on foals. He would insert the tube into the foal's nose, down the throat, and into the stomach. Then we would pour the life-giving fluid into the tube, and the foal would receive its first milk and her mother's colostrum. On his way out of the barn, Edgar said, "What shots did you give the mare during her pregnancy?"

"Shots?"

"Yeah, injections—you know—to prevent abortions and such," Edgar said, stopping and turning around. He was seriously annoyed. "It's a series of three shots that must be given at regular intervals during the pregnancy. When did you give them?"

"I didn't know the horse was supposed to have any shots," she admitted.

"And she should also have had TEWF—that's tetanus, eastern and western encephalitis, and influenza vaccine." His voice was louder, angrier, and he turned toward the truck in search of the foal stomach tube.

Mrs. Dreck's ignorance of horses and breeding them would not damage her or any other human, but it certainly made life difficult for the poor animals. And if the foal did somehow survive, how would the woman halter-break her? Foals should be broken to the halter within two weeks. If she couldn't get into the stall with the horse, how in the world would she halter-break her—a task that required a lot of patience and some strength and stamina. No one would even want to buy a horse that had not been halter-broken. My mental picture only became bleaker as I realized that an unhaltered, untrained horse was only good for pet food.

Edgar came back into the barn. "What about your other two mares out there?" he indicated, pointing. "I see they're pregnant. They need rhinopneumonitis shots, too. Didn't the owner of the stallion or anybody explain to you the need for injections for pregnant mares? Who is your regular vet? Who confirmed the pregnancies, anyway? That person should have recommended the injections."

"The breeder didn't tell me a thing about shots." The woman clung to the side of the stall, her knuckles a ghastly white against the red fingernails. "And *you* are my regular vet."

"I am?" Edgar gulped. "I know I haven't been up here in well over a year. I didn't even know these mares were pregnant. Haven't you been getting even the yearly shots—rabies, TEW, and so forth—for all your horses?"

"No," she admitted somewhat sheepishly. "I haven't called you for well over a year."

"Then that's why I didn't know about the pregnant mares. Otherwise, I would have given them their injections. But the breeder who owns the stud, too, should've told you about the shots."

"No—he didn't," she said. "No, he absolutely didn't tell me shots were necessary."

"Well, they are," Edgar growled. "We could be having all kinds of problems with these animals because they didn't get the vaccines. After I'm done here, I'm going to give your other pregnant mares their shots. It may be too late for this foal, but it's not too late for the others."

When Edgar was angry, he moved at a rapid, staccato pace. He coiled the foal tube around his neck and walked with determination to the stall, where he quickly stepped inside with the foal and mare.

"Gay, you steady the mare with your other hand so that she doesn't get upset when I grab her baby. Whatever you do, don't spill that milk; it's the only bit of colostrum we have. After I get the tube down the foal, attach this funnel, line it with this gauze, and carefully pour the milk into the funnel. Then hold the end of the tube high in the air so that it all goes down quickly."

Edgar was a master at tubing a horse quickly. The faster it's done, the less stress on the horse. He stuck one end of the plastic tube into his mouth and leaped at the foal. The unsuspecting animal tried to escape around the side of her mom, but Edgar was too quick. He grabbed the foal around its waist, and the two of them fell in a heap in the corner of the stall. Then, with all the expertise of someone who has done the same procedure time and again, Edgar began stuffing the free end of the stomach tube into the foal's left nostril. Beneath his weight the foal struggled, throwing her head and trying to rise—a natural reaction. But she wasn't having much success, especially in her starved and weakened condition and with legs so flimsy and knuckled over. She just wasn't strong enough to put up much of a battle.

Edgar continued to push the hose down her nose while blowing and sucking on the other end to insure that the milk would go into the stomach and not the lungs, which would cause a foal to drown and die in minutes. Edgar restrained the foal for perhaps three minutes, pushing the length of hose and blowing and sucking until he was sure he was in the animal's stomach. Then he pulled the other end from his mouth and gave it to me.

"Okay, Gay." he said. "Pour the milk into the funnel. Then hold the end of the tube up over your head."

Carefully I attached the funnel, lined it with the gauze to filter out any dirt and poured the rich liquid into it. Then I held it aloft, and we both watched as the milk flowed down the tube and into the foal.

"Oh, my goodness," Mrs. Dreck said in horror. "I never saw that done before. Is the foal all right?"

I removed the funnel from the end of the tube and passed him the free end. Edgar blew hard, clearing the tube of any liquid, and quickly pulled the hose out from the foal's nostril. Once free of the hose, the baby stopped struggling. Edgar got up, and the foal scrambled to her feet. "The foal will be a lot better now that she has something in her stomach," Edgar said.

As we left the stall, Edgar turned to Mrs. Dreck. "All right. We're finished with the foal. I've examined the mare; she's not torn behind or anything. That's surprising considering the size of the baby. You're very lucky a foal this size made it through the birthing all right. It could easily have gotten caught inside the mare. With nobody watching, it would've been the end for her. Now where's the afterbirth?"

"The afterbirth?" she said.

"Yes, where is it? You should always save it to make sure it's all there and that there's not some parts of it left in the mare. It gets toxic if it's inside her over twelve hours."

"I buried it," she said, wincing.

"Well, unbury it. I need to see it."

Mrs. Dreck left the barn, a shovel in hand. In a few minutes she called that she had exhumed the afterbirth. Edgar went to examine it and luckily found it all intact. A mare that had retained part of the placenta could founder—a deadly condition that horse breeders were well familiar with. They always knew to save the afterbirth.

Edgar took the metal pot and motioned to Mrs. Dreck. "Come in the stall with me. You have to learn to milk the mare because the foal's not nursing on her own," he said. He was speaking to her as if she were a child—firmly and unequivocally. "There's no other way but this," he said. "After I tell you how to do it, I want you to go to a drugstore and buy a human baby bottle. Make the hole bigger in it for the foal. Then every two hours that foal needs to be fed its mother's milk. Come in here, now, so that you can strip out the mare. She's easy to work with—not nasty or anything. You don't have to be afraid."

I glanced at Mrs. Dreck, still clinging to the stall wall. At first she made no attempt to move, but she couldn't refuse Edgar's insistence. Excuses were not acceptable anymore: no fear of the horses, no hospital alibi or other lame reason. The woman was responsible for creating a life, and this life depended on her now for survival. If she had no previous sense to arm herself with the proper information about mares and foals, then she would get a few quick lessons about them now, whether she wanted them or not. Neither Edgar nor I were going to leave this barn without knowing that the woman was going to accept responsibility for her animal. She was going to get in the stall with that mare—like it or not. If she couldn't summon enough gumption to take responsibility, then this was a case for the Humane Society. I would report her myself.

Mrs. Dreck timidly grabbed hold of the stall latch and slid open the door. She tiptoed inside and stood like a naughty child next to Edgar and the mare. I was surprised that she didn't complain or resist.

"Here's how you do it," explained Edgar, hunching down next to the mare's flank. "Come on—bend down." The mare stood still as stone as he began to work the teats, one at a time. "You feel for a little lumpy kind of thing at the base of the teat, not the tip. Feel here. See where my fingers are?"

Mrs. Dreck bent down and looked where Edgar was pointing. She nodded.

"Okay, now take your thumb and index finger and squeeze that lump—that's the teat cistern that has milk in it—down to the end of the teat. The trick is to start farther up the teat—at the base—and then pull the milk down toward the tip." With that, a large stream of milk rang into the steel pot. "Now you try it."

Mrs. Dreck reached toward the udder. I saw her wrist move but didn't hear the familiar "tinkling" in the pan. Edgar demonstrated again and offered her encouragement to try again. Soon a very faint "ring" sounded into the dish. Then another one. Then another tiny squirt.

"There—now you're getting it," Edgar said, obviously pleased. "Okay, since you're not used to doing that, it's going to take you a while. It takes practice. Just keep at it until you get about a cup's worth. Then transfer it from the pot to the baby bottle. You need to feed the foal every two hours."

"Okay, I'll try," she said. Then she stood up, glanced at her nails, and quickly headed for the outside of the stall where she stood beside me like a spectator at a zoo.

"I'm going to put a little more iodine on that umbilical cord," Edgar said and left the stall for his truck.

I took his absence as an opportunity to stress the importance of all this to Mrs. Dreck. I looked at her clinging to the stall wall, quite sure that she had little intention of being diligent with this foal's feedings. "You know, no matter how afraid you are, you must, absolutely *must*, strip out the mare and feed the foal."

She looked away from me and out the barn door. She didn't want to hear it.

I continued, "You have no other choice. The foal will die without your feedings. Her legs are too long and weak to let her get to the udder. Until she masters use of them, you need to keep her strength up. You have no choice. You *must* do it."

Mrs. Dreck turned toward me. She looked me in the eye for a moment and then said reluctantly, "Yes, I will. I promise. I just don't know why the breeder didn't tell me about all those shots and stuff."

After Edgar drenched the umbilical cord again, he massaged the foal's poor buckled knees, patted its head, and left the barn. I followed, trailing bits of equipment like the iodine bottle, the stomach tube and funnel, and the empty enema tube. Mrs. Dreck lingered behind, gripping the metal pot.

Back at the truck Edgar said, "This woman is absolutely clueless. I know she won't feed the baby—I can tell she won't. And without milk the foal won't make the night. I'm going to ask Carlin to come out and check the baby again around nine this evening. Maybe then we can take a blood sample to see if she got enough colostrum. And when we get home I'm calling the breeder. I can hardly believe he didn't tell her about the injections a mare needs. He's been breeding horses for a long time. I'm also going to recommend that he get up here and help this woman. After all, it's partially his responsibility since he has the stud. The woman has no one to assist her, and even though the mare is very good, she could still use an extra hand while she tries to bottle-feed the baby. I've never seen anything like this before." He shook his head. "Someone like that breeding horses is a sin—sickens me."

Presently Mrs. Dreck came around the side of the barn through the smoldering fog of the garbage heap. Once again Edgar explained the milking procedure. He reiterated how she should massage the foal's knees, and he suggested she find a neighbor or someone who could help her with the feedings and care. She said she had no one—her husband didn't care for horses—but that she would manage herself.

"I'm sending my associate up later this evening to check our little girl," he told Mrs. Dreck. "Let's see if we can get her through the night." Then Edgar climbed into the truck, and we slid back down the mudflow of her driveway.

"Why in the world didn't she read a book about breeding horses or something?" I said as we started away. "She can't blame it entirely on the breeder not telling her about the injections. She had the responsibility to keep herself informed on the care of mares and foals. There are tons of books out there for people who need information like that. I can't believe she didn't at least read a book."

On the way home Edgar must have worried the situation inside and out, for when we pulled into our driveway, he immediately went into action. First, he telephoned the stud owner and explained the situation. He replied that all the material about mare injections was written in the breeding contract Mrs. Dreck had signed. Obviously, he said, she must not have read the contract. But he said he and his wife would give Mrs. Dreck a hand with the foal.

As Edgar's vet associate later reported, that evening the stud's owners had visited the Dreck farm, but seeing the foal in such a dire condition, they suggested the foal and mare be moved to a large horse facility nearby where the foal would have round-the-clock care.

Once the mare and foal arrived at the thoroughbred horse-training farm in New Jersey, a whole slew of folks went to work on them.

Edgar's assistant, Carlin, had already contacted Dr. Vaala, the neonatal intensive care specialist at Mid-Atlantic Equine Hospital in Ringoes, New Jersey. On Dr. Vaala's recommendation Carlin developed a medical protocol for the foal. Her bloodwork showed no antibodies, so there had been no colostrum in the milk Edgar and I had fed her earlier through the tube. Carlin administered two units of plasma and one liter of 5 percent dextrose and water because the starved foal was rapidly becoming hypoglycemic.

Things were not looking very good for the filly. Shortly after she arrived at her new home, she lost her suck reflex—a dire condition for any baby. Another blood test showed the foal, because she had no vaccinations, was becoming septic; her white blood cell count had dropped from 12,000 to 2,000 in a matter of hours—white cells were out in the body fighting disease somewhere. Luckily the plasma would help the sepsis. Carlin also gave the foal two different antibiotics and Banamine, an inflammation reducer. Finally, she gave the baby steroids for shock.

Edgar and I anxiously awaited news about the foal the next day. She was still hanging on, but things still didn't look promising. And our suspicions about Mrs. Dreck had been right: she had no intention of feeding the foal or massaging her legs. She still refused to get into the stall with the mare and foal, but she agreed to run to the drugstore for the baby bottles or for Kaopectate when the foal developed the runs. In the next two days the baby's condition became worse despite being fed every two hours. Carlin reported that it was much weaker, still had no suck reflex, and could not stand for any length of time.

Over a critical two-day period the foal received numerous IV fluids of dextrose and water. Mrs. Dreck, we heard, would consent to be the "gofer," running for materials, but she wouldn't lay a hand on the foal. Even with an entire barn assisting the sick foal, not enough help was available; round-the-clock nursing care was hard to find.

"How's the Dreck foal?" I overheard Edgar asking Carlin the third morning. Uh-huh. That's all, huh?" He was scowling. "I'm going to check her again myself this afternoon—see if I can't do anything more."

I looked at Edgar as he put the phone in the cradle. He said, "Not good."

I stared through our picture window into the woods beyond. My eyes unfocused as if trying to see a shape in one of those illusion drawings. Suddenly, in my mind I was running on the path alongside our woods.

As I rounded the curve, I stopped where I had seen the deer the day before our end-of-summer party. I turned off my headphones and stood still for several minutes. Finally I realized that something was odd, really strange. I peered at the hill over which the deer had fled, and I glanced into the woods at my left. Then it came to me: except for the oak and ash trees and underbrush, the woods was curiously devoid of life: no squirrels chattering in the trees; no groundhog peeping from its hole; no birds singing; no insects buzzing.

I was alone at woods' edge. No other being, no animal accompanied me on my run. None of my cats were around to chase me up the path, and the wildlife had disappeared altogether. My animal family had deserted me.

And I was scared.

Marion

THE NEXT DAY WE DROVE IN SILENCE to New Jersey to check Mrs. Dreck's foal. When we sped up the long driveway to Running River Farm, we didn't know what we'd find. But when I ran from the truck to the foal's stall, I was pleasantly surprised.

The foal was standing.

Shortly a petite, ebony-haired woman walked into the pen. She was smiling, but she looked a bit ragged, her pony-tailed hair hanging tangled at the side of her head, her eyes dark and circled. "Hi," she said, wiping sleep-spit from the corner of her mouth with a shirttail. "I was just trying to get a few winks before the foal's next feeding. I can't seem to get any sleep. But look!" She beamed at the foal standing on shaky legs. "Doesn't she look a lot stronger?"

Just then Edgar walked, stethoscope in hand, into the stall. "Wow! She's standing!" Relief was all over his face. "She's definitely getting stronger. Has she nursed on her own yet, Sally?"

The young woman smiled, "She's been trying awfully hard. Still difficult for her to bend her knees to get under mom to the udder."

Edgar looked around and said, "You look pretty beat. You doing the foal all by yourself?"

Sally sighed but smiled anyway. "Yeah, everybody around here lost interest about two days ago, so I had to go it alone. I was determined this foal would live. I sort of camped out in the tack room. Things like this shouldn't happen, and people like that Mrs. Dreck shouldn't be allowed to breed horses. It's criminal."

"We couldn't agree more," I said. "But I think with your help and Carlin and Edgar's she's going to make it now."

Edgar put his stethoscope to the filly's chest, and this time she got away, skipping around to the other side of her mother. "Look at that," Edgar laughed. "She's much stronger than yesterday. Almost a miraculous change. You did a great job, Sally. I don't think you'll have to be quite as vigilant anymore. The mother's udder is not nearly as full now. And I'll bet it's because the baby's getting strong enough to start nursing on her own. All you should have to do is supplement her for a few more days until we're absolutely sure she's out of the woods."

"A few days, huh?" Sally laughed with an exhausted look on her face. "Well, that's better than a few months, anyway. I'll go heat up another bottle." In her scuffed English riding boots and smudged riding pants, Sally trudged up the aisle and disappeared into the tack room.

A week later Edgar and I visited the filly. What we saw made us ecstatic. The filly and her mother had been moved into a nicer, larger stall. The foal, a miniature of her mother, who was a chestnut with a blaze and four stockings, skipped and danced circles around her mom. In only seven days she had learned to control her stiltlike legs. The knees were no longer so bulged and knobby-looking.

"She's doing fine now," Sally said as she closed the door to the tack room. Her ponytail looked refreshed and rested. "I only feed her once or twice a day because I know for sure she's nursing."

"You've done a great job, Sally. Mrs. Dreck ought to give you her foal. After all, you saved it."

Sally snorted. "Well, we all know that won't happen. I'd buy her, but I can't afford what Mrs. Dreck wants. But that's okay. As long as the foal lives and gets a decent home, that's all I care about. I did my part, and I feel good about it."

Edgar and I left abruptly when an emergency call came through from the Trexler Game Preserve. On the way I thought about the Dreck foal and all those people, especially Mrs. Dreck, who should have shared responsibility for the sick baby: the stud owner and his wife, Mrs. Dreck's husband, the other boarders and riders who soon lost interest in the two-hour feedings. From beginning to end, people had all "crapped out" on the foal—except for Sally, whose diligence and genuine concern for the animals gave me some cause for hope. But considering all things, I felt too betrayed—by people and by my idealistic dream that maybe all animals and humans can somehow live together in harmony. Maybe my wish that people and animals can eventually live amongst each other with consideration and mutual respect was an impossibility, an empty theory that could not be made real.

Edgar reached for the truck phone. Tony LaPorte from the game preserve said that Marion hadn't eaten for a few days and looked rather bleak. Could Edgar come out and look at her?

"Who's Marion?" I asked, picking my cuticle. We bounced over a rut, and I grabbed hold of the door handle.

"The new bobcat," Edgar said. "They just got her from a zoo in Maryland." He swung the wheel, and we turned toward Schnecksville. Pulling into the service entrance to the game preserve, we beeped the horn and then drove to the bobcat house.

Edgar stopped the truck, and we got out, climbing the fence that surrounded the cedar-shake hut that was Marion's home. We looked in through the wire screening at a hunched form straddling a tree limb. From the branch a bleak-looking bobcat gazed down out of the shadows, her eyes sunken, drool running from the corners of her mouth. Bloody pools of urine stained the bottom of the house, and the air smelled of ammonia. Marion's hair was matted at her hind end as though she hadn't bothered to clean herself for days. A cat that didn't clean itself was in pretty bad shape.

Tony and Rich pulled up in a rusty Ford truck and, hopping the fence, ran toward us.

"Looks pretty bad, huh, Doc," Tony said.

"Very depressed," Edgar agreed. "Hasn't eaten for days, right? Bloody urine. She looks about on her last legs."

"What can we do—anything?" Rich asked, his thumbs in his pants pockets.

"I won't know until I examine her better," Edgar said. "Can you

guys catch her? I think we ought to take a blood sample and check her
hydration and temperature. Most likely it's some kind of infection. I
need to check her out, but I'm worried about someone getting hurt.
We don't need anyone being bitten or clawed. And by the way she
looks, we can't really stress her too much 'cause that alone will kill her."

Tony nodded as we watched the sick animal. Marion stared back
with great somber eyes. She had lost a lot of weight recently. Her loose
flesh hung over the branch like an emptied sack.

"I guess we need the rabies pole," Edgar said. "Let's just hope she's
too sick to struggle. Doesn't look as though she's going to make it anyway; I think we're probably too late. Whatever's got ahold of her does-
n't look as though it intends to let go, at least not while she's alive."

Rich went for the rabies pole, and when he returned, the men ral-
lied. Tony and Rich crept into the bobcat house with the rabies pole
and handed it slowly to Edgar.

I stayed outside the bobcat compound. There were already enough
people helping; they didn't need me in the way.

Marion watched the men's every step, with one eye on the rabies
pole, but she was too sick to move. Quickly Edgar rushed forward and
flipped the wire noose up and over her head. Still, she showed no reaction. Very sick cat, I thought. Too ill to defend herself. Edgar tightened
the noose and coaxed Marion off her branch. Obedient because she
had no other choice, she crawled off her perch and sank onto the
ground on her knees. I winced, feeling an imaginary tightness around
my own throat. But Marion did not seem to mind. Perhaps she sensed
we were there to help her, though I really doubted it. It was not like a
wild cat to be calm while restrained. She lay in a heap on the floor
without even enough energy to hiss. Not a paw did she raise, nor did
she growl or threaten in any way. She merely lay sprawled like a trophy
rug as the two men gently restrained and examined her.

"Two cc's of penicillin, Gay," Edgar called.

I ran to the truck, pulled the antibiotic vial from the refrigerator, and
filled a syringe. I rushed back and passed the syringe through the wire cage,
and Edgar injected the solution into Marion's hide. She made no sound.

Edgar pinched a piece of her skin up into a tent and let it pop back
into place. But it didn't. It just stayed in a little hill. After a minute or
two it slowly melted back around her body. She was very dehydrated.

"She needs fluids," Edgar said. "In fact, fluids might be the only thing that could save an animal this far gone."

"Geez, we just saw her this way this morning," Rich said. "Yesterday she looked fine." He couldn't help feeling partially responsible for her condition, though he couldn't have known she was that sick.

"Wild cats are hard to diagnose because they try to hide their illness," Edgar assured him. "Any kind of illness in the wild is a sign of weakness, and the ill and defenseless themselves become prey. Often with wild animals it is too late once you see the signs of disease. She's probably been sick for about a week already, but she just didn't show you the signs. Okay, let's get her to the service hospital."

Tony and Rich went to work, setting up the catch cage to transport Marion inside where she would be more comfortable and out of the elements. There they'd be better able to administer fluids, and she'd also be warmer until she recovered—if she recovered.

Very carefully while Edgar worked the rabies pole to make sure she wasn't choking, Rich and Tony lifted her inside the catch cage. Then the three hoisted her into the back of the pickup and drove to the service hospital.

Settled into her hospital cage, Marion again submitted, unflinching, to the administration of the fluids although the men still had the

Marion

wire noose around her neck in case she tried to bite. But she was so close to dying that Edgar let up on the tautness of the snare. She hardly needed restraint at all.

"She's not going to make it," Tony said. "I can tell." He stared dourly at the bobcat panting on the floor.

Edgar drew two vials of blood—one for a white count, the other for a chem screen. Then he took her temperature.

"Temp's high," Edgar said. "Most likely an infection. We'll see what the bloodwork shows tomorrow. Doesn't look good, I'll admit," he agreed, shaking down the thermometer. "But you'd be surprised what fluids can do. Sometimes they act a miracle; in fact, that'll probably help her more than the antibiotic at this point. Give her the night, and we'll see what we have in the morning."

That afternoon Edgar and I drove home in silence. The blood test showed a high white count, indicating an infection. The antibiotics would help, but we were both wondering if Marion was strong enough to ward off the infection and live into the morning.

The next morning the telephone rang. It was the game preserve. Marion was still alive. "In fact," Tony told Edgar, "she looks reasonably bright. She even sat up on her front end. A couple of minutes ago she tried to eat some raw liver."

"Great," Edgar said, "glad to hear it. But Marion has to get penicillin twice a day. Can you handle that? Okay, then. I'll leave things up to you."

A few days worth of penicillin treatments passed. As the bobcat started feeling better, she began to resist the rabies pole with all her animal instinct for self-preservation.

After one incident Tony called, frantic, about Marion's nasty behavior. He shouted into the phone, "She's become a fury. How about stopping the antibiotics? She seems almost her old self."

"No, Tony," Edgar warned. "It's not a good idea to stop them prematurely. The bacteria could regenerate if the disease isn't completely eliminated. Then she'd be worse off than ever. I'm afraid the antibiotics must be finished, even though she is much like her old nasty self."

So Tony and Rich struggled to give her her medicine. They had long ago abandoned using the rabies pole because she fought it with her very being. So each day they had to sneak up behind her and use the jab stick to administer the antibiotic as quickly as possible. Each time Marion grew more resentful, screaming with furious gurgles and slicing the air with her claws.

In a few days we arrived at the preserve for a follow-up exam on Marion. Tony met us with tempered annoyance at the hospital's entrance. Edgar asked what was wrong.

"You made Marion feel like the Queen of the Serengeti," Tony said. "She's impossible. We can hardly handle her at all. She's been threatening to shred us into the likes of human string cheese every time we approach her with the needle."

Edgar smiled. "Feeling a lot better, is she? That's great! Thought there for a moment she wouldn't survive at all."

"That's an understatement. She thinks she's up for a role in *Born Free*." In the background a worker hummed the tune from that famous movie. I laughed.

"Well, today we'll just have to get an extra good grip on her with the rabies pole," Edgar said. "She looks so much better now that in a few days we can stop treatments."

Tony sighed. "Good—because one of us is going to get sliced into lunchmeat if we don't."

"Okay . . . , let's get this over with," Edgar said as Tony slinked into the bobcat's cage. Immediately a much healthier-looking Marion backed into the corner, and the hackles raised on her back. A warning look came into her eyes, and her lips wrinkled back from her teeth in a Halloween grimace. She knew what was coming.

Edgar slowly approached with the noose. Marion hunched, coiling herself much like a rattler, and just as I thought she might spring, Edgar slipped the snare snugly around her neck. With that Marion did leap into the air, but Edgar held the pole and her head away from him and the rest of the animal crew. Then he gave the pole to Tony. Tony stood rigidly holding the cat, her head in the noose, into the corner. Even so, every few seconds Marion's body flipped and bounced like a fish on a hook. I hated seeing her struggle but knew it was for her own good. She thrashed for a few seconds and then lay exhausted on the floor.

"She's still fairly weak yet. Notice how she has given up struggling—all tuckered out," Edgar said. "Let's hurry up and give her a final shot."

I handed Edgar the injection through the wire fencing. He took it, crouched low over the bobcat and lifted a hind leg. Then he darted the needle into her thigh and depressed the plunger. Marion gave no reaction.

Next Edgar checked her hydration. The hillock of skin melted immediately back to her body—another good sign. Last, he looked at Marion's eyes to check for color and reflex.

No reflex. The eyes were dead quiet.

"NO!" Edgar yelled. He tapped the corner of the eye again—no blink—no reflex.

"What the hell!" he shouted. He lifted her lips to see her gums.

Her gums were purple.

"The noose!" Edgar hollared "Loosen it! We're strangling her to death!" Tony released his grip on the snare, and the cat went limp. Quickly Edgar tapped the eye again for a reflex. There was none. He pried open her mouth. The tongue was a leaden color. Then he whipped his stethoscope to her chest.

No heartbeat.

"She's dead!" he yelled. "Christ, what happened?" He began pumping her chest to encourage the heart. He squeezed, massaged, and coaxed it, but there was no response. Edgar bit his lower lip. Over and over he kneaded Marion's heart. But I could see the filmy glaze of death coating the bobcat's eyes, which had been wide and alive only ten minutes ago. My fingers flew to my mouth as I hoped for a miracle.

Marion's chest wasn't moving. She was, indeed, dead.

"Come on . . . , come on—breathe, Marion," Edgar pleaded. He squeezed the bobcat's heart again, but it was no use. She had choked herself—*we* had choked her—to death. I felt sick knowing that she had been a spunky thing before we got here, and that probably because of us she lay dead. Certainly the illness may have compromised her, but ultimately we must have accidentally strangulated her with the rabies pole. Because of us she lay lifeless.

I felt sick in my guts.

Suddenly the animal gave a great gasp. Then she exhaled, and a wheezing sound resonated in her chest. It could be an agonal response, but I was hoping it was life coming back. I wrung my hands and bit my lower lip.

Edgar put the stethoscope to her heart.

"I've got a heartbeat . . ., but it's faint."

Tony stood weakly by, the offending rabies pole dangling from his hand.

Marion gave another harsh cough, and then she opened her eyes.

"Sounds stronger now," Edgar said as he listened to the heart. "I think she's out of the woods." Quickly he injected the last antibiotic shot.

"Actually, I think she'd rather be 'in' the woods," I said. Edgar smiled but didn't take his eyes off the cat. He massaged the imprint on Marion's neck made by the rabies pole. Then, as she regained consciousness, he and Tony took the rabies pole and stepped out of the cage. In a few minutes Marion staggered to her feet. She dragged herself to the corner and lay down—a drunk in a stupor. I could almost see the life flowing back into her as minute by minute she began to look like the bobcat we had first seen.

"We damned near killed her," Edgar said, wiping his brow. "That was real close."

"Hell, we did kill her—for a few minutes at least. She was absolutely dead as far as I'm concerned." Tony shook his head and rubbed his chest as though easing away a pain.

Marion pouted in the corner, and she had every right to. She looked suspiciously at us, and we took the blame like adults.

"I had no idea she was strangling herself," Tony said. "Didn't really notice anything until you yelled."

"Yeah," Edgar agreed. "I had no idea the noose was that tight. I didn't want any of us getting hurt, but we didn't want to hurt her either. These exotics are real touchy creatures," Edgar admitted. "First, they disguise their illness so that we don't even think anything is wrong with them. When they are really hurting, we need to stick them a couple times a day with antibiotics. Then they begin to feel better to the point that they want to kill anyone with a needle in his hand. These animals just don't understand what's going on, and the whole thing snowballs from there."

I couldn't help smiling now, especially since Marion had recovered. "Hey guys, you all know where the swan pond is, right? While you're on a roll, why don't you try walking across it?"

Hicks's World

AUTUMN, WITH ITS WIND AND BONE-CHILLING DAMP, roared in with a vengeance, sweeping to the ground all the leaves that the animals and I had taken shady respite under only months before. The pigs were in their glory, for with the birth of fall came the bountiful fruit of the oak trees: those piglicious acorns. I spent every waking moment raking and burning leaves, and I was weary of smelling like a charred thing.

Fall melted uneventfully into winter. The pigs and I once again holed up in front of the woodstove while the wind ripped outside. On winter-bleak days the pigs cheered me with their usual sunny personalities, always eager for a belly-rub and adult conversation. They were never at a loss for words, grunting and chirping when I walked into the room, so happy with my company. And I always offered them an afternoon snack of juicy grapes.

Christmas and the millennial New Year's Day came and went, and we and all our animals managed to survive the Armageddon forecasted by the doomsayers. We hadn't saved up any drinking water, nor had we so much as gone to the gas station to fill up our tanks in case of a global computer glitch. In fact, we didn't do anything out of the ordinary in preparation for the turn of the century, which turned out rather ordinary.

We celebrated at a party, but I was sure none of my animals even noticed the old year had magically turned into a new one. Edgar and I blandly clinked our champagne glasses together, tried to look excited, kissed, and wished each other a fine and dandy year 2000. We wished our friends lots of luck and health, and then we left. We hardly noticed the roads icing on our way home. Thus far the winter had been bone-dry boring; in fact, the dramatic change to sleet and ice proved the most interesting development of the New Year's Eve. The ice storm was only a prelude, we would discover, to hefty snowstorms to come.

The late snowfalls were really something to celebrate. Winter had arrived in her ravishing crystalline gown after a comparatively nude first month without precipitation. We rang in the new year with a hike through the alabaster-cushioned hills and valleys behind our house—the Catholic seminary's property. Our land abuts the Mary Immaculate Seminary and its 500 acres of woods and fields. The area has become a wildlife refuge for a large herd of deer and all kinds of squirrels, birds, rabbits, and other interesting critters. The acreage is a haven for hikers able to tackle the rocky hills there or take the easier paths the deer have carved. A few of the cats set out on the trail with us, but after a while, guessing where we were headed and what an arduous trip lay ahead, they headed back home.

The air was crisp and moist that Sunday as we climbed over a couple of fallen oaks and skirted a natural pond at the seminary's edge. Canadian geese pecked along the pond's shore, and a few mallards swam, ducking for morsels in the shallows. Edgar and I stopped, taking in the view, listening to the snow-muffled sounds, and tasting the unpolluted, frosty air through open mouths. We heard no cars, saw no other persons, houses, or any other accouterments of human existence—only uplifting, invigorating silence.

When our fingers and earlobes became cold enough to snap, we headed back, trudging up our old, treacherous toboggan run, affectionately named Himmy Hill. It had been the site of many thrilling runs and just a few minor injuries—smashed fingers and overturned ankles. Halfway to the top we paused on the hump in the middle of the nearly vertical hill. Catching my breath, I said, "Remember when we sailed the toboggan over this mogul, Edgar?"

"Yep," he laughed. "How many feet did we step off? Didn't we figure the toboggan must have been airborne for at least fourteen feet
before it touched down again?"

"Fourteen it was," I agreed. "Boy, did we hit hard, too, when we
finally caught ground. My ass hurt for several days after. But it was
worth it. What a ride!" We both turned toward the dizzying bottom of
the hill. There the electrical tower with its humongous, humming
power lines stood staunchly—a grim reminder. "And remember when
we almost slammed into one of the legs of the tower?"

Nodding, he continued my story. "I remember the snow was blowing over the front of the sled and into our eyes—so hard, so thick. We
couldn't see a thing, remember? We were blind things speeding down
this mountain on a mere splinter of wood. And screaming our guts
out. The only things that kept us from hitting the tower leg were a
bunch of sticker bushes. The twigs and bushes—and let's not forget the
thorns—slowed us down just in time to veer away from it. We only
missed that tower by half a foot, remember?"

"It was scary, but it was *extreme*," I said, licking my lips. "Those
used to be the days. I'd love to try it again sometime."

"No, thanks. This hill is *really* dangerous. We were crazy to try it in
the first place. The one in back of our woods is more my speed these
days."

"What?" I kidded, "In these days of creeping old age?"

"Yep, that's it," he smiled. We trudged the rest of the way up
Himmy Hill, looked back down the steep slope at the tower, then
turned around and headed for home.

A week later we had another six inches of snow on top of the original foot, but we never did get up enough nerve to venture out onto
Himmy Hill and dare the hill on a final toboggan run. My husband
and I weren't kids any more. The foray down Himmy Hill long ago
had occurred while we were in our mid-thirties. Now in our forties, we
try to guard ourselves a bit better—for our own benefit and for all the
animals out there that need our care. We're no good to ourselves or
anybody else if we're all beat up and broken down.

Winter was Edgar's slower time of year, so he did his calls leisurely,
assigning the bulk of the work to his two associates. In spring the
reproductive work would pick up, and then all three of the vets would

be combing the countryside breeding mares and giving spring vaccinations. In the winter, however, he usually worked the morning, and in the afternoon we ran errands. In fact, we had gotten into the nasty habit of going to Assante's Italian restaurant for lunch—like a couple of old folks. That would have to stop before we both grew bigger than couches.

Over the past twenty years Edgar's veterinary practice has evolved into a kind of artistic stew. He had begun his career treating cows, cats, and dogs. After a while he shifted to working primarily with horses. He still specializes in equine medicine, but in the past few years he has expanded his repertoire to include many more exotic animals such as deer, elk, buffalo, and monkeys. The change entailed a shift in thinking that can be best described as doctoring animals with an artistic approach.

When I imagine a painter who has best represented from his imagination the kind of world we work in, I picture Ed Hicks and his work, *The Peacable Kingdom,* in which all manner of species share the same canvas, their tranquil eyes in a unified stare that soothes peoples' souls and endears them even more to the world of animals: unflustered, unique, and primitive.

If I could become Hicks for a few weeks, my painting of our veterinary practice would be similarly colored with a variety of species. Of course, I would feature all the animals we have ever cared for: the cat and dog; the cow and horse; the pig and sheep and goats. I'd scatter them across a moss-covered, Early American landscape, perhaps add a stone house and fenced pasture for the domestic animals to frolic in and add a few naked humans to complete the package. But eventually the scenery on my canvas would transform from its tamed, domestic corner into one of a more wild and mysterious breadth. Here, amid a tropical forest and African savannah, would roam more recently and semi-domesticated wildlife: skunk, deer, elephants, buffalo, ferrets, and monkeys. Their eyes, painted with fine pointillistic brush strokes, would glint a touch of ferocity. The final triad of the painting would depict, amid Egyptian sands and polar caps, animals of pure, undomesticated savagery such as the bobcat, the fox, the lion, the zebra, and the tiger.

These days I still imagine myself as Hicks, adding with each passing day yet another strange beast with great expectant eyes to the imaginary canvas of our patients. Such a mixed-up conglomeration of wild and tame animals exists in our practice, the treating and doctoring of which becomes, in the end, the work of art itself. For a veterinarian to figure rare diagnoses and treatments that span the animal world from dog to lion requires an artistic and imaginative quality seen only in the greatest of thinkers and creative beings. It also requires vigilance—an awareness and willingness to keep one's knowledge up-to-date and to read and study the medical literature as varied as the number of species itself. The veterinarian must assume the character of a detective, sleuthing out the scholarship that describes treatments for swans, aoudad, wolves, and other strange creatures. Like bats.

"Bats!" I exclaimed. "Where?"

"There's a bat exhibition in Bethlehem this winter," Edgar said. "I thought you might want to go along. One of the bats keeps falling off the ceiling and hitting the floor. She has trouble climbing back up, too."

"Does she yell 'I've fallen, and I can't get up'?" I laughed.

"Ah-ha! Very funny. Do you want to go?"

"Wouldn't miss it, Ramar. This oughta be something I can write about—not everyday you get to work on bats."

It was an icy winter's day, but we had no trouble getting to the bat building with our four-wheel-drive. The day was cornea-searing bright with the sun's brilliant reflections off the snow and ice patches. But the temperature was so bitter cold that I doubted the sun could melt much of the ice anyway.

We arrived at the bat exhibition an hour before it opened. The heap of bats in "Bats—Masters of the Night," as they were billed, were bundled up on the ceiling in a sleepy mass, just settling down from an active night. We peered through the window of their cavelike room, the size of a Porta-Potty.

Edgar shined his flashlight through the glass. The swath of light sent the pack into a trembling, blinking panic. They threatened momentarily to take wing. Quickly he turned the light away, then directed it toward the floor—no bat. The one that had fallen must have found its way back to the security of the group.

"Wow," I said like a kid at his first bat exhibition. Indeed, when it concerned animals, I was like a kid, and this was certainly my first bat exhibition. "This is cool."

"Yeah," Edgar nodded, "real cool. In fact, it's a bit *too* cool in here, especially for bats. They're very sensitive to temperature changes." He shined his light at the wriggling bat mass on the ceiling. "See that. There's the proof. See them huddled on the ceiling together?" With the light in their eyes, their little leathery wings pulsated and flicked in discomfort. Their tiny ebony eyes blinked and shifted, and some dipped their heads behind a companion's wing to hide from the glare. "They're trying to keep warm," Edgar said.

"Uh-huh. They're all one on top of another." The bats huddled in a mound about a foot in diameter.

"I just want to stand here and observe their behavior for a while," Edgar said, cupping his chin.

The bat exhibition was a child's treat. And it was spooky. The entrance, formed from papier-mache, resembled the foyer of Dracula's castle with candles and medieval furniture draped in cobwebs and chiaroscuro shadows. To enter the castle we had to cross a foreboding drawbridge and hunker down through a dimly lit tunnel which ended in a clearing resembling a rainforest. All was in shadows—real kid-spooky.

More displays were set up within the forest atmosphere. There was a model of a cave used to demonstrate echolocation in bats. Kids could poke their heads inside, yell, and hear their echoes. All kinds of touchy-feely boxes were scattered here and there so that a person could stroke a piece of material resembling the surface of a bat wing and feel the delicateness of bat toes.

In the next room microscopes were set up with bat parts: bat brain cells, bat blood, bat hair. A bat dining table featured dinner plates with various foods palatable only to bats: bananas, citrus fruit, seeds, pollen, simulated blood, and insects. And a bat skeleton as large as a human skeleton stood inside a large glass case so that kids could compare bats' bones to human humeruses and other appendages. Across from this display case was another where hung a giant, six-foot robotic bat with its baby. I hadn't noticed it until all of a sudden the wings began to flutter and the head and ears swiveled side to side. Goosebumps rose on my skin at the eerie robotic whining and grinding behind the glass.

As we observed the trembling mammals through the window, the bat boss entered, greeting us with a friendly voice. "Seems that bat is all right now," he said, shining his own light into the cage. "She hasn't fallen off her perch yet this morning."

"It's a little cold in here," Edgar said. "I was researching material on bats last night in one of my journals. They have a hard time regulating their body temperature. Perhaps you could try to rig up a space heater to warm their room up a little."

"Yeah—ya know, when we close this place in the evening, we do turn the heat down in the whole warehouse. It probably gets pretty nippy overnight."

"I'll bet that's the problem then. The one bat probably has less of a tolerance for erratic temperature changes. Try setting up a space heater with a fan to blow some warmer air into their little enclosure. Is everyone else okay?"

"Actually," the manager said, "I need you to look at Stella's eye. I think there's something wrong with it."

"Which one is Stella?" Edgar said, shining the light onto the trembling group.

"You'll recognize her by the eye. It's cloudy," he said.

"Can I get in the little room there with them. I'd like to examine them closer," Edgar said.

"Sure—step in from the back of their case. They aren't real active this time of morning. Don't shine the light on them too long, or they might start flying around."

"Come on, Gay. Want to go in with the bats?" Edgar offered.

"Is the Pope a Catholic?" I said.

We first slid behind some black, webbed sheeting designed to catch any stray bat that escaped from the closet-sized room. Then, very quietly, we pushed a heavy door inward into the bat room. First, Edgar stooped and stepped inside, and then I followed. We were both cramped, hunkered down inside the telephone booth-like display case. I avoided stepping on their breakfast, a piece of cantalope, and faced the quaking, quivering mass of bats.

"They're constantly moving," Edgar said, directing the light again onto the heap of animals. I could see tiny, black, bony feet clinging to the wire mesh that provided a foothold for them on the ceiling.

"How many are there?" I said. Their tiny dark brown eyes reflected Edgar's light. The mass wriggled and squirmed like a batch of worms in the uncomfortable glare.

"About seventeen altogether," he said. "See how they move?"

"Yeah. They seem to be switching positions."

"That's right. The center of the group is where it's the warmest, so they all want to be in the center. Of course, they all can't be in the middle at once, so they take turns. That's why the mass is constantly shifting. When the ones on the outside get too cool, they worm their way into the middle of the pack. Now, where's the one with the cloudy eye?" Edgar asked.

All the bats were staring at us: hard, beady eyes—clear, glass-like. They were beautiful. But then I saw one with a white eye.

Edgar had seen it at the same time. "There she is," he said. "Stella." He looked closer. "It's just a cataract, by the looks of it. Okay. That certainly can't be treated. She'll have to learn to live with it."

"Well, what does a cataract do to a bat?" I asked.

"Probably not much. She has one good eye to see with; besides, bats pretty much react in synchrony with the rest of the group. She'll just follow the others, and I'm sure her radar and echolocation will keep her from colliding with other things, too."

Edgar shined the light into the cloudy eye, and the whole bat brigade quaked with discomfort. "Yep—that's Stella Luna, then. She's got a cataract, but the other eye is perfectly fine. Okay, let's go. Did you see enough?"

"Yeah—take the light off them. They don't like it. They're very pretty—very delicate looking. They have such fine features, almost like mice." I looked one last time at the writhing mass of bats. "They're real big on togetherness, aren't they? What kind are they?"

"They're Egyptian fruit bats."

"Hm-mm. Their faces resemble miniature foxes. What kind is the robotic bat in the other room?"

"That's, I believe, a model of a flying fox bat. They can grow fairly large. Some have a wingspan of six feet. Altogether there are around a thousand species of bats. Then there're the vampire bats. Vampire bats are only in Central and South America, but they are a big draw with kids—the Dracula thing and all that, ya know."

"Yeah—guess that's the reason for the castle when you enter, huh?"

Edgar told the manager that Stella had a cataract which shouldn't compromise her functioning within the group. On the way out of the exhibit, I stopped at the Bat Boutique to buy a bat pop-up book. Collecting pop-ups was a passion of mine. The gift shop was a virtual bargain basement of batmobilia. Last, I stopped in the batroom.

Two weeks later Edgar and I had occasion to check the bats again. This time it was for health papers. They were being sent to their next location—the Bronx Zoo. Again, as I watched from the plate glass window, Edgar squeezed himself into the bat booth. Again he shined his light on the bobbling bats, befuddled by the brightness. He checked their tiny nostrils for "crusties" and their eyes for alertness. He checked their breathing. It was a health test on a furry mass—not one individual could be discerned, so packed together and constantly shifting were they.

In moments Edgar declared the bat bunch healthy. Then he signed the papers that would allow them to board the bat bus to the Bronx.

I said good-bye to the brooding bats, and on our way out I noted the sponsors of the exhibition: the Junior League of the Lehigh Valley and, of all organizations, the Miller Memorial Blood Bank.

I howled with delight.

But several days later Edgar received a letter from the owner of the bat exhibit; he had botched the traveling regulations. His bunch of bats were not destined for the Bronx as he had originally thought. Instead, they were going on display to, of all places—Kuwait!

"Kuwait!" I exclaimed when Edgar showed me the letter.

"That's what it says," Edgar laughed.

"Don't the Kuwaitis have any other bats to borrow that are closer to their country?" I said.

"Guess not," Edgar said. "There's also a lot more paperwork to fill out because it's an international move. And what a long trip for those guys, too."

"Boy, being a bat is a bitch," I added, snickering.

"Yeah."

"And it would've been more poetically aesthetic had they been going to Bhutan or Britain, or Burma, or even Bermuda. But Kuwait?" I laughed. "It just won't fulfill my alliterative expectations!"

A few weeks later I had a radio interview about our life doctoring animals. The radio announcer asked me what the strangest animal was that my husband had ever worked on. I told him, that, as a matter of fact, he was checking the strangest animal at the very moment that we were talking on the radio.

"What is it?" the announcer questioned.

"A bat," I said mysteriously.

"A bat? What is wrong with it? he said.

"Well, he's rechecking her because she was having trouble clinging to the ceiling. She was always falling off and hitting the ground," I volunteered.

"Oh, yeah? Well, maybe she was just a ding bat!" he quipped.

Not to be outdone by a wise-ass radio person, I retorted, "Possibly. I really don't know what kind of noise she made when she hit the ground."

"Touche!" the announcer retorted, and then we finished the interview.

While the Bethlehem Bat Exhibit housed what must have been one of the most exotic of all creatures Edgar has ever worked on, the Trexler Game Preserve certainly was no slouch for presenting us with uncommon animal species and nerve-wracking situations. We've stitched up an elk gored by another elk, TB-tested monkeys, captured the zebra for treatment, and examined the owl's sore wing. Working with animals of this sort demands a certain amount of caution and more than the average torso's worth of guts.

Last summer the yearling wolves were due for their check-up. On the "to-do" list were such tasks as cleaning their teeth, checking their coats and treating them for ticks and fleas, administering vaccinations, drawing blood for a chem screen, taking a fecal sample for worms, trimming their nails, weighing them, and swabbing the dirt from their ears. Since a wolf wasn't likely to just hop up into the cosmetician's chair and sit still for her manicure and prophylactic treatments, we started the day by prepping the tranquilizer gun. While it may sound like a harsh method for clipping a few nails and sprucing up a wolf's breath, using sedation was easier on both the wolf and the caretakers. A sleeping wolf is unlikely to remember and hold a grudge against its zookeepers. It makes for a better relationship all the way around.

When we arrived at the game preserve, Tony, head of the animal crew, was in his office caressing the brand-new tranquilizer gun. He smiled proudly, and I congratulated him on his new acquisition.

"Yeah, well," he said, putting it back into its velvet case, "this is just in case the jab stick doesn't work. We always used the jab stick because we could always hit the target accurately—you just walk up to the animal and put it in the leg muscle. Our old tranquilizer gun tended to misfire, and you could never guarantee aim. Still, I don't like to shoot 'em with a gun unless we have to."

I looked at the jab stick lying across Tony's desk. It was a wooden rod about a yard long with a syringe and needle ingeniously attached to one end—a McGyver tool if I ever saw one. A string was attached to the outer part of the syringe, and once the stick sunk the needle into the hide and the string was held taut, the stick plunger pushed to inject just the correct amount of fluid.

Tony showed me with a quick demonstration. Tony was appropriately dressed in his reversible khaki safari vest. Probably fifty pockets decorated the garment, and in two tiny pockets two 12 cc syringes rode. To compliment the rugged outback jacket, Tony wore a matching set of khaki shorts.

"Hey, Tony , . . . er, rather, Sahib Tony. Looks like you could put Marlin Perkins to shame in that outfit."

Tony laughed. "No, not Marlin. My all-time hero is Steve Irwin."

"Who's that?" I said.

"The snake man on the Discovery Channel. I love him. Don't you just love the way he wrangles those snakes? He's orgasmic over snakes."

I snickered.

Suddenly Tony went into his Irwin imitation. In an Australian accent that was more British than Aussie Tony said, gesturing with his arms wide, "Just look at this beauty, folks. Isn't she lovely? She's gorgeous (he pronounced it "gar-jus"), simply beautiful. This, my friends, is the most poisonous snake in the world, and can you believe it—she is living right 'ere—right 'ere, mind ya—in me garage." Then Tony said in a half-whisper that Irwin is well-known for, "Ooh, ooh, look folks. She's pregnant, so I want to be very careful with 'er. I'm just going to put 'er back in me toolbox, so she can 'av 'er babies in peace."

I laughed. "Now I remember him—the crazy snake guy. Hey, you do a great imitation of him."

"I think he's love-ly," Tony crooned in his Aussie accent, "and I want to be just like 'im when I grow up."

Tony picked up the jab stick again and worked the string back and forth.

"Hey, that's pretty slick," I said. "But how do you get the wolves close enough to you to inject them?"

"Believe me, they don't come looking for us. As part of their training, Brent and I always feed them in their holding pens. That way, if we need to treat them for any medical condition, they go right in, thinking they're going to be fed. And they're also used to my standing around and watching them. I'm sort of their buddy, especially Storm. He seems to like me. Now Thunder prefers Brent. Both are already in their pens sleeping. We gave them their breakfast there, and now they're snoozing it off."

"Still, how do you manage to inject them?" I wondered.

"When they're down resting, Brent distracts them, and then I just sneak up behind them and jab them through the chain-link fence with

Storm and Game preserve keeper Tony LaPorte

the syringe. Ya got to be quick, but most times they think they've been bitten by a fly or something. At least they don't seem to put the blame on us."

"Okay," Edgar said, coming into the zookeepers' office with the "to-do" list. "Let's get going. Hear you have a problem with one of the kangaroos, too?"

"Yeah," Brent said. "A swollen jaw. You can take a look at her later."

"Okay," Edgar said, stuffing the paper into a clipboard. "Have you decided how we're going to do this?"

With that Brent entered and sat down in Tony 's chair.

Tony reached atop a tall filing cabinet and grabbed two walkie-talkies. He handed one to Edgar. "I don't want anyone going into the wolf pen with Brent and me until I have those guys out like lights. We don't need a crowd hanging around to make them any more nervous. First, I'll try the jab stick. If that doesn't work, I'll use the gun."

"Two-point-four cc's of the xylazine and ketamine cocktail with a three-to-one ratio of ketamine to xylazine. Depending on the temperament of the animal, you might need to use a bit more than two-point-four—perhaps another point-eight cc," Edgar advised. "We can always reverse them to wake them up sooner if we have to give a higher dose."

"That's what I was planning on giving," Tony agreed. The rest of the animal crew, including Diana and two college students, Jeff and Tony, who were summer part-timers, walked into the office, ready to help once the wolves were sedated. Tony grabbed one of the walkie-talkies, and he and Brent headed out the door. "Everybody stay here until we call and give the okay. And don't anybody call us, or you might scare the wolves," he called. The door slammed behind them.

We all waited anxiously in the zookeepers' office. Finally, static sounded on Edgar's walkie-talkie. Edgar snapped up the walkie-talkie and pushed the button. "Tony, do you read? Over."

A voice erupted from the box, "Yeah, Storm is going under real fast. I just jabbed Thunder, so he ought to be ready by the time you guys get here. Over."

"Okay, we're coming right now. Out. Let's go!" Edgar yelled. The veterinary technician interning for the summer grabbed the pouch containing the autoclaved dental tools and a fecalizer to test for worm eggs. Armed with curry combs, blood tubes, a muzzle, and the rabies pole, we hurried outside and jumped into the truck. Diana, Jeff, and Tony climbed into an old pickup and followed behind as we sped through the preserve toward the wolf pen.

Tony and Brent already had Storm laid out on the concrete stoop the wolves used as a lookout. "I want as few people inside with the wolves as possible. The less stimuli, the better," said Tony. Jeff, Tony, and Diana waited outside the chain-link fence until we needed them. Tony had already given me permission to go along inside with the wolves, but I didn't want to be in the way, so I lingered behind. I considered it a privilege to be able to assist with what everyone there regarded as the trophy animals of the preserve.

Edgar quickly went to work on the sedated Storm, who was breathing deeply under the effects of his xylaxine and ketamine cocktail. He shaved a patch of hair from a foreleg, tapped for a vein, and drew blood into a 12-cc syringe. Then he quickly transferred the blood to red and purple capped tubes. I approached quietly, took the tubes, and put them in my pocket.

While he had been drawing the blood, the veterinary technician had spread out the dental tools. Tony pried open Storm's mouth and inserted a mouth speculum so as to better see and get at the teeth. Then the veterinary technician began scraping the plaque off Storm's incisors. Those were big teeth—the biggest and whitest I had ever seen—but, surprisingly, they weren't as dirty as we thought they would be. We were all amazed at Storm's relatively clean choppers.

"How's Thunder doing over there?" Edgar called to Tony, who had gone back and kneeled down beside the half-tranquilized brother of Storm.

Thunder was still sitting up in his small rectangular pen. But he wasn't tranquilized. He was panting heavily, and his head was drooping. Every once in a while he caught himself and jerked his head to an upright position. He was fighting the drugs with all his wild instinct. Just as with humans, different individuals of the same species can react differently to the same drug dosage. Thunder was more high-strung than Storm, too. He had already had his maximum allotment of cocktail, but he was almost as awake as we were.

"He's only half out—fightin' us all the way," Tony reported.

Thunder dragged his face along the chain-link fence and snarled, his lips curled menacingly around his teeth.

"Oh, yeah," Edgar laughed. "He's mighty pissed. Let's just let him alone and see if he goes down any farther. Maybe if we can convince him there's nothing to worry about, he'll relax and go to sleep."

The vet tech had finished scraping Storm's teeth. She took out the mouth speculum and pushed his slack tongue back in his mouth where it would stay cleaner and more moist. He continued to sleep, completely unaware.

Edgar checked Storm's fur coat. The mange Storm had had months ago had fortunately disappeared. "Must've been the Frontline," Edgar said. "We'll give him another dose right now." And with that he smeared a few drops of the flea and tick killing chemical between the wolf's shoulder blades.

"What kind of wolves are these?" I asked in a quiet voice.

"They're Arctic wolves," Tony offered.

"Yeah," Edgar agreed. "They're actually the same as timber wolves, but these guys are stockier and white."

"Storm sure hasn't shed out very well yet," I said. "Would you like me to comb him to remove some of that thick fur? He'd probably be a lot more comfortable in this hot weather."

"Sure, go ahead," Tony said. "Knock yourself out."

And so I went to work on Storm's fur, plucking and pulling out loose tufts, both with my fingers and with a horse shedding blade, making sure I didn't dig into the soft skin underneath. While I was providing Storm with a new, more fashionable "do," the vet tech was swabbing out the wolf's ears with alcohol and cotton. His ears were as immaculate as his teeth.

We had been working for perhaps fifteen minutes when all of a sudden Edgar said, "His weight! We forgot about weighing him. We really should have a weight on them. Damn. We should've done that first thing when he was good and asleep. We have to hurry if we're going to do it. I think he's starting to come out of the anesthesia: his breathing is becoming more rapid and shallow. Still, we should have about ten minutes left."

"Diana," Edgar directed. "Why don't you and Jeff and Tony run Storm up to the service center and weigh him on the grain scale?"

Diana rolled her eyes, clearly not anxious to drag a half-awake wolf uncaged through the preserve. She didn't answer.

"It's okay," Edgar assured her. "He'll be out for at least ten minutes, and when he wakes up, he won't have much control of himself anyway. He'll hardly have the energy to bite anybody. You'll be okay. He'll be goofy for quite a while. Trust me; I know how these drugs work.

"Diana, you and the two guys," Edgar pointed to the college students on the outside of the fence, "come inside here and pick him up— now. Hurry. Take him to the service center in the back of the pickup. Let's get a weight on him." He motioned for the three to come into the wolf pen. "And don't forget the muzzle."

I stopped combing the wolf as the three put their arms underneath Storm and lifted him. "Support his head!" Edgar warned. "Don't let him choke on his tongue. Now take him—that's it—on the back of the pick-up, and. . . ."

Thunder and Storm

And before he could finish his sentence, the three were off and running with Storm bobbling helplessly in their arms. A minute later the pick-up started up and raced up the hill toward the service center. I was a little concerned about the wolf waking up while they were transporting it; as they were carrying him away, I thought I heard a half-hearted snarl from his lips.

"Boy, I hope they make it," I said.

"I think they'll be okay. He can't do much of anything anyway even if he should wake up. They did take the muzzle, didn't they?"

I looked down at the pile of equipment. There it was lying amidst the hair combs and brushes. "Nope. Here it is. We all kind of forgot about it in the rush."

"Too late now. They're gone. I'm sure they'll make it. Now, how's Thunder doing?" Edgar asked, walking over to the other wolf pen.

Thunder was lying, his legs tangled, in his pen, but he wasn't totally out of it, because when he was poked, he jerked his head around to bite. He was still a danger to people in his half-tranquilized condition.

"We can't give him any more tranquilizer, that's for sure," Edgar said. Weighing the options, Tony stared at Thunder. "Get the rabies pole from the back of my truck, Tony. We're just going to have to snag his head and pin him to the floor while we work on him. We'll try to get as much done as we can. What we can't we'll just have to do another time."

In a minute Tony had returned with the rabies pole. Edgar opened the back end of the cage just far enough to insert the pole and loop it around Thunder's head. When he saw the rabies pole out of the corner of his eye, Thunder jumped, but the drugs were keeping him glued to the ground. Edgar snugged up the loop around Thunder's neck and gave the end of the pole to Tony. Then Tony held Thunder's head against the floor of the pen.

From the opened back of the pen, Edgar snagged a hind leg and had the blood drawn in seconds. Thunder snarled, jerking his head toward Edgar, but Edgar persisted until he had the tubes completely filled. "It's okay, Thunder," Edgar said in a soft voice. "We just want to make sure you're doing all right here in your new home." Next he reached in his pocket for the flea and tick medication. He broke open the neck of the vial, parted the fur, and rubbed the solution into the shoulder blades. Thunder growled wolf threats by the hundreds, but Tony had his head pinned into the corner. Thunder would be hurting no one.

"His coat looks pretty good. He doesn't even need to be shedded out," Edgar said, observing the wolf from the outside of the pen. "Eyes clear—so is the nose. We can't clean his teeth or ears, obviously. Next year we'll make sure we give him an adequate dose of tranquilizer, and we'll do him first."

We were so focussed on Thunder's checkup that we almost didn't hear the pickup pull to a sliding stop next to us. Diana jumped from the truck cab and raced for the gate. She yelled, "Hurry up, guys! I got the gate open! Just get him the hell back inside! Run!"

We couldn't believe our eyes. Storm was just about out of his anesthesia. Jeff and Tony looked scared bloodless, but they were pumped with adrenaline. In a flash they had hoisted Storm out of the back of the truck. Then they galloped toward the gate with the 76-pound wolf.

"Oh, my God!" I said, my hand over my mouth. "The wolf is awake."

"Not totally, but mostly," Diana yelled. "He's growling like mad and snarling. Hurry up—put him right in his little pen, guys!"

The students rushed the wolf along the outside of the pen and barreled through the gate. Storm's body was twitching, trying to fight back, and his head was jerking and spitting bubbles. He was madder than hell.

I ran to open Storm's pen just

Thunder

in time for the guys to set him on the floor and slide him in. When the gate shut with a loud bang, Storm rose on his front legs and leaped around to snap. Luckily he only caught air.

The guys stood back puffing. "That was real close. Real close," Jeff fumed. He looked drained of any body organs.

"Cool," Tony said smiling. "Far out. Do we get to weigh the other one now?"

Edgar laughed, "No, not this one. He didn't really drop for us. He's about the same size as Storm, though. So, I think it would be fair to guestimate his weight."

"Good," Diana said. "That was pretty hairy. Storm started waking up just as we set him on the scale. He nearly crawled off the damn thing, he did. I really didn't think we'd be able to get him back without him taking an arm or two off us. But we did it. Thanks, guys."

Jeff and Tony stood smiling, obviously quite proud at having accomplished the mission.

"Next week we do the two adults—White Cloud and Spirit," Edgar said, checking his list. "Now let's go back and check out the aoudad and kangaroo, and I'll change the bandage on the bobcat. Good job, everyone. Everything went without a hitch."

"Sure," Diana chirped.

Then suddenly Edgar exclaimed, "Oh, no. I forgot to do a fecal on Storm." He ran back to Storm's cage, tore a rectal sleeve from his hind pocket, and put it on. Then he called out, "Three" at which time Tony pulled the rope that hauled up the door on Storm's cage—number three.

Storm was sitting up on his elbows, but he looked pretty dizzy. Edgar inserted a finger in Storm's rectum and brought out a fecal ball the size of a nickel. "There," he said, brandishing the evidence, "I got some. Shut the gate. Someone gimmee the fecalizer."

A final injustice for Storm, I thought, as we climbed back into the truck. Brent and Tony stayed back with the wolves as they were waking up, just to make sure they wouldn't get their legs caught beneath the fencing. We gathered all the blood tubes, dental equipment, horse combs, and muzzle and headed toward the kangaroo pen to check a sore jaw.

Normal Square

ONE MONDAY MORNING, despite hairy winter driving conditions, we headed west into the heart of the Pennyslvania Dutch country.

Normal Square was a small village established centuries before by Dutch ambition. As anyone could guess by its name, the town was as simple and unpretentious as its 18th-century Dutch founders. Main Street, the town's busiest thoroughfare, boasted two five-and-dimes featuring household products right out of the 'Fifties. No one shopped there for computer software, palm organizers, DVDs, or high-tech audio equipment, but one could certainly shop for the basics at bargain-basement prices: Levi overalls, John Deere rubber boots, denim work hats, cast iron pots and pans, Ball canning jars, rag mops, and dairy farm supplies like shovels, pitchforks, and slop buckets.

Simple, nourishing, but rather fatty foods appealed in a practical sense to the farmers in need of sustenance after a day wrestling cows and pigs on the family farm. Ham hocks the size of cement blocks and army-sized containers of sausage and ground beef loaded the refrigerator sections of the Food Fair. Pennsylvania-grown potatoes and summer and winter squashes filled the produce department along with red net bags of onions and countless crates of sweet-smelling cantalope and watermelon.

The Food Fair had no seafood section, but the deli was loaded with Dutch delights such as scrapple, which, for breakfast, could be fried to a crisp and loaded with pancake syrup until it flowed over the plate and pooled on the table top. Instead of a gourmet food section, the Dutch folk preferred such staples as souse, its gray, vinegary gelatin holding together a variety of unidentifiable meat products, and cow and steer tongue, a Dutch delicacy when sliced thin. Rolls of bologna, blood pudding, and liver pudding snaked eerily along the inside of the deli case, in and around blocks of farmer's cheese and head cheese, which is not really cheese at all, and whose ingredients could nauseate one of my pigs.

The baked goods section was scant at best, but the delicacies there could fuel a Dutch person's furnace. Sugar-coated crullers glistened behind the bakery window, beckoning children and old folks alike. Vanilla and molasses sugar cookies showed alongside chocolate cup-cakes bloated with cream cheese. The most tempting of the baked stuffs, though, were the wet-bottom shoe-fly pies stacked one atop another. Together they gave the bakery section a pungent aroma of molasses.

To the town of Normal Square, which seemed altogether normal to Edgar and me since as Dutch descendants we love basic, fatty foods, we headed out to give yearly vaccinations to a couple of mules and to clean the sheath—the penis casing—of another. But there was one condition: I would only help out if Edgar promised to stop at the Amish store for a shoe-fly pie. I'd had a deficit of fat grams in my diet lately and could afford the extravagance. Only an Amish-made molasses pie, a gooey, dark sugar syrup covered with a sparse layer of flour, sugar, and butter crumbs, would satisfy me.

"Okay," Edgar snickered when I presented him with the ultima-tum: no pie, no go. "I'll buy you a shoe-fly pie."

"Wet bottom?"

"Is there any other kind?" he kidded. Then he winked and gunned the engine.

We crested over the top of a hill that led to Bonnie and Sterling Heckenbrodt's farm. Winter was easing its grip on the area, yet the ground was semi-solid with ice chunks and crystals that prevented yesterday's downpour from completely sinking into the earth. All was slick greasy, slippery, icy mud. As we began our descent, Edgar gripped the steering wheel. We slewed down the first part of the drive, our wheels spinning in the slime, gripping, losing purchase, then grabbing again.

The truck slid around the first bend, which Edgar somehow managed to navigate successfully, and from the top of the hill we could see a red brick house in the distant valley. Behind it sat an aluminum-sided pole barn. Edgar shoved the truck into four-wheel-drive to gain purchase on the muddy lane and maneuvered the truck down the slick cow path. I sat upright gripping my door handle as if that would help Edgar stay on the road.

So slowly we descended, yet the truck felt beneath us as if it were wearing ice skates. Even with the four-wheel-drive, the truck's rear end was trying to catch up with its front end, and I bit my lip as Edgar turned the wheel in the direction of the slide.

We passed a small herd of cattle, all of whom stared in disbelief as we slid awkwardly past them. After another few hair-raising moments, Edgar brought the truck to a sliding halt just short of colliding with the electric-wire fence. The house and barn stood before us.

"Wow," Edgar said. "That was close. Good we have four-wheel-drive. I hope we can make it back up the driveway. That was a pretty steep hill. But Sterling has a tractor that could pull us up if we get stuck." He turned off the engine.

I released my grip on the door handle.

"Oh, look," Edgar said, pointing to the pasture within the fence. "Those are our two patients."

I squinted and eased down from the truck. Two equines were muzzle-deep in the mud. "They only *sort of* look like mules," I said, walking up to the fence. "That one must be a cross of some sort."

"Yeah, he is. His name is," he said, pointing to the stocky chestnut, "Hacksaw."

"Hacksaw?" I laughed. "What a name!" The red-bodied horse looked up from the mud-splattered pasture when he heard his name. Then he and his partner went back to sniffing the icy field for vagrant weeds.

"Hacksaw," Edgar said, "is a special mule; he's a Paso Fino and donkey cross. He really ambles when they move him up in his gaits."

I watched the mule picking amongst the stones and mud balls in the pasture for something edible. Then I heard a door slam, and a man came running over the slippery drive toward us.

"Hey, Doc," he called. In his hurry the slimey mud propelled him forward much like a first-time figure skater, and his arms wheeled frantically. Incredibly he managed to catch himself just before falling on his dog, who was peddling furiously to steer clear.

"Dutchess, naw get awt off the vay, oncet even," he said to the dog. "Ya gonna make me fall, naw," he yelled in a Dutch accent. But try as they might, he and his dog weren't slowing up at all—and they were headed right toward our truck. That would stop them—sure enough. "My gudtness, I can hardly stop oncet, this ice iss so badt," he hollered.

"Take it easy, Sterling," Edgar called. "I'm not in a hurry. I don't want you to kill yourself in your own driveway."

"Vell, I vasn't really in much off a hurry, but the slippy driveway gave me momentum right when I stepped awtside on the porch," he laughed as he skidded to a stop beside the truck. The dog slid past us, his legs skittering in the mud, and then he dashed over to a downed tree branch which he lapped into his mouth and began to wrestle.

Sterling was an average-sized man sporting a set of denim coveralls designed for someone three times his heft. Of course, he probably wore a full set of street clothes underneath it, but the outfit still hung away from his frame, the legs billowing out around him like sewer pipes. Little did he realize he was in fashion with the male youth of the day who wore their pants similarly: loose enough to squeeze a small sequoia down each pantsleg. Sterling looked to be in his forties, and he had cultivated a beard that hung as limply from his chin as did the pants around his body. He looked in good physical shape for his age, something the huge pants belied.

"I'm Edgar's wife and helper," I said. "It's nice to meet you."

"Oh, so this iss the missuss, iss it?" Sterling grinned. "Nice to meet ya."

"Now, exactly what are we doing here to your guys, Sterling?" Edgar said.

"Vell, chust give Hacksaw and Cody all their shots, whateva they need, naw. Ya know, Bonnie and I take 'em inta da voots for huntin' trips, and sometimes we meet up vit other horses on da trail. I don't want 'em to pick up somethin' contagious." He pronounced it "kun-tay-chuss."

"Okay," Edgar said, "then I recommend vaccinating for Eastern and Western encephalitis, tetanus, influenza, and "rhino," rabies, and Potomac Horse Fever—just in case you get in with some animals that are infected with those diseases."

Sterling nodded.

"I don't remember seeing you with glasses before, Sterling. When did you get them?" Edgar said. He remembered things like that about people, along with the color of their eyes; whereas, I couldn't recall if a guy wore a moustache or was bald.

"Oh, cheessus. Dese are chust my big ol' safety goggles. Before you came, I vas hammering an old mailbox together, and I forgot to take 'em off. I alvays vear 'em when I work—to be safe, ya know."

"Yeah," Edgar mused. "I didn't think I remembered you with glasses."

The dog was off at the corner of the barn twirling the large branch over his head and running circles with it in his mouth. Periodically the heavy end of the branch dug into the mud and brought the dog to a screeching halt, whereupon he resituated his grip on the thing and took off with it again.

"Guess I'll go awt there and get the two mules for ya," Sterling said. "Dey're eassy to catch, naw. They alvays come to me cuss they know they're gonna get a peppermint stick." Sterling smiled.

"Peppermint stick?" I said.

"Yep," Sterling said. "Those mules chust love candy canes. And dey doan't even haf to vait for Christmas, oncet even."

"Get awt," I said in appreciation.

"Here haf one, too-a," he said as he opened the gate. And with that he fished one out of his huge pants pocket and threw it to me. Only by luck did I catch it, and then I ripped off the paper and sucked on the curved end. The flavor sparkled in my mouth.

"Here, Doc. Here's von for you, too-a." A candy cane sailed through the air.

By the looks of his lumpy pockets, Sterling must've carried a real load of candy canes around in his pants. Just how many he stored in those huge drawers, like a chipmunk's loaded cheeks, would probably remain a mystery.

Immediately the two animals approached as Sterling reached into his bulging coverall pockets for the peppermints he and they knew were hidden there. Their pace quickened, their steps steadfast and sure. They were on a mission. But they were no sooner within arm's reach of Sterling than they came to a skidding halt, sat back on their muddy haunches, spun off their hind legs, and bolted away, pieces of mud, stones, and ice spraying and clattering noisily behind them.

"Vhat da hell vas dat all abawt naw," Sterling said flabbergasted, a peppermint stick dangling weakly from his fist.

"That's strange," Edgar said. "I thought they were coming right to you."

"They neffer run away. They alvays come to me and Bonnie—on accawnt off the peppermint, ya know. They chust love peppermint. Let me try again, oncet." Off Sterling skipped in the direction of the mules. We watched from the fence, and I could see that with a little coaxing, Sterling had managed to grab Cody by the halter. When he brought the mule through the gate, the animal was busily munching his candy cane. He snorted as he passed by, and I could smell the good, clean smell of his breath.

"Vell, naw I godt to get da udder von." So out to the pasture he went again, slipping and sliding through the mud. It's a good thing he was wearing his high rubber mucking boots, I thought.

But this was a case of Sisyphus and his grapes. Sterling proffered the candy and Hacksaw, with his foot-long ears and pointy nose, approached so close as to be able to snatch the mint out of Sterling's hand. But the minute Sterling went to take him by the halter, Hacksaw whirled on his heels and retreated to several feet away.

In a few minutes Hacksaw approached again. Sterling put out his hand with the candy cane. Clearly Hacksaw was focused on the mint candy. He came closer, tempted.

"Here ya go, Hacksaw," Sterling said. "Come get your peppermint stick."

Hacksaw approached to within a foot of Sterling's hand, and then, like a frightened cat, he darted away.

"Huh, that's funny," Edgar remarked to me, watching. "His mules always come to him. They never act this way. They almost seem afraid of him. Even the one he first caught still seemed scared when Sterling led him to the barn."

The scene played itself for what was probably the sixth time, and then Sterling, dejected, trudged empty-handed back through the gate.

He shook his head, muttering, "I chust doan't know vhat's ailin' him. He's never done thadt before. He's afraid off me for some reason. I chust doan't know why, though."

"Do you think I could catch him?" Edgar volunteered. "Maybe he'll come to me."

Sterling shook his head. "Oh, I dawt it, naw. He doan't usually take too vell to strangers. But vhat the hell. I sure didn't do any gudt tryin'. Maybe you can get him." And then Sterling handed Edgar a candy cane. "Here, this'll help maybe."

Edgar slipped through the gate and marched out to the pasture where Hacksaw stood, his huge ears pointed toward him like focussed antennae. Edgar offered the peppermint, and with that Hacksaw stepped right up to him, wrapped his long lips around the end of the stick and allowed Edgar to take him by the halter. In a few minutes Edgar and Hacksaw were walking calmly through the gate.

"I'll be damndt," Sterling said in a wondrous voice. "Vhat's vit dadt animal, anyvay? Here, I'll put him in his stall." And as Sterling walked up to his mule and extended his arm, Hacksaw's eyes widened to the size of drinking coasters. But Edgar wouldn't let go. He held tight as the mule plunged backward. In the melee Hacksaw lost his balance and sat right down in the mud on his rear end, pulling Edgar toward him through the debris. But Edgar tightened his grip on Hacksaw's halter and planted his heels. Instinctively Sterling backed away, and then, the threat gone, Hacksaw stood up, a picture of tranquility.

"It's definitely something about *you*," Edgar said to Sterling.

"He's never done dadt before, naw," Sterling said in a sad voice. He adjusted the glasses over the bridge of his nose. "I doan't know vhat's wrong. He's my best animal."

"He's scared to death of you," Edgar said.

"But I doan't beat him or nothin'," Sterling said with apparent guilt.

"No, of course you don't beat him, Sterling. But what could it be? Why is he so afraid of you?"

Sterling thought and thought. He took off his glasses and rubbed the steam out of them. Then slowly he put the thickly-paned goggles back on. I looked at him and noticed for the first time that his eyes seemed exceptionally large behind the spectacles—enlarged as if behind a close-up lens.

"Could it be your glasses?" I shouted. "Maybe he's not used to seeing you with glasses on."

Sterling looked incredulously at me, his eyes as big as cue balls behind the bottle lenses. "I'll betcha dadt's it!" he blurted.

"Take them off, and see how he reacts to you," Edgar suggested.

Sterling folded the glasses into his shirt pocket and walked over to Hacksaw. Edgar held the mule tighter.

Nothing happened. Hacksaw stood still as moss.

Taking Hacksaw by the halter, Sterling said, "Naw vas it my glasses (he pronounced it "classes") that scared ya, Boy? Dey're chust my safety glasses." Then Sterling smiled and led Hacksaw into the barn and to his stall. He was obviously relieved that his horse was able to recognize him again.

"I'll be damndt," Sterling repeated. "It vas the glasses! Isn't dadt the veirdest thing, naw?"

We followed Sterling and Hacksaw into the barn where Edgar set up his vaccinations and deworming medicine. Sterling continued to rub Hacksaw's brow while Edgar filled the syringes, and I readied the dewormer tubes.

"This guy is somethin' else, ya know," said Sterling with admiration. "He's chust a bik baby, is all. Scared of hiss shadow, but, boy, iss he a gudt huntin' mule. I can take him inta da voots to hunt 'coons, and when he knows I'm gonna shoot, he chust freezes (he pronouned it "freess—uss"), so I get a perfect shot.

"And vhat a trail mule he iss! He goes through anything; he can scale glacier boulders bigger dan the barn. He does real gudt for me. And, belieff it or not, I ride him with a treeless saddle, and it's like I'm sittin' in my oldt armchair at home." He looked in Hacksaw's eye and smiled proudly. "Ridin' him is like floatin'."

Edgar drove the vaccination home so quickly Hacksaw wasn't even aware what happened. Then, while Sterling steadied him by the halter, I handed Edgar a paste wormer.

"How does he like these wormers, Sterling?" Edgar asked.

"Oh, vhy he'll eat most everythin'. He'll gobble dadt up, too-a. Cripes, von time he had a badt cough, so I gave him a gudt dose of pine tar. He ate it like it was ice cream." Sterling laughed.

I cringed—another deadly home remedy that an animal luckily survived.

Sterling patted Hacksaw on the neck as Edgar pushed home the plunger on the wormer tube. Hacksaw licked the corners of his mouth and swallowed the paste willingly enough.

"Yop, I can remember vhen vee brought him back from the trainer. He was so vild, he gave me the shits. He'd go any damndt vay he'd want to go, no matter vhat I told him. I'd be barely hangin' on yellin', 'Whoa-oa-oa, you son-off-a-bitch. Whoa, naw.' But he chust kept goin' vherever he vanted to go. But naw, he's like ridin' a big, ole armchair."

Edgar was looking underneath Hacksaw's belly at something that obviously concerned him, but he was letting Sterling finish his story. Soon Sterling noticed Edgar staring at Hacksaw's sheath, the sack from which the penis extends and contracts.

"Oh, yeah, I vanted to ask you abawt that. Does it look a little svollen to you?"

"Yes, actually, it does. That's what I was looking at. It may need cleaning. When was the last time you cleaned his sheath?" Edgar said.

"Vhy, acshally, it vas last veek. Bonnie and I cleaned it real gudt." Then he looked again at the swollen underside and said, "Vell, maybe *too gudt,* the vay it looks."

"I think it's a bit inflamed," Edgar said. "What did you use to clean it?"

I was hoping he was not going to say Ajax, and he didn't, thank goodness.

"Vell, Bonnie used some of her dishvashing liquidt, and we got up there real gudt with a rag and all."

"A rag!" Edgar blurted.

At least it wasn't a Brillo pad, I thought.

"Yep, an oldt rag Bonnie had. Oh, doan't vorry—it vas clean and all. Hacksaw didn't seem to mindt at all. He put it right awt for us, and we scrupped it real gudt. Then Bonnie went all the vay up hiss sheath with the rag and cleaned awt the inside. She vent up so far she hadt to get on her knees," he laughed.

Edgar winced. "Next time you go to clean his sheath, use a milder soap, like Betadine scrub, and don't use a rag or anything. Just use clean, soapy hands. Afterwards rinse it out with warm water. Then I like to grease it up real good with baby oil. For now, though, I'm going to give him a shot of lasix to get rid of the swelling, and I'll give him a steroid shot, too, to reduce the inflammation."

"Sawnds gudt, Doc," Sterling said.

We administered Cody's vaccinations and deworming medicine, too, while Sterling bedded the mules down with fresh hay and water. He gave each mule a peppermint stick and said good night. Then he slid the large garage doors shut, and we walked toward the truck. Sterling's dog had long ago tired of the tree branch, which lay abandoned in the backyard.

We climbed into the truck, and Edgar started the engine. He kicked it into four-wheel-drive and pressed the pedal until the truck pulled us from the mud. Slowly we clawed our way around the curves, past the gaping cattle to the top of the hill, then pulled onto the macadam road and wound down back into the town of Normal Square.

I begged Edgar to stop at the local five and dime, not only for a shoe-fly pie but also because I had another curious hunger for a candy cane.

"Why didn't you just ask Sterling for an extra one?" Edgar said, pulling into the parking lot.

I was back in minutes with my packages and sucking on the end of a peppermint stick already. I handed Edgar one, too. Then when we backed away and onto the road I smiled at the thought of Hacksaw and Cody enjoying their daily candy canes. To be sure, those mules are the Heckenbrodt's kids. They receive excellent vet care on a regular basis, and they enjoy weekend excursions into the woods with their owners. The mules are true family members who relish candy the way any human does.

I sighed and crunched the end of my candy cane.

Thumbelina

WE ACQUIRED SOPHIE, A MAMMOTH YEARLING JENNY, as partial payment for a veterinary bill. Her former owners had named her Flopsy because when she was first born her huge ears hung limp as a lamb's, draping her head like a Russian scarf. At a year old the chestnut-colored donkey easily reached 14.2 hands, and that didn't include her skyscraper ears, which added an additional foot to her stature.

Born and raised in the ghetto of a hack stable in the Poconos, Sophie had no taste of the good life. Her only experience was living amid a crowd of overworked mules and worn-out horses who wore their saddles and bridles eight hours a day and carted overweight, unfriendly big city tourists on rides through the woods. At Jason's Hack Stable, Flopsy was just another number among the fifty or so animals that shared the meager offerings of oats and grass hay thrown to them twice a day. One as young as Flopsy was always at the bottom of the equine pecking order, left with only sprigs of hay for her supper.

Flopsy had lived in a barren pasture and led a life barren of friends, human or otherwise. The mules and horses were too tired to pay her much attention and the people too busy. Unusable for another two years, when she would take her rightful place at the hitching post, she was considered little more than a nuisance by her owners. Daily from her mud lot she watched the strings of mules, weighted down with the tenth round of tourists, marching wearily out from their hitching post positions. In an hour she watched them plod back to their position where the rider slid awkwardly to the ground and walked away without even a pat.

The first thing I did when Flopsy arrived muddy and thin was change her name to a human one. Thereafter she would be known as Sophie, after our loving, long-haired calico cat that had been killed on the road. For an animal that had been so neglected for the greater part of her life, Sophie was surprisingly calm and well-mannered. For example, she had no idea what a curry comb was, but she obviously liked the feel of it along her back. And she allowed us to groom her ears and pick her feet with no complaint.

Sophie certainly enjoyed all the attention showered on her those first few days: the brushing, the ear clipping and cleaning, the apple treats, and the petting. At first she didn't know what to do in our lush pasture and stood outside with the llama and Scotch Highland steer watching them eat. It didn't take her long, though, to figure out that what she was standing on was edible. In just a few short weeks her ribs disappeared behind a layer of fat and muscle.

Sophie had no worries about getting enough to eat, for Larry the llama was a delicate eater. In contrast, Scotty consumed with the best of his breed, but there were more than a few acres for him to sate himself on. And every day Edgar went out to the barnyard offering Sophie a grain biscuit and discussing the day's happenings with her. Sophie was in paradise.

Little did Sophie or we realize that in another year a playmate would show up on our doorstep and share her life—another payment for a veterinary bill. An old rickety horse trailer backed up to the barnyard one day, and out bounced a Sicilian donkey. Benjy was a diminutive guy—around eleven hands—and more resembled a Shetland pony than a horse. He was a brownish-gray mini donkey with the typical Sicilian racing stripes over his back and a few spots of white between them. He had come from a farm whose owner had raised miniature species. Benjy, however, didn't size up too well when it came to being used for breeding stock; he was too large for the breeder's liking. He was a castoff, and that's how he came to us.

Giant Sophie, who had grown to sixteen hands, and tiny Benjy avoided each other at first, but in a few weeks they had become friends of the field. It was nice for Sophie to have one of her own kind for company instead of an alien like the pointy-lipped llama or the nose-licking Scotch Highland steer.

Benjy, however, found life not entirely idyllic on the old Balliet farm. Once Sophie became used to him, she laid down a few rules of the pasture that all equine family members needed to follow. Rule number one was that Sophie was the boss and Benjy her vassal. He would obey unquestioningly—penalty: a kick in the ass of the ass by the ass. Benjy learned his position fast and well. Vassalage suited him; he seemed to enjoy his dominatrix.

Though he had plenty of food, company of all kinds, and a clean stall, Benjy still found adjusting to his new life a bit daunting. Along with learning to obey Sophie, he also had to deal with physical hazards he hadn't been accustomed to: a pond, creek, steep hills, and barbed wire fencing.

In fact, a few months after Benjy arrived, he managed to snag one of his long ears on the barbed wire. That day when I stopped for the mail, I told Edgar of the ragged ear, "Benjy caught his ear on something. It looks pretty nasty."

Edgar peered over the fence into the pasture. Benjy raised his head from the grass, apparently none the worse for wear. His ear had a large, blood-encrusted gash a quarter of the way through it.

"Better fix that before it gets infected," Edgar said. "Guess I better castrate him while I'm at it, too. I meant to castrate him when he first came, but he was pretty wild then, ya know. Remember—we couldn't catch him. At least I think he'll walk up to me now. You can help me with it, okay?"

"Sure," I said. With that he went to find a lead rope.

In a few minutes Edgar had coaxed Benjy over to him just long enough to slip a pony halter over his little head and clip a lead rope to it. Benjy didn't seem to mind being haltered. Then Edgar led him into the clinic where I talked to him while Edgar slipped him the sleepy juice.

The cleaning and stitching of the ear was done in about ten minutes. Then Edgar castrated him, which was as uneventful as any castration he had ever done. We waited for Benjy to sleep off his anesthesia, and within twenty minutes he hopped to his feet. Edgar and I could steady such a small, low-to-the-ground mini very easily. We must have looked like two bookends supporting the whoozy donkey. In another couple of minutes, we released him back into the pasture—deeds accomplished without incident.

Many months later, we watched the barnyard crew devouring their dinner of alfalfa and oats scattered on a few choice hay bales and ledges devoid of snow. Benjy and Sophie stood together munching hay, now inseparable buddies. I laughed at the difference in size between them. Benjy sported a myriad of colors: brown stripes on a red background interspersed with white spots, while Sophie was a faded redhead with only one stripe down her back. But the striking difference was their build: the top of Benjy's head only came up to Sophie's hocks. He was of petite, slight stature, while she had a solid, large-boned, mule-like body. He was a jelly bean next to a jaw breaker, a snowflake next to a drift, a kumquat next to a honeydew, a Cessna 150 next to an Airbus.

To be sure, Sophie was a giant compared to him, and she ruled the roost with a gargantuan personality as well. Benjy knew not to mess with her; he rarely stepped out of line. If he didn't behave himself, Sophie issued him a swift and carefully placed kick in the butt or side. For days afterward the little guy walked the pasture with a hoof print tattooed on his hide, a souvenir of Sophie's tyranny. Benjy was Sophie's ward; he was her subject, tied by his ears to her imaginary apron strings. Benjy walked a wide berth around Sophie when he passed, avoiding the kick he knew was sure to come. Their relationship, it seemed to all of us, was that of wicked stepmother and obedient stepson. At times I pitied Benjy as he tiptoed carefully around the pasture, such an obsequious thing. Yet, for all Sophie's bullying, they were always together in the field.

One day while Sophie and Benjy stood ankle-deep in the snow lapping the good hay off the rocks, Edgar's mother happened by. She, too, rested her arms upon the wooden barnyard fence and watched them eating. Then she proclaimed, "Sophie's pregnant."

"Pregnant!" the word shot from Edgar's mouth. "Impossible.

There's no stallion here to *make* her pregnant." He laughed and shook his head at the silly prediction.

"Well, I don't care. I think she's pregnant. She's larger in the belly than she was last year," she sniffed.

"Well, that's because she's eating too much. But she's not bred. That I know."

"Says you," his mother smiled. "I know you're the vet—I'm not—but she looks bigger to me in a motherly way. I don't think she's fat; she's pregnant. Ya know, I have a sixth sense when it comes to pregnant people or animals."

"Well," said Edgar with a smirk, "Who do you think the father could be? It's certainly not the llama or the steer, and Benjy only comes up to Sophie's hocks. He'd need to mount her from a ladder or something." He laughed, then looked at me. "Hey, Gay, Mom thinks Sophie is pregnant. Now who could be her suitor? Benjy the gelding? And how do you think he reached her? Hey, maybe he stacked a couple of rocks together and climbed aboard!"

"Ship ahoy!" I yelled, laughing.

Edgar laughed, too.

But Edgar's mother smiled wisely and said, "Go ahead and laugh. I still say she's in foal."

"It would have to be some kind of immaculate conception or something," Edgar answered. "Besides his being too small to mount her, he's castrated. You can't get blood out of a stone, and you can't get offspring out of a castrated donkey."

"Mark my words," his mother warned.

In January we were vacationing in Costa Rica when a phone call came through to our hotel room. It was Edgar's mother. Was something wrong at home?

"I told you so," she said mysteriously.

"You told me what," he said with knitted brow.

"About Sophie," she said.

"What about Sophie? Is she all right?" Edgar looked worried, and I stopped brushing my teeth so that I could hear more of his conversation.

"She had twins last night," Edgar's mother declared.

"No way!" Edgar shouted loud enough to wake up the entire hotel.

"Yes sir!" she laughed. "Unfortunately the larger twin was stillborn, Carlin said, but the smaller one is still alive—only weighs maybe thirty pounds. Carlin checked her out real good, though. She's fine. It was a girl by the way."

"I don't believe it," Edgar whispered. "How did it happen?" Then Edgar told me the news.

"Get awt!" I shouted from the bathroom.

"Told you so," his mother repeated.

"Is the foal nursing?" Edgar asked.

"Yes. Carlin says she stood up and was drinking from Sophie. They're out in the pasture with the rest of the herd. Is that all right?"

"Sure, as long as the other animals are tolerating the foal and not chasing her."

"Well, Sophie is protecting her really well. Poor Benjy got close one time, and as usual she kicked the you-know-what out of the poor guy. She didn't want him near her baby."

"What does the baby look like?" Edgar said.

"She looks just like Benjy."

"Benjy. Benjy. But he couldn't possibly be the father. I castrated him, and he is so small. How did he get to her?"

"Told you so," she repeated. "Maybe he did the deed before you castrated him—obviously he must have. Maybe he stood on a chair or stacked a couple of egg crates. Maybe she kneeled. 'Where there's a will, there's a way,' I always say."

Edgar laughed. "But she always was so nasty to him."

"Love works in strange ways," she said. "Anyway, I'd thought I'd add to your vacation with the news. I'm hanging up now. One last thing . . . I told you so."

By the end of our vacation I had decided upon a name for the new foal. In honor of Benjy and his "beating all the odds" I would call her by a diminutive name, as tiny but mighty in concept as he: Thumbelina. Edgar liked the name from the beginning.

We came home a few days later, and dashed down to the old farm to visit Sophie and see Benjy's new baby. She was so tiny—a mini donkey that mirrored Benjy. To be sure, the name "Thumbelina" fit her extraordinarily well because she was a miniature mix of Sophie and Benjy—so frail, so fragile looking. She shared her father's stature but her mother's color—a heathered chestnut with a stripe down her back.

Yet, already at that age she displayed a likeable personality. Thumbelina was curious in every sense of the word. Instead of being afraid of the humans who fussed over her and cooed baby talk to her, she approached us all with no such nervousness. At such a young age, she had the courage of an aged soldier. She loved rubs on the forehead and offered no objections to Edgar's examining her with a stethoscope and otoscope. She was a fearless, outgoing animal with an appreciative nature.

A day later while I was straightening up the house, Edgar bolted through the door.

"Hurry!" he yelled. "You have to help me."

Why?" I said. "What happened?" I could see he was upset.

"It's the foal—Thumbelina. She broke her leg. One of the other animals, maybe even Sophie, stepped on it. It's not a compound fracture, but she just drags it behind her when she walks. She's bearing no weight on it at all. I could kick myself—guess I should have separated them from the rest of the herd. I didn't think that would happen."

"Which leg and bone is it?" I asked.

"Hind cannon. I think I can cast it all right, but I need someone to help."

Minutes after confirming the break with an X-ray, tiny Thumbelina was lying asleep under anesthesia on the surgery table in the clinic. Quickly Edgar shaved the leg, wrapped it with heavy gauze and cottons and molded the wet fiberglass casting material around the hoof and leg all the way to the stifle. I stood by with the scissors and handed him the materials while he manipulated the broken bones back into place. He took a radiograph to make sure the bones were aligned correctly within the cast. Then we waited for her to wake up.

"You're going to be all right, Thumbelina," I whispered in her ear as she tried to focus on the walls around her. "This is only a minor setback."

In half an hour she was completely awake, and once she climbed to her feet, we carefully steered her out of the clinic and back into the barnyard dusted with a thin coating of snow. Sophie brayed a happy greeting. Surely she must have thought someone had kidnapped her firstborn. Sophie nuzzled her baby, almost knocking her on the ground in the process.

We had been worried that little Thumbelina might have problems getting around the pasture with such a cumbersome cast. After all, she was only a frail thing and had a hard enough time controlling her unsteady legs, let alone getting around on one hampered by an unyielding weight. But though she walked stiffly, she followed Sophie down to the creek as if the cast was part of her.

"Do you think we should have separated Sophie and Thumbelina from the rest of the herd?" Edgar said as we watched the two move slowly out to pasture.

"I don't know. Maybe. But it's possible that they'd get stir crazy cooped up in a stall for weeks. I think we're okay with letting them outside."

As it happened, however, our decision to let the two outside with the others was wrong. The next day we walked down to the farm to see how the mother and new baby were doing. Sophie was in the barnyard hovering over her foal. Thumbelina was just lying there. She didn't look right.

"There's something wrong with Thumbelina," I said, rushing over to the fence. Sophie honked a greeting but wouldn't leave Thumbelina's side. Thumbelina did not attempt to rise, unusual for so gregarious a baby.

"Oh, no," Edgar moaned as he climbed the fence, all the time looking at the newly cast leg. He ran over to Thumbelina, who lifted her head to greet him. She whistled a couple notes of hello through her nose but still didn't offer to stand up. "She's broken her femur," he said in an ominous whisper.

I rushed after him into the pen. The large upper bone between her hip and her stifle was broken. I winced at the bones grating as Edgar manipulated them to see where exactly the break was.

Edgar stood up and just looked down helplessly at the poor baby. The same leg that had the cast was now broken above it on the large upper bone—the equivalent of a person's thigh bone.

"I have an idea. This is too big a problem now for me to handle. She needs a large animal facility. We've got to call Quakertown. Maybe

Randy can do surgery on her. Get the Jeep ready. You've got to take us down."

"In the little Jeep Wrangler? Aren't we going in the horse trailer?"

"No—she mustn't move that leg at all. She only weighs about forty pounds, so I'm going to put her in the back of the Jeep and hold her in my lap the whole way down. That way she can't move the leg and hurt it more."

I ran back to the house for the Jeep and was back down at the farm in minutes. Edgar hoisted Thumbelina into his arms, and I opened the gate for them. Sophie followed behind, desperate to be with her baby, but I had to push her back out of the way. She couldn't go along. She didn't understand that she would be no help to her foal.

The trip to Quakertown took an hour, and I tried my hardest to give the two the smoothest ride a Jeep Wrangler could offer. Edgar sat in the wayback with the foal in his lap while she leaned against his chest. Together the two faced backward, looking out the rear window. Every time I looked in my rearview mirror, I saw the outline of two heads—Edgar's and Thumbelina's right beside his. I would have

Benjy, Sophie, and Thumbelina

laughed had the whole situation not seemed so pathetic. For that solid hour's ride Edgar talked to Thumbelina and braced the broken leg against all the bumps and dips. Not once did she try to get up or struggle against him.

Randy was already expecting us, and when we pulled into the clinic's parking lot, the tall, good-looking surgeon stood before the doors to the large animal clinic. He walked over to the Jeep and peeked inside.

"My God, she's so small," Randy said with a worried look.

"Yeah," Edgar said, still supporting the broken leg of the foal. "She's only about forty pounds, if that. First, one of the other animals had stepped on her cannon bone and broken it. I cast it, but either the cast was too heavy and broke the femur or another animal stepped on that bone, too."

"Quite possible the mother herself stepped on it," Randy said. "I've seen many foals with broken legs. The mothers are so protective they don't realize they're standing too close to where the foal is lying. And, of course, straw may have been covering the leg, too. Mares aren't real careful about not stepping on their babies."

Randy helped Edgar and Thumbelina out of the back of the Jeep. Together they carried Thumbelina into the clinic. We all gathered round as Randy examined the fractured femur. He poked and prodded the appendage, which Thumbelina didn't appreciate but tolerated well enough, considering the pain she must've been in. As he proceeded with the examination, Randy's face became set, determined.

"I can't do much about this," he declared finally.

Edgar looked as though he had been punched in the mouth. *"You can't* do surgery on her?" he asked incredulously. "You *can't* fix it?"

"No, *I* can't, but my wife might be able to."

"But she's a small animal surgeon. She doesn't work on horses."

"I know she doesn't," Randy smiled. "But we have a small animal here, right? I'll go find her and see what she says." With that he disappeared through the clinic doors toward the small animal section of the hospital.

Edgar and I looked doubtfully at each other. Thumbelina lay between us on the floor, and I knelt down to pet her.

It was at times like these that I always felt so helpless and vulnerable to forces beyond my control. When a loved member of the family, which each of our animals happened to be, was in desperate need of help that Edgar or I couldn't provide, I developed a sense of complete futility. And shortly thereafter birthed the feeling of dependence on Edgar—or in this case, Randy—relying on him to come across with his expertise that, alone, would help my animal. But when we got to Quakertown and Randy had pronounced himself nearly as unable in aiding Thumbelina as we, I really became worried.

Certainly I had no skills to help the little donkey. Edgar had already tried to fix her leg, but the problem had grown worse, so that, he, too, probably felt somewhat ineffectual. He, too, was depending on Randy. But now Randy couldn't remedy the situation. I felt weak. Would Randy's wife come through? Surely this trip wouldn't result in our having to put Thumbelina to sleep—right here, in the next few minutes. I swallowed hard.

Finally Randy came back with his wife. She leaned over Thumbelina, palpated her leg and said assuredly, "I can fix it."

I felt strong again.

She continued, "Yes, I think I can fix that fracture with screws and wire. Of course, I'll only know if that's possible after I've taken the X-rays, but I think that sounds like a plan. I'll make a long incision right here," she said, demonstrating with a finger on Thumbelina's leg, "and I'll just use screws and wire. I don't think a pin would be appropriate in this situation. Again, the X-rays will give me a more definitive answer."

"What do you think?" Randy said to Edgar.

Edgar said, "You guys are the experts. Just fix her up. She's quite a character. I want her to pull through this."

Randy's wife added, "Also, I think I'll splint the cannon bone, so that it's not so heavy for her."

"Good idea," Edgar said.

We left her that day in the hands of two of the area's best veterinary surgeons. From what I knew about Randy and from how he handled our horses' colic surgeries, I knew Thumbelina would come through the surgery just fine. If Randy and his wife weren't successful, then no one would be.

That afternoon we drove home, leaving Thumbelina in very good hands.

Four hours after we got home the phone rang. It was Barb, Randy's wife. She said Thumbelina's surgery went fine. Her cannon bone now had a splint, and the femur had been repaired, just as she planned—with a couple of screws and wire. Thumbelina, she said, was recovering nicely in one of the dog kennels and had already tested out her repaired leg. She had no trouble standing. Barb recommended we pick her up the next day. One of the technicians would feed her overnight with milk replacement every three hours.

Early the next morning we set out for Quakertown Vet Clinic. Edgar wrapped his arms around Thumbelina and lifted her carefully into the back of the Jeep. Randy wasn't around, but his wife saw Thumbelina off. She advised us to keep the foal and her mother separate from the herd until the leg healed completely. And she advised us to help her up to nurse every four hours.

Barb said, "She is going to need to nurse at least six times a day until she finds out how to get up and maneuver that leg better. In a few days she should be able to get up by herself."

"Yes," agreed Edgar. "Of course, once she's up, she'll be able to nurse anytime she wants to. It's the getting into the standing position that's the trick. And foals do lie down a lot."

"Yes, they do,"

"That's all right. I'll see that she gets the help she needs. She's only a peanut. Anybody at the clinic can help her if we're not around."

I said, "I'll just make sure I'm around to help, too. I'm sure it won't be long until she figures out how to maneuver herself into a standing position."

"No, it shouldn't," Randy's wife said.

We thanked her for her help, and then Edgar took his place beside Thumbelina in the back of the Jeep. I drove Edgar and Thumbelina home, Edgar sitting with the foal in his lap and supporting the newly repaired leg. As I drove, I marveled at the docility of the mini donkey. Perhaps she was behaving well because she trusted people not to hurt her. Or maybe she knew somehow that she had a bum leg and needed all the help she could get.

Whatever the reason, she was a good, calm little animal, and her demeanor probably contributed to her recovery nearly as much as the expert surgery on her leg.

Fortunately, Thumbelina required help to stand every few hours for only about a week. She soon figured out how to wield her leg around and raise herself. The rest would be only a matter of time, and a long time it was for Thumbelina's leg to heal. Mother and filly were not ecstatic to be confined in a back stall of the barn, but they had each other, which was enough. Thumbelina was a resilient, intelligent animal who knew how to take care of herself. For two months she and her mother lived in a cozy, straw-lined stall, and then one beautiful spring day, we released them into the pasture.

That morning Thumbelina tiptoed out to the edge of the barnyard, glancing all around her. Sophie followed her, careful not to rush her foal beyond her capabilities. When they came to the boundary of the barnyard and saw the other animals down by the pond, they both took off at a slow trot, eager to join in the fun.

To this day Thumbelina has the screws and wire in her femur. She is well healed and much older now, and she is still the trusting, appreciative, friendly creature that had ridden with Edgar in the back of the Jeep.

Josip and His Circus Tigers

HAD I KNOWN THAT IN SPRING we'd be called out to examine a family of circus tigers, I could have told the radio interviewer who joked about the "dingbat" that my husband also risks his life examining wild jungle cats. Certainly the DJ could have made a wisecrack on that subject like, "Hey—was the tiger's name Tony, and was he a real flake?"

That day, as we entered the Trexlertown shopping center that hosted the Clyde Beatty Cole Brothers Circus, we were accosted by well-meaning animal rights activists protesting the circus's cruelty to animals. They marched back and forth, pumping their placards up and down and yelling at families in vans—telling them not to patronize the circus. As we drove into the complex, a protestor, yelling into our window, flashed us his sign reading: BOYCOTT THIS CIRCUS—CRUELTY TO ANIMALS.

I didn't understand, even though the signs were perfectly clear.

"What do they mean—cruelty?" I asked, craning my neck as another demonstrator shouted into our truck window. "Is there something going on here that we don't know about?"

"Animal rights people are always picketing circuses: standard practice, I guess. I'm not exactly sure of their agenda. I guess they're against caging animals and exploiting them for human entertainment."

"That sounds reasonable," I said. "I don't know much about it all, but I'd probably agree with them. Animals should live in an environment that is natural to them." As we drove past the protestors, I felt immediately apprehensive; after all, they were yelling at our truck—at us, at me.

"They're yelling at me!" I blurted as we drove past the protestors. "I don't like them yelling at me!"

"They're not just yelling at you; they're yelling at everybody," Edgar reminded me.

"So what! They're still yelling at me. I'm not hurting any animals! Why should they holler at me? I haven't even seen the animals yet!"

"Ignore them," Edgar said.

At home that morning I had been as excited as any kid to see animals in the circus. I was anxious to see the tigers, elephants, and trapeze artists perform. It would be a fabulous experience, one long overdue.

But once we had driven through the gates and been assaulted by the protestors, I began to wonder. Why were they yelling at me as if I were, in some way, contributing to their problem? And what exactly were they so angry about?

Was I naive? Had I tripped through life up until this time unaware of the animal abuse that pervaded all circuses? What, exactly, were we driving into, anyway? Would all the animals be emaciated? Would the tigers be rail-thin, lethargic, and confined to tiny, dirty cages? That's evidently what the protestors were claiming.

It was a beautiful day, and I had been looking forward to some fun; I didn't want it ruined by having to see sad animals. Then I began to feel guilty for two reasons: first, I was acting a bit selfish worrying about the sight of suffering animals destroying my fun, and second, somehow, being associated with the veterinarian called to the circus, I was in some way in league with the evil circus managers: Would I be "guilty by association" if I assisted the vet who came to help the abusers? In reality, of course, I was not—not in any way. In fact, I was more on the protestors' side than any of them yelling at me realized. Little did anyone know, except for Edgar, that if I felt any animal in that circus was a victim of abuse or cruelty, I would cause even more of a stink than the animal rights activists. I would be the first to report neglect to the authorities and would follow through against any animal maltreatment.

In the distance and behind the strip mall, we spotted the main circus tent. Its white dome protruded like a snow-capped mountain, and hoards of circus-goers swamped the entrance. We drove under the red and gold banner welcoming us to the Clyde Beatty Cole Brothers Circus, and when Edgar questioned the gatekeepers as to the whereabouts of the tigers, I felt more than a little uneasy.

As circus workers directed us toward the tiger compound, I worried that I might, indeed, become the snitch against the very people who had called us for aid. I also knew that Edgar wouldn't appreciate my contacting the humane society to complain about his circus client. He would probably feel it unethical, unless there was evidence of gross negligence. I reasoned that we were there in the capacity of caregivers and that the probability of witnessing cruelty to the animals was unlikely, considering that *they*, the tiger trainers, had called us to help their animals. But, being the existentialist that I am, I would certainly inform the proper people—no matter who tried to persuade me differently—if I felt abuse existed.

Still I wondered what could be wrong with the tigers? Would Edgar be treating any cuts or scratches that had been caused by whipping or beating? Had the tigers' trainers disciplined them too harshly, bad enough to require veterinary medical attention? Had they withheld food and water to "teach them a lesson." We didn't know. The answering service had only told Edgar that tigers at the circus needed immediate care. I decided to wait and see for myself before letting my imagination run away with my reason.

The first animal we saw on our way to the tigers was an elephant giving pre-show rides to groups of children. The elephant wore a glittery silver and purple headdress and had a large wooden box strapped to its back. Round and round it plodded within the circle, and the half dozen kids in the box wiggled and jerked with the elephant's every move. The elephant didn't look especially happy, but then I supposed beating the same old path for an hour wasn't much of a hoot for an animal that would rather be out exploring the bushveld in Kenya. I sighed heavily: Could this be considered a part of the abuse thing?

On the way to the tiger area, we passed the big top, a flurry of activity in preparation for the upcoming show. The public was already lined up at the entrance, and lots more folks and kids were gathered around the ticket box. Set up all around the backside of the main show tent were the exhibitors' travel campers and animal enclosures. The public was free to walk around those areas behind the big top. There the animal trainers lived and tended their animals, but many trainers protected their privacy by fencing off their personal areas and their animals with orange tape. Without the tape, nosey folks might peer through their camper windows in search of a clown or magician. Others might even wander into the carnival folks' yards to pester the animals in their pens, as if the animal trainers and their animals had no sense of home and privacy.

Soon we came to the llama and camel compound. A camel wearing a red halter with a long red tassel was lounging on the grass in a large, portable metal pen, chewing his cud with nonchalance while his llama consorts stood next to him watching the crowd from over the fence. Piles of hay lay untouched around them. The llamas and camels were housed comfortably right next to their owners' camper from whose stoop I saw a woman in a flashy belly-dancing outfit descend. She wore gold and crimson "Aladdin" pants with a matching cut-off top. On her head was a beaded and sequined tiara with a veil that draped her face. As we passed, she entered the llama pen to ready her animals for their segment of the show.

We pulled the truck to a stop alongside a silver "bullet" mobile house trailer beside which approximately twenty tigers lay under a large, airy tent, each tiger in its own large cage, all lined up in two perfectly straight parallel rows. Each cage was hooked to the one in front and behind it. Behind them was their traveling tractor trailer, minus the truck. Quickly I glanced around. Some of the tigers were flat out asleep while others were sitting sternally, curious of the folks and children passing by. They seemed in good flesh, their eyes and noses clear, their demeanor content. I sighed. So far, so good.

The first row of cats in their carts, I would find out later, were the star performers for the evening. They lay with all the elegance and grandeur of their species in their single-file cages on new, clean sawdust. These tigers were as varied in pattern and color as butterflies. A few were white with gray stripes; some sported beige or red coats with darker brown stripes—such a beautifully variegated group. Their coats were sleek, shiny, and healthy. The giant cats gazed around with interest, surveying their surroundings with snouts pointed and enjoying the breeze that blew through the huge tent canopy. On such an unseasonably warm spring day I was glad to have a little shade myself, so I walked through the grass and under the tent while Edgar knocked on the door of the house trailer.

How unfair it seemed. I had been set up by the protestors to expect some kind of neglect, so I approached the first line of tiger cages half expecting to see some indication of abuse. Careful not to get too close to the large cats, I appraised their living conditions, whether they had food and drink in front of them, whether their cages were clean and safe. I assessed their body conditions—athletic, not ribby, not fat. I analyzed their body language for a clue to their overall condition: relaxed body positions, quiet tails, normal set to the ears, eyes not in slits, content expressions. Finally, I would be able to tell a lot about their treatment from how they interacted with their owners.

Shortly Edgar and a middle-aged couple walked over to where I had become mesmerized before a cage containing two tiger kittens. The young cats rolled and played together, nipping and pulling on each other's loose skin. Edgar introduced me to the trainer, Josip Marcan, who had lived most of his life in Frankfurt, Germany, and his American wife, Cheryl. Josip had been a veterinarian at the Frankfurt Zoo for seven years before he decided to work exclusively with tigers. Then he came to the United States, met Cheryl, and started a private tiger ranch in Ponce de Leon, Florida, on the Panhandle, where they continue to breed, raise, and train fifty to sixty tigers. Their vocation revolves around the tigers they lease out for different events: circuses, TV commercials, movie stints, and safari parks.

Cheryl noticed my interest in the kittens, and as I reached out to tweak the gray tiger kitten's paw that was poking between the metal bars, she warned me to be careful. "You can get away with touching the kittens like that, but, please, don't try it with any of the other cats. They don't know you and will just as soon take your hand off as let you stroke their paws. They wouldn't do it to be nasty, but instinct won't let them trust strangers."

"Yikes!" I said, backing away from the kittens' cage. "I'm sorry. I should have known better, but they're so irresistible and so playful." I laughed at my own ignorance. "They also look so very innocent. But it's all a big act, isn't it? I have to remind myself they're wild animals."

Elise, one of the tenders working with the Marcan's cats, walked past pushing a wheelbarrow. She was making a manure-cleaning round just before the first string of tigers would be wheeled into the big top for their show. She stopped at the kittens' cages and grabbed the kitten's foot I had tweaked.

"EE-ee-eek!" Elise squealed with an impish grin as she lightly squeezed the paw. With that the kitten's eyes went wide, and his mouth shot open with a look of delighted surprise. Quickly he pulled his paw back inside his cage and then lunged, mouth wide, in a mock attack that was clearly for fun.

"That's Buljba. Buljba, you're my baby, aren't you, Sweets?" Elise cooed. She opened the cage door and reached inside to the other kitten, a white tiger cub, who looked at her with big, expectant eyes. "You get a hug, too, Taras. You know I never forget about you. You're my baby, too." She rubbed his belly vigorously, and he rolled over and grabbed her entire hand with his two paws, biting and gnawing on it as if it were a toy. "Okay, Taras, give me my hand back," she said, and she gently removed herself from his grip. "See you guys later," she told the kittens. Then she closed the door and wheeled the barrow to the end cage.

"How much do they weigh?" I asked.

"They're about thirty five pounds now," Cheryl said. "We hand-raised them."

"Will they eventually be performing in the circus?"

"That we'll only know once they're older. If they continue to have a nice temperament, we'll train them for the act and see how they take to it. They seem to have the personality we need at this point, so it's likely they'll eventually join the troupe."

"Who's the one with the problem, Josip?" Edgar asked.

"It's Ramu, Doc, right here in the second line in the cage next to the kittens. He's real sick."

Edgar and I peered into the cage. A large white tiger, whose color is properly called melanistic white, weighed approximately 150 pounds. He looked wiped out, the way I visualized myself with the flu. The tiger merely stared through droopy eyelids, and he seemed clearly disinterested in us. He just lay on his side, flat out, his third eyelids nearly covering his eyes—the true sign of a sick cat.

"It's calici virus," Josip said.

"Did you see the sores?"

"Yep. Ramu, open your mouth and show us your tongue," Josip coaxed. But Ramu just lay there conserving his energy. "I know this guy. He's pretty sick. Ya know, cats disguise their illnesses 'cause in the wild if they don't fake normality they're more vulnerable to attack by other cats. I have a feeling Ramu's been sick for quite awhile before he began showing it today."

We watched him for a few minutes, Edgar observing his respiration and looking at his nose for ulcerations and pus. Ramu yawned, and all four of us quickly squatted down to get a glimpse into his mouth. There, in no uncertain terms, were the telltale ulcers of calici virus. He had a big sore on his tongue and a few smaller ones on his gums.

"Did you vaccinate him for calici virus?" Edgar asked.

Josip said in an exasperated voice, "I've vaccinated them all with *five strains* of the virus to get the maximum protection. But we travel a lot, and somewhere they must be picking it up, maybe from the ground when we let them exercise in their pens. If any household cats with the disease had been in the vicinity or defecated in the area where we let the tigers run, I suppose they could pick up all kinds of different strains."

"Yeah," Edgar agreed. "Well, you know as well as I 'cause you're a vet, too. It works like people flu. We get vaccinated for certain viruses, but those viruses can mutate, and then we have no protection against them. Do any of the other tigers show signs of it?"

"Not so far that we can detect, but Ramu's neighbor, Apollo, here, isn't behaving quite right either. I think he may just be starting with it. He's not himself today. He just is not curious about his surroundings, seems to not have much interest in anything. Also, this morning he didn't eat much breakfast."

"Did Ramu stop eating?"

"Yes, almost entirely. He ate all right last night, but he refused everything today. He doesn't even want to drink anything. That's what worries me the most."

"Yeah—that's not good. We've got to keep him hydrated," Edgar said. "Do you have any liquids, like warm chicken broth or something to entice him to drink?"

Cheryl indicated a large pot next to their camper where floated about fifty raw chicken carcasses.

She said, "We do have chicken juice. I could try to get him to drink some."

Edgar said, "That would be great if he'd drink it. He needs to be started on amoxicillin right away, and so does Apollo, if you say he doesn't seem right. I'll check them both for a high temp, rapid respiration, and other signs of illness, but with those sores in the mouth, I definitely think we have a case of calici virus, in which case, you can really only give supportive nursing care and antibiotics for any secondary infection antecedent to the virus. Calici just has to run its course—probably about four days."

"I usually have a good supply of amoxicillin on hand for problems like this, but I ran out several weeks ago. Of course, I can't buy my own because I'm not licensed to practice veterinary medicine in the United States. Maybe I could buy a few bottles from you, especially since we are having a problem right now with calici," Josip said.

"Sure, I'll get you a couple, and I'm going to draw up a syringeful right now to give Ramu." With that Edgar headed back to the truck.

While Edgar readied the injection, I stayed with the two sick tigers. Calici virus, as I knew from its effects on domestic cats, was a serious illness that left the tongue ulcerated and painful to the extent that the animal refused to eat, but it was seldom deadly. I was glad that the tigers had something treatable, and not something like leukemia that was contagious, untreatable, and fatal. As long as the Marcans encouraged the animals to eat and drink, they would be all right in a few days. I looked at Apollo, the one who was behaving oddly but had no overt signs of illness, and just then he yawned. I quickly squatted, and there I saw the marks of the calici virus. Yep, just as Josip thought—he had it, too.

In a minute Edgar was back with the syringe of antibiotic. He explained the correct dose to Josip, but Josip already knew how much to inject. Since Josip was a vet and was most familiar with his own cats, Edgar left it up to Josip how to dispense the drug.

"You can't go *in* the cage with him, Doc." Josip. said. "Even though he's not feeling too well, he won't tolerate a stranger in his pen. One look at you, and he'll eat you alive—despite his lack of appetite. Usually we have to give injections on the sly, so to speak. As they are lying in their cage, with their back and hind end against the bars, we just sneak up and slip the needle in, at the same time injecting the medicine. Would you like to try it, or do you want me to do it?"

"Well," Edgar said, hesitating, "I'd like to try it, if you don't mind. The more experience I get with these kinds of animals, the better I'll be to help the next one that needs it. He seems pretty mellow right now—almost looks asleep. I think I could slip it to him without his realizing much. I'd appreciate the experience, if you don't mind."

"Okay," Josip said, walking to the front of the cage. "I'll try entertaining him at his front end. Whatever you do, be quick about it. These guys can react like lightning, even when they're half dead."

"Good advice," Edgar said. With that Edgar bit the cap off the end of the syringe, pushed the air out of the end until the fluid leaked from the needle, then walked along the line of cages to the other side where Ramu's back was leaning up against the bars of his cage. Josip was already sweet-talking the big cat, as much as the sick animal would let himself be sweet-talked in his weak condition. Ramu seemed vaguely interested in his owner's conversation. Edgar aimed at a muscle in Ramu's hind end and jabbed the syringe in, at the same time pushing the plunger.

Almost instantaneously Ramu let out a surprised yell. In a split second his upper body shot up and twisted backwards while his giant arm raked the air behind him. It all happened so fast it was a blur. But I certainly saw clearly enough Edgar's equally surprised expression. The cat had been fast, but, fortunately for Edgar, he had been faster. The pie-plate sized paw hooked, not onto Edgar's hand, but onto one of the metal bars of the cage where it caught for just a few seconds. Then, with the injection over, Ramu forgot and lay back down in a heap of weakness.

"Good job, Doc," Josip said. "It was pretty close, but you're fast for an old guy like yourself."

"Thanks a lot," Edgar laughed. "I'm just glad I still have my hand. Boy, they're quick."

"I'll start Apollo on his antibiotics tonight. The tigers will be all right, I'm sure," Josip remarked. "Right now I've got to get ready for the show. Before you go, though, please, just check the rest of the tigers, and give Cheryl the bill. She'll pay you right away. But I must get the first line of tigers in the tent," he said turning around to them, "and get them a little acclimated in there before we begin our program." He pulled two tickets from his pocket. "Thanks for coming all the way out here and on such short notice. If you and your wife would like to see the show, here are two complimentary tickets for you."

Edgar looked at me. I smiled and said, "Of course, I'd like to see the circus. Who wouldn't?"

Josip hailed the tractor that had already backed up to the first line of tiger cages. He waved to the driver, and the whole line of tigers began to roll out of the low-ceiling tent. In anticipation of their act, the tigers stood up in their cages, their faces pointed into the breeze. We watched the line of tigers round a bend toward the main tent into which a minute later the last tiger cage disappeared.

"Aren't you going inside with Josip?" I asked Cheryl. "Aren't you part of the act?"

"No. I help train them, and I take care of them. But I have to stay here with the other tigers while the first line is showing. We always have two people with them at any time. You never know what the public will try to do to these animals. Some people don't respect the fact that these animals are wild and can be dangerous. People have already gone up to the cages and poked their hands inside as if they were house cats. People just don't act sensibly, so we have to stay with the cats at all times. And we are always on the lookout for kooks who could slip them something they shouldn't eat. People are weird these days. These guys are like our kids. We don't want anything happening to them."

"Josip wanted me to check the rest of the tigers. Where are they?" Edgar said.

"They're in the tractor trailer right there," she said pointing behind the tent. "It's cooler for them in there; otherwise, they're outside with the ones showing. If you can, just walk up that wooden board into the trailer. Don't get too close to them, now. They might take a swipe at a stranger."

Edgar and I walked the plank to the high tractor trailer. It was, indeed, cool in there, and each tiger seemed perfectly content, asleep or half asleep on his or her clean sawdust bed. They had each other to look at and talk to—one big satisfied family, as far as I could see. Edgar glanced into each cage, careful not to approach too close, and he tried not to stare into their eyes because wild cats consider that a threat and become upset.

"Nobody in here looks sick. No one's respiration is elevated. I guess I really shouldn't touch them, but I'd like to feel at least one paw to see if they feel overly hot," Edgar said.

I looked down the line and saw a couple of toes protruding from one cage. They were from a hind leg, and their owner was fast asleep. I pointed to the dangling toes, and Edgar quietly approached. The tiger lay in dreamland, his whiskers twitching, the tip of his tail lifting and jerking to his mind imagery. Edgar sneaked to the edge of the cage and lightly felt the pink pads on the foot. The tiger hadn't stirred. Then Edgar backed away, breathing heavily.

"I don't feel any fever in that one's foot," Edgar said, obviously proud of himself for having felt a tiger for a fever. "He's healthy, and the others in here look pretty good, too. But I'm certainly not going to go around feeling all the other cats' paws.

"Before we see the show, I must give those couple of bottles of amoxicillin to Cheryl, and I want to check Ramu and Apollo once more."

So we carefully climbed back down the plank and stopped once more at the trailer. Cheryl was scooping out chicken blood and juices from the big stewing pot of raw chickens she had purchased at the mall's grocery store.

"It must cost an awful lot to keep all your tigers," I said, noting that the amount of chicken could have supplied a company barbecue.

"Yes, it certainly does. I'm always going to the grocery store for meat, mostly chickens. That's what they prefer."

"Other than the two that are sick, they certainly look well cared for," I said.

"Yes, they are. Actually, they're quite spoiled. They're our babies, and they're more work than babies are, too. This group is going back to Florida in a few weeks for R and R. Josip and I are looking forward to a vacation, too."

"Oh, where will you be going?" I asked.

"Nowhere—as usual. We can't get away from the tigers. They need constant care, and other than Elise, I don't really trust anyone else to take care of them the way we do. If Josip and I ever do go on vacation, we go separately so that one of us is always with the tigers. And when a group of tigers are to be leased to a circus in Europe or somewhere, we train people months in advance to become familiar with that particular group of tigers. The tigers must feel comfortable with their trainers, or it'll be a complete disaster. It makes for a somewhat confining life for us, but we're used to it."

"They are really beautiful animals," I said, observing the lone row of tigers. Still the kittens wrestled with each other. Their cage rocked back and forth as they played and made threatening growls at each other. Edgar was peering into Ramu's cage, and then he stepped down to Apollo to give him one last look.

Edgar examines a tiger kitten

Cheryl said, "Josip has been researching tiger coat color for about twenty years now. He's really interested in color genetics. He breeds for the rarer colors, like that tiger in the end cage there. That's Assam; he's a golden tabby Bengal. They're rare." Then she pointed to the next to last cage. "Assam's neighbor is Jasmine; she's considered a beige with brown stripes. Then Tora—that's Japanese for "tiger"—is a melanistic white with gray stripes. We have another group that is on lease to the Ringling, Barnum, and Bailey Circus for the next four years. As a matter of fact," she said, checking her watch, "they're on a ship right now headed for Hawaii. There are three melanistic whites in that group. We trained a girl from Switzerland to work with them. She gets along really well with them. She loves them."

"Your tigers sound like very sophisticated, accomplished travelers," I said.

"They really don't seem to mind traveling. Another group of tigers we raised has been leased to a safari park in Vienna for a few years; they aren't trained in circus acts or anything. They just lounge around in the park all day while people drive by and admire them. We had another group just come home from a stint in Europe. They were there for four years. They worked hard and deserve some playtime. Here comes Josip. The show's ready to start. If you want to see Josip and our tigers perform, you better find your seats."

"Oh, yes. I want to see Josip's act and all the others, too. It was very nice meeting you and all your charming animals. I hope Ramu and Apollo get better quickly. Actually, I'm sure they will. And thanks for the tickets. Maybe we'll see you again sometime."

"It was nice meeting you, too," she said. "Thanks for helping our guys."

Edgar walked over and handed her the amoxicillin. "Ramu and Apollo look about the same. If Ramu should get worse, please give me a call. We can try some pain relievers perhaps. But right now he looks as if he's tolerating the virus well enough. Offer him some of that chicken juice to keep his hydration up. I'll give you a call in a day or two to see how they're doing."

"Well, we're moving out of here tonight. We have a few nights in the Poconos, but then we'll be back in Phillipsburg, New Jersey. I'll call you when we get there if there are still problems."

"Do that, please. I'd like to know how they're doing and how long the virus lasts. I'm sure they'll be better soon, probably even by tomorrow already. Don't hesitate to call if anything comes up," he said. "Come on, Gay. Let's see the circus."

I took one last look at the tiger kittens, and then we walked into the big top and found a couple of seats right in front.

Josip and his tigers were the first to go on. Josip wore tight silver pants and a purple satin sleeveless top with gold trim. First, he introduced each cat to the audience, then he began to put the cats through their routines. When each tiger did his trick, Josip rewarded him or her with a treat and a pat on the head. The tigers did the usual stunts. They ran and lay together, one next to the other, until the last one jumped over the whole group. They sat obediently on stools, stood up, pawed the air, pivoted on the stools, and stood together as a group. Josip had them stand up as a group on their hind legs and leap into the air. He danced with one, and another gave him a hug, wrapping its arms completely around his body. The way those tigers worked with Josip in the ring demonstrated, clearly enough for me, their respect and love for their owner and trainer.

The tigers performed willingly, as if they enjoyed it. They didn't act irritated or move sluggishly as if bored with routine work. They dashed out of their cages and jumped on the stools—feline play behavior if I'd ever seen it. They were having fun—most notable in the stance of their tails, their facial expressions with their alert eyes and ears, and their energy. Wouldn't a miserable cat have expressed reluctance at performing for the hundredth time? Wouldn't he have worn a grouchy expression and pushed the trainer away with his paws?

Was this the abuse the animal rights people were protesting? Of course, it couldn't have been, for anyone only slightly aware would have agreed these animals were anything but abused. It wasn't a whole lot different than asking my cats or pigs to perform tricks for my and their own entertainment. While Josip's cats didn't have the ability to roam a savannah after their performance, they certainly didn't have to fret about finding prey to sustain themselves. Cheryl would be doling out raw chickens for dinner at the usual hour. Likewise, they didn't have to worry about finding a protective cavern or bush to ward off other, more dominant tigers that would threaten them during the day or night. And their chances for contracting life-threatening diseases were reduced as captive animals.

While their life outside the show arena was probably blasé compared to living in the wild, it certainly assured them food, protection, medicine, exercise, and occasion to play and socialize. From what I had seen, all the tigers Josip and Cheryl had in this circus were cared for very well and were respected and loved, even by the workers that tended them. There was no neglect or cruelty going on.

During the act I also noticed that Josip never touched one with his whip—similar to the way horse people carry a whip while riding but don't use it. It merely serves as a reminder. The animal knows it's there, and that's good enough reason for him to behave. Certainly Josip cracked it when he wanted the tigers to move, but I really think the crack of the whip was meant more for the audience's expectations than for controlling the wild animals. After all, the cats had done the same routine probably hundreds of times before. They didn't need any reminders to behave.

Of course, no abuse existed with Josip and his tiger act. But what about the other animal acts? I had not had the opportunity to assess the well-being of the rest of the circus animals—the ponies, the horses, the camel, the llamas, the chimpanzees.

I thought for a moment about human life and the abuse inherent in everyday living. Just in a day's work, people may wrestle with math problems, shop for groceries, cook meals, wash cars, drive on the highway, shop for Christmas presents, survive bridal and baby showers, travel by air and be hassled in airports, put up with teenage sons' and daughters' crises, and tolerate bad-tempered in-laws. Compared to all that, I decided animals performing in a circus were hardly abused. Perhaps the animal activists at this circus should help protect the tortured human animal instead—the one that appeared to be truly suffering in this world.

Edgar and I watched trick horses wearing head plumes of pink, purple, and white. They were all nicely rounded, perhaps even a bit too fat. They obviously were not starved or neglected. They were groomed beautifully, and their tails were all untangled, more than I can say for my own horses when I have neglected to comb or wash them for a while.

I had to admit, happily, that the abuse and neglect that the activists decried at the mall's entrance was absolutely not apparent at this circus. These animals, though they were performers for human entertainment, were well-cared for. They were plump and feisty, not thin and sluggish. Edgar, too, agreed that these were not suffering beings, and we knew enough about animals to be sure. They appeared to enjoy the company of their owners and the appreciation of the crowd.

Before the next animal act came onstage, we enjoyed the trapeze artists from Russia, a couple of clown acts, jugglers, sword swallowers, and fire gulpers. These were humans abusing themselves, I thought with amusement. The camel and his llama friends we had driven past earlier paraded into the ring. The animals looked in good health and flesh. Not one was coughing during the performance, nor were they sluggish at all. Again, never was one touched with the whip. They went through the motions, the llamas running through the camel's spread legs, jumping over the camel, lying down beside the camel. They

Josep Marcan riding a tiger in his circus act

weren't asked to do anything outrageous like climb a rope or balance on an orange. They all did things that came rather naturally to them: running, lying, stepping, jumping.

On our way out of the mall, we noticed the protestors had left. They had probably come out for the start of the show—to wreck business for the circus. What those people hadn't thought of was that in persuading folks to turn away, they were really snatching the food right out of the mouths of the animals they were hell-bent on protecting.

Certainly I can't say with any assurance that other circuses are not neglectful of or cruel to their animals. I would be the first to admit that, according to the laws of probability, there most certainly have to be ones that mistreat their animals in some way or another. I had only witnessed that one Clyde Beatty Circus. But not *all* circuses are abusive, as the animal rights activists would have everyone believe.

I am not an anti-animal rights person. In fact, I am in favor, always have been, of animals being given rights by humans. I largely dislike rodeos in which calves are roped around the neck, thrown to the ground, and tied up. The calves exhibit tremendous fear, and some are choked to death by the rope. I also have qualms about some zoos that don't provide large enough and clean enough pens for their animals, but I believe open-air zoos are havens for many species and aid those rapidly reaching extinction.

I also do not think an animal should be forced to do something that comes unnaturally to it. For horses, I believe steeplechase and stadium jumping is abusive. One of the first things Edgar learned in veterinary school was that a horse was not a jumping animal—thus the many injuries jumpers endure at the hands of trainers and riders. When one thinks about it, a horse has a hard time jumping something the height of its head—unlike a cat that can leap to the top of a refrigerator with little problem.

For the animal rights people to have singled out that one circus is wrong. They are right, however, to protest groups like circuses, zoos, farms, laboratories, slaughter yards, and rodeos in which animals openly display fear and anxiety overload. As in anything else, the matter boils down to what is fair. It would have been fair for the protestors to inspect the animals before they lit out for the mall entrance with their signs. Only by behaving fairly and reasonably will the animal rights people gain acceptance and favor from concerned individuals. People tend to disbelieve those who condemn without evidence, who overreact with hysteria and extreme measures. Behaving in such ways, the animal rights people are delaying, possibly even hurting, the bid for rights for animals.

We watched the rest of the circus with fascination: the tightrope walkers, a group who rode motorcycles on a thin wire, trapeze artists, dancers—all rare artists. We had to leave early to attend another animal patient, but we left feeling assured that a host of very talented animals and their owners were happy and content with their life as a traveling troupe.

On the way home I thought of all the various family relationships existing here at the circus. On the largest scale the public, performers, and animals come together in a familial way during the interactive performance. Offstage, other family ties are obvious in the entire human circus family, from the trainers to the tent erectors to the clean-up crew to the food concession people. They're in it together to make a decent living. Too, the circus is comprised of individual families—mothers, daughters, fathers—living in mobile house trailers, each member of the family contributing, in some way, to the work.

Likewise, the different animal species interact and behave toward each other with respect and tolerance: horses, dogs, camels, llamas, monkeys, and bears. Different species learn to live together harmoniously. Humans and animals in the circuses make for the most satisfying display of family, from the trainers and performers to the muckers, feeders, grooms, and maintenance personnel. The humans were there specifically to care for and comfort the animals. As I saw with Cheryl's and Josip's tigers, the animals were their friends and family. And the tigers themselves also had their own families with their own kittens, who were destined to become part of the traveling troupe.

Kenya

SINCE THE CIRCUS'S NEXT APPEARANCE was nearby in the Poconos, Josip would have called us had his tigers' condition gotten worse. He never phoned, so we assumed Ramu and Apollo recovered without incident. No news was good news.

A few weeks after we had seen Josip's circus tigers, Ivy Mae, one of my young pot-bellied pigs, was lounging alongside me when Edgar walked into our garden room. He was bursting with anticipation. "Do you want to come along while I examine an elephant?"

"An elephant?" I exclaimed. It couldn't be at the Trexler Game Preserve where he tended most of his exotic animals. They didn't have an elephant.

"Yeah," he said, bursting, his cheeks red. "It's with the Shriner's Circus over at Stabler Arena."

Stabler Arena was the area's largest entertainment complex, host to shows like the Ice Capades, the Lippizaner horse extravaganza, and numerous rock concerts, and circuses. The Shrine Circus was a big attraction in the area.

"Wow," I yelled, fumbling for my shoes. "This could prove exciting. You've never worked on an elephant before. Of course I'll go along." I assured Ivy Mae, who was basking in a sun ray on her cedar pig bed underneath my table, that we would be returning within two hours and that I would give her a little extra dinner for being such a good girl. One thing about a pot-belly: she, like my other pigs, never made a mess in the house. They were fastidious. I grabbed a light jacket, and we climbed into the truck and took off down the road.

There usually isn't a whole lot of conversation when Edgar and I head out on one of his calls. He is contemplating what he's likely to find at the end of the trip, how to approach the animal and, from the phone conversation with the owner, what could be wrong with it. Meanwhile I am pondering whether the call might contain an element of adventure or action. To be sure, we could stand a bit of entertainment. Other than the circus tigers, we hadn't experienced the thrill of working with an unpredictable exotic animal lately. We both needed something to break up the routine of our equine practice. The lure of an action-packed veterinary call was as tempting as white-water canoeing: with the danger came the attraction. Temperance was nice, but on a daily basis it became the equivalent of wearing the same T-shirt everyday; sometimes a person just needs a change. Secretly I was hoping the elephant might provide us with a situation challenging enough to write home about.

In 45 minutes we were at Stabler Arena in Lehigh University's athletic complex.

We had no sooner parked the truck than an olive-skinned, long-haired stocky man dressed in denim coveralls and chewing on a stogie introduced himself in a Southern accent, "Doctor Balliet? Y'all're here to see my elephant, right? She's right this way," he indicated, pointing.

"You can call me Ed," Edgar said, shaking his hand.

"I'm Lancelot—Lancelot Ramos. You can call me Lance."

I almost choked. Lancelot?

Edgar shook his hand, "Nice to meet you, Lance. What are we going to do with your fella?"

I bounded from my side of the truck. It wasn't every day the vet and his assistant were summoned to treat an animal of the bushveld. Perhaps the elephant would provide us with a bit of fast-paced drama of some kind. Of course, we didn't need anything so dramatic as the beast using Edgar for an ottoman or making a wall hanging out of him. I didn't want anyone to get hurt, but a narrow escape might offer a well-deserved "rush."

Lancelot, his wavy hair flowing like Fabio's, eyed me with interest.

"Hi," I piped, anxious to greet our patient. "I'm Dr. Balliet's wife. Can't wait to see your elephant. They're fascinating animals."

Lancelot nodded, smiling, and decided I was innocuous. He turned to Edgar.

"What I need you to do is do a general kind of check-up on Kenya and fill out a health certificate. Do ya'll know anythin' 'bout exotics?" he drawled. When he talked, he took the inch-long cigar from his mouth and gestured with it. The mouth end was black and gooshy-looking from all the sucking and chewing. It looked slimey, too. I swallowed hard. Then he put it back into his mouth.

"Well," Edgar said, "I do work with exotic animals at the Trexler Game Preserve in this area; it's a small zoo about twenty miles from here. So I know a little something about working with them. But I have to admit I don't know a whole lot about elephants—only what I read about them before we came here."

Lancelot pulled the stogie from his mouth and waved the mushy end in the air. "That's quite awl right, then. You'll be able to see that my girl's a strappin' elephant, and that's all I need. I just have to prove that she's healthy, that's awl; there's no animal here healthier than my girl, no sirree," he said. His Southern drawl was strangely pleasant, so fitting for a person of bovine temperament as he appeared to be. He was just the calm type that should be working with wild animals.

"Yeah," Lancelot continued, pulling on the cigar, "I need the papers for a New York City company that just called y'st'd'y wantin' to use Kenya—that's my elephant's name—for a commercial. Last year's health certificate is out of date, so I need another one anyway."

"A commercial!" I yelped. "In New York? How cool! What's it for?"

He reluctantly removed the cigar and said, "I don't know, really. All I know is that they want to put a hat on her and take a couple of pictures."

"Wow!" I said, rubbing my hands together. "An elephant celebrity. Far out!"

"Let's take a look at her then," Edgar said. He went to the back of the truck and fished out a stethoscope and a thermometer.

"She's already loaded in the truck along with all the rest of my guys. We're leaving tomorrow, so that's why they're all ready to roll. Otherwise, we keep them in their cages or tied under a big tent. You'll be able to get at 'er from a small side door, though," he said. "Folla me."

We walked around the outside of Stabler Arena. Parked in the lot alongside the building was a huge, white tractor trailer. It had an extended cab that stretched probably seven feet behind the driver's seat. Attached to the cab, then, followed the gigantic trailer.

"The elephant's in there?" I gasped.

"Yep—and so are my eight ponies and twelve cats. Kenya's in the last section here," he said patting the end of the tractor trailer.

"Cats?" I questioned.

Kenya close-up

"Yep—tigers, leopards, lions. They're all my trained cats."

Lancelot pulled open a small metal door, just big enough for a human, on the side of the trailer near the back end. It creaked and grated as he pulled it open, and then he hinged it back to the outside. Immediately an elephant's long, bristle-haired gray tube of a trunk poked through the doorway and fingered the air. Lance slipped his hand over the end of the trunk as a greeting, and Kenya twisted the end around the hand to assess that it, indeed, belonged to her owner and friend.

I was spellbound, being that close to such a large and unfamiliar animal. I instinctively reached out to touch the trunk. Kenya released her grip on Lancelot and poked the end of her trunk into my hand. The touch was surreal—warm and alive, yet sporting four-inch, sparse, wiry hairs. The tip of the trunk, where the nostrils were, twisted around to smell my hand and crawled worm-like up my arm to give it a thorough examination. She gave me goosebumps. The nostrils were wet and pink as the inside of a seashell, in contrast to the dry, leathery, metal-haired skin of the trunk.

"Wow, an African elephant," Edgar said. "Look at the size of her ears! You know, Gay, African elephants are seldom used as performers because they're more high-strung than their Indian counterparts. She must be very different from other African elephants."

Enamored of the great beast, I was only vaguely aware of four cats on the opposite side of Kenya's compartment, each partnered with another cat in a barred cage. One cage in front of the door housed a dreadlocked male lion plus a full-grown tiger. Next to them was a cage with two younger cats, a new type Lancelot called a tabby tiger, and its companion, a Siberian white tiger. The tigers seemed as enthralled with us as I was with them. Both the lion and tiger had stood up when the metal door was opened and begun pacing their cage, one in front of the other, in anticipation of some action. They were intensely curious about us. One sidled up to the end of the cage, twisted his head to the side, and roared in a soft, inquisitive voice, sliding his huge incisors against the bars. The huge cats' motion set the wheeled cage to rocking. *Squeak, squeak, squeak* the cage went as the two big cats paced back and forth.

While the cats commanded my attention, Edgar had been observing the elephant. He explained to Lance what he was looking for as far as signs of health or illness in the elephant. Again Kenya steered her trunk out the people door, and before she could retract it, Edgar grabbed the end of it. She clearly didn't appreciate that move, for the trunk writhed and twisted uncomfortably beneath his grip. But he only needed a moment to check the nostrils for any bacterial discharges or other abnormalities. If Edgar had ever learned one thing about treating or examining exotic animals, it was that speed counts. Know what you're looking for and get a glimpse—fast. Likewise with the treatment: the quicker, the better, the safer.

"Nose looks good," Edgar said, letting go the trunk. "No mucousy discharge or anything. "Throw a flake of hay to her so that I can see she has a good appetite."

Lancelot tossed a flake of hay through the hole, and immediately Kenya wrapped her nozzle around a clump and stuffed it into her mouth. Her tiny eyes blinked appreciatively.

"Nothing wrong with her appetite. What's her stool look like?" Edgar looked toward the back of the truck where the elephant manure lay. Piles the size of African termite mounds lay at the back of the trailer. Each load was easily half a wheelbarrow full. I couldn't imagine anything making a lump of waste that large, but then, I guessed, everything was relative—big elephant, big shit. As if he were looking at a gaggle of yummy fruit pies, Edgar said, "Oh, yes, they look very nice— well-formed, not runny or anything—just right." I swallowed hard; I couldn't get excited over elephant shit. Then Edgar took his tiny flashlight from his pocket and shined it on one massive load. "Great! Don't see any mucus, either. That's good."

I was a little disappointed to think that the examination was all going to take place passively outside the trailer. I wanted to get inside with the elephant, even if it was only to touch her on the flank. Edgar, Lancelot, and I gazed in at Kenya while Edgar watched her sides move with every breath. He was checking her respiration visually.

"Respiration is normal," he declared.

I sighed with disappointment then turned to the cats pacing in the neighboring cage. Both the felines were consumed with curiosity. Surely we smelled different from their owner and his stogie breath. Maybe they were entranced with my perfume, which had probably lingered since morning. Then, too, maybe they smelled Ivy Mae, my pot-belly, on me, in which case, it was probably making them ponder a nice, fatty snack. We probably also smelled like horses, cows, and other good-tasting wild cat prey.

Mesmerized by them and their rhythmic pacing, I found it hard to believe these agitated cats would stoop to obeying a human and per-forming tricks for him. Somehow, I thought, that must be beneath such a royal, dignified animal. Yet I could tell that Lance was not mere-ly an animal trainer but also a friend to his menagerie. It was evident by the way he conversed with them and how they responded to his conversation. It was apparent by the familiarity with which he touched them through the bars of the cages. They didn't shrink from his hands.

Edgar had completed his visual examination of the elephant. He paused and said, much to my delight, "I'd like to get in there with Kenya to listen to her lungs, if I could." I was hoping I would be allowed inside with the elephant, too, if only to shine a flashlight where Edgar needed it.

The cats continued to pace their cage, intent on their human visi-tors. At every turn the lion slid his teeth against the bars and roared in a kind of cat whisper. He had attic breath.

The large felines had charmed me, and I stood still as moss before them, totally enamored, totally enchanted, like a possessed thing. For several minutes I stood glued in place, spellbound by their rhythmic pacing, their wide clear eyes, their hoarse questioning. What I didn't know, however, was that they had taken like pleasure in me as I in them.

I was standing still as a tree stump, mouth hanging open in awe, when suddenly Lance yelled, *"WATCH OUT! HE'S PISSIN'!"*

At first I didn't react, so fixated had I been on the pacing lion and tiger. I stood before them like the Venus de Milo.

But in a second, what Lancelot had shouted finally registered. I wasn't exactly sure who "he" was, but suddenly I had a suspicion it was one of the cats. Reacting simultaneously, we all hitched left, and, sure enough, like a missile, a stream of urine shot past us and into the park-ing lot—to a whopping distance of *fifteen feet*.

After I regained my senses, I giggled, "He sure has good aim. I've never seen an animal pee like that. Quite a feat." The scene had reminded me of the tiger at the Allentown Fair that had come to like

me and decided to claim the human monolith as his own. I had narrowly escaped being hit by that one, too.

"He ain't exactly peein', ma'am," Lancelot said in a matter-of-fact voice.
"He's claimin' territory. He thinks ya're mighty fine. Likes ya terribly."

Flattered, I giggled.

"Okay, Lance. Now do you think I can get in with Kenya?" Edgar
said, hitching his stethoscope around his neck.

"You can get in there if ya want to," Lancelot smirked, "but she'll
probably kill ya." His voice was deliberately blasé.

Edgar's eyebrows shot up. "That so?"

Lancelot chuckled, "If ya go in at all, ya can only go inside with me.
I'm her big daddy, and she knows if I bring her a visitor, that person is
okay cause he's with me. Then she won't hurt ya."

I bit my lip. Well, that does it for me, I thought. I don't need a
change of pace that badly. Was it really that necessary for Edgar to listen to Kenya's lungs? She was breathing pretty steady, by the looks of
her. Being pulverized to a pimple between an elephant's ass and the steel
walls of the tractor trailer might be a bit uncomfortable.

"Okay, then. Let's go," Edgar said.

I winced and stepped dutifully forward.

"No, not you, Gay. You stay outside," Edgar said. I stepped back
quickly and breathed relief. But I was worried for Edgar.

With that, Lancelot hoisted himself up through the tiny door, and
Edgar followed, Lancelot pulling him up by the hand into the straw-
lined compartment.

First, Lancelot assured Kenya that it was he—her daddy. He talked
quietly and assuringly to the elephant, and her tiny eyes looked past
him toward Edgar. I watched as Edgar gently put a hand to Kenya's
side. Her skin shuddered under his touch, but Lancelot, our hero in
unshining denim armor, stood close by should Kenya decide she needed to defend herself against the stranger in her compartment.

I gazed up at Kenya, whose head, elevated in the trailer, was high
above me. She regarded me with eyes so teeny—relative to her large
African elephant ears, stovepipe legs, and boxcar torso. The little
brown peepers darted back and forth, then straight at me, assessing me
as a potential threat or danger. I didn't move or speak for fear of alarm-
ing her.

When Edgar slid the stethoscope dish to her chest, she reached down slowly with her trunk between her front legs to touch the person and the instrument at her side. The trunk stealthily approached to within inches of Edgar's hand and the tip of the stethoscope. There it stopped, poised.

What could she have been thinking? Was she comparing Edgar's smell to her daddy's? Was she analyzing his touch compared to Lancelot's? Certainly she was able to see that this fair-skinned man with short thinning hair didn't look anything like her thick-set, wavy-maned owner. Slowly the trunk twisted past Edgar's hand and toward his body as if with a mind of its own.

Lancelot saw the questioning appendage at once. He simply said in a stern voice, "*HEY! HEY! TRUNK!*"

With that Kenya quickly withdrew her nosehose from between her front legs and curled it up and over her head as if to say, like a mischievous child, "I didn't do anything. See—here's my trunk, just hanging above my head doing nothing. I'm not doing anything bad with it." But as Lancelot became more preoccupied with Edgar's examination of his elephant, Kenya gradually lowered her nozzle and, ever so quietly and slowly, directed it through her front legs again toward Edgar and his stethoscope.

Again Lancelot caught it. "*AY! TRUNK!*" he yelled.

Again, she withdrew her schnozzle, but this time she didn't attempt a retry. She knew her trainer was wise to her. She probably also realized that if the stranger standing at her side had not done her any harm yet, he probably wasn't planning to.

I held my breath, though, until Edgar stepped away from the elephant and leaped out the door to the pavement below. Then Lancelot jumped down beside us.

"Everything looks good," Edgar said. "She's as healthy as I've seen them."

I smiled at the confirmation.

In the meantime the squeaking of the tiger cage had become mere background music as the tiger and the lion with his mane like a golden halo paced back and forth, back and forth in their cage. They sniffed the air upon which the wind, no doubt, carried my scent—of various barnyard animals and my own domestic felines at home.

Suddenly Lancelot yelled, "*LOOK OUT! HE'S GONNA PISS AG'IN!*"

This time it was too late.

I was standing right in line with the cats' cage, and I didn't have time to run. All I could do was duck, like a foot soldier under fire. Bent over, I craned my neck to see the cat's stream of urine spray over me in a perfect arc. I had hunched down and wrapped my arms over my head, but I wouldn't escape completely. Cat piss rained all around me. I cowered in the urine shower as the droplets hit my windbreaker.

Tic—tic—tic—tic—tic—tic—tic—tic—tic—tic, the drops pelted the nylon of my jacket.

And as quick as the shower came, it ended.

I wiped the pee from my hair with my sleeved arm and noticed Edgar grinning and shaking his head as though he couldn't believe my luck.

"Sorry about that," Lancelot said. "I tried to warn ya."

It takes a lot to gross me out, and usually it's human leavings of some kind: an itinerant's mucous ball on the sidewalk, baby barf, baby poop, a pusy finger or toe. Human waste gags me, but I'm no stranger to animal waste—no, not at all. I've walked barefoot in it when there was no time to put shoes on and I had to catch horses before the next lightning strike. I've cleaned cat piss and shit off my kitchen and living room floor with cheap paper towels that disintegrated and leaked the mess onto my fingers. I've helped Edgar clean retained placentas in cows, and I've assisted in the bloodiest of operations.

A little cat piss bath was hardly anything to get upset about.

"It's really no big deal, Lance. I've endured worse, believe me," I laughed. "Besides," I added, "I consider it quite a compliment to be marked by a tiger. He likes me. He is claiming me as part of his family, I bet."

Before we all headed back to the truck, Lancelot, his hand to his temple in deep thought, said, "Oh, yeah, Doc. I 'most forgot. Would ya'll take a look at Lukas? He's got a might of a sore on his right paw. Just keeps lickin' and lickin' it—seems ta have no chance ta heal." Lancelot turned toward the cat cage and opened a barred hatch about the size of a tissue box.

"Which one is Lukas?" Edgar said, following. I brushed the remain-

ing drops of piss from my jacket and peeked into the cage with the lion
and tiger.

"He's the African lion," Lancelot said. "You don't hafta worry 'bout
him now. He's just like a big kitty." Then Lancelot tapped on the bars
of the opening. With that Lukas turned around and slid his big, hairy-
rimmed face against the steel bars.

"Down here, Lukas," Lancelot coaxed, tapping the hole.

Lukas lowered his head towards Lance's finger. He was looking for
a treat, and his tan nose thrust through the opening. Edgar moved
slowly toward the cage. I could already see the red and inflamed sore
on Lukas's paw.

"Gimme yar paw, Lukas," Lancelot said. Lukas had sniffed the hole
for goodies, but finding none, he decided to feel for any treats. When
he stuck his big paw out, Lancelot motioned for Edgar to quickly take
a look. If Lancelot grabbed Lukas's paw, the animal would probably
jerk it away. So, while Lukas batted Lancelot's finger, his owner cajoled
him, tickling the underside of his big paw. That's when Edgar got a
good look at the sore.

"Lick granuloma," Edgar said firmly, stepping back from the cage.
Lancelot looked alarmed at the diagnosis. Edgar quickly dispelled his
worst fears, "It's no big deal, really. More of a nuisance than anything
life-threatening." Lancelot sighed with relief then dug in his pocket for
a treat and slipped it into Lukas' mouth. Then, not to be ignored,
Lukas's cage-buddy thrust his nose out the opening for a treat, too.

Edgar shrugged his shoulders, "Lick granulomas are common.
They're sores kept alive by the animal's constant licking and irritation.
Sometimes they're buggers to get rid of, but I'll give you a tube of
Panalog. It's a salve that has anti-inflammatories, a fungicide, and
antibiotics. Apply it, if you can, to Lukas's sore at least two times a day!
Afterward, try to keep him busy so that he doesn't lick it off right away.
Only for about ten or fifteen minutes—until it has sunk into the
wound somewhat. That should take some of the heat and swelling out
of it—reduce the inflammation. He should stop licking it once the
inflammation goes down, and then the hair will eventually grow back."

"Good 'nough," Lance smiled. "Won't be no problem treatin' him.
He's a big pussy—plays with me awl the time. I'll be able to put that
stuff on 'im, no sweat."

"That should take care of it in a couple of weeks," Edgar said.

Then Edgar and Lance and I had headed toward the truck where Edgar filled out the health certificate on Kenya—bland and routine work. While they were busy, I crawled back inside the truck cab and thought of the exotic family all packed within the tractor trailer, ready to hit the road with their stogie-smoking daddy. I scratched my chin. For sure, that family, like Josip's circus tiger family, was geared for entertaining and interacting with human families all over the United States. Maybe humans and animals could respect each other as most human family members do after all. The full realization of my dream might take time and numerous, perhaps thousands of, Josips and Lancelots with their animals to set a good animal/human family example, but, what the hell—if we don't have time, we don't have anything.

Looking back on the afternoon, I had had my action-packed experience all right, though it wasn't exactly what I had in mind when Edgar asked me if I wanted to go along to check an elephant. There had been no narrow escape from a beast fifteen times larger than a human; there were no bloodied body parts or scrapes or bruises to tell friends and relatives about.

On the contrary, all I had to show was a dotted-up coat and the scent of wild cat piss in my hair.

Edgar swung the wheel of our vet truck, and we rounded the corner out of the grounds of Stabler Arena. At that hard right turn I clung onto the "chicken handle" above my door as the turn pulled me toward the center of the truck.

"Well," I said, looking up at the truck ceiling. "We certainly aren't lacking for interesting subjects these days."

"No," he laughed, stepping on the accelerator. "This next call won't be nearly as exciting. Got to palpate a mare for pregnancy."

"Geez," I pondered. "I always thought we've worked on the strangest animals."

"We run the gamut, don't we?"

Suddenly I was in my own little world, revisiting all the creatures great and exotic that my husband tends in our world of veterinary medicine—the monkeys, the elk, the muntjac at the Trexler Game Preserve, not to mention the buffalo. Let's not even bother about the number of deer we see. Then we've checked barnyard animals—cows, pigs, and sheep at the fair. Even roosters take their toll on us, like the one at Guy Barry's place. I smiled at the thought of Josip and Cheryl and their brood at the circus and Lancelot's tractor trailer full of beasts, each one of which was a part of his family. As we pulled onto the Hatch's farm where Edgar was to examine a mare, I replied dreamily, "The veterinary gamut. Yep, that's right. You tend them all: steers, llamas, elk, bats, and wolves." I smiled, thinking, "And lions, and tigers, and mares."

"Oh, my!" Edgar yelped and jumped from the truck.

Fairyland

SURVIVING THE CAT URINE SHOWER fulfilled my need for adventure for a while. Yet we were destined for more amusement when, on a late spring day, we set out for Fairyland, the "enchanted" farm.

"We're going where?" I laughed, imagining all of Shakespeare's nymphs peering at us from around every pitchfork and straw bale. "Gee, do you think we'll meet Ariel? What about Oberon and Titania? Maybe they'll treat us to a little bit of their magic—turning us to moss or something, huh?"

"Ha, ha—very funny," Edgar said, retrieving an old syringe from his shirt pocket. "Just because the place is called Fairyland Farm doesn't mean any sprite is going to waste her time casting spells on us, though I wouldn't mind a new hairline myself. Fairyland is a small family farm; the Millers raise sheep and a few pigs. We need to castrate the lambs born last year, and I need to do a few health certificates for some going to a show."

It was late spring. The forsythias were winding down their golden extravaganza. The Chinese cherry trees had reached their grand finale and were "snowing" all over the ground and alleyways. The late-bloom-ing magnolias and some of the peach and pear trees, however, had only begun to bud. At home my tulips stood proudly, over seven hundred of them, quite a display—tangerine, salmon, white, crimson, black, lavender, and candy-cane striped. I just loved springtime, the natal leaves on the deciduous trees, the wild redbuds peeking through the woods along the highways.

I enjoyed driving along with Edgar on his calls in the springtime, too. In fact, thinking about it, I appreciated most all the seasons. Well, except perhaps summer, which was simply green with manicured lawns and lazy, over-weighted ash and oak trees. Summer in Pennsylvania could often be hot and muggy, and it was always buggy, especially in the cow barns.

In fall Edgar and I savored the multihued leaves changing throughout the different sectors of his practice: the Poconos would be the first to start showing color. We could spend the day tending animals in the Poconos and be enthralled with the technicolor landscape, but then we'd drive home, quite a bit south of the Poconos, to monochromatic scenery painted in greens, olives, and chartreuse. Then, perhaps two or three weeks later, our area began showing its fall foliage: the maples turning peach and pink, the ash turning gold.

We enjoyed driving in winter, past the ski lodge where we could see the skiers braving the snow-covered paths like Lazy Mile and Main Street on Blue Mountain. And there was adventure in tending to an emergency during the middle of a snowstorm or ice storm. We really didn't have to worry too much about our safety, for the most part, because Edgar's truck was a four-wheel-drive, three-quarter-ton pickup. It plowed through just about the worst of snowy conditions, and we, indeed, felt as though we were performing a public service by helping a sick patient in a blizzard.

Then, just as we tired of the bone-chilling cold and the gray, bleak landscape, we welcomed the crocuses and daffodils attending winter's demise. We relished the profusion of hyacinths, daffodils, azaleas, moutain laurel, and rhododendron with such varied patterns and hues.

We left the town of Lehighton and headed farther into the north country. Fairyland Farm was situated in what came to be known as the Western Poconos. It was fairly close to Beltzville Dam, where, characteristically, hordes of people looking to escape the heat of summer congregated for boating or lying on the beach. Summer picnics and band jams made the Beltzville Dam a happening place.

When we pulled into Fairyland, I was immediately saturated with a mixed tableau. On our right was the tiny country store that Bobby Miller's wife ran. It was only about fifty feet long and fifteen feet wide and sported only one front door over which hung a narrow green awning. A throwback to the Fifties roadside grocery, it was a convenient place to pick up sausage or steak for dinner, and Mrs. Miller made one hell of a good luncheon hoagie as per each customer's specifications. When we drove up and announced our arrival at the service door, Mrs. Miller was already placing the last of the tomatoes on a heap of lunch meats and cheeses lining a roll.

"Haw're ya?" she yelled in a Dutch accent through the door. "Go on up, naw. Bobby's (she pronounced it "Boppy's") waiting for ya at the bik barn."

"Okay, thanks," Edgar called. "Oh," he said to me, looking straight ahead, "I see Bobby right there. Remember that year you helped me here, I told you that Di, their daughter, was an artist. She used to work for Slocum Publications, but now she helps out the rest of the family on the farm. She's really into her kids learning the 4-H stuff and everything."

Ahead of us in the driveway a large, stocky man of sixty-something was sitting atop a John Deere tractor. Behind the tractor was attached an empty manure spreader. When he saw us approaching, his broad, outstretched hand went up in the air, and a giant smile erupted on his face. As we passed to park in front of the long barn, I waved back, and big Bobby nodded and grinned like a jack-o-lantern. That's one happy guy, I thought. Maybe farming in Pennsylvania had been kinder to him than to the many struggling farmers we knew. Most had been run ragged to make ends meet and were still working endless hours. It seemed they rarely had time to play.

We got out of the truck while Bobby backed the manure spreader under the eaves of a garage across the way. Soon he hurried over to us, flanked on either side by a young woman in denim bib overalls and a man in gray coveralls. Bobby himself wore the true trademark of any hardworking Pennsylvania farmer: the New Holland suspenders—green straps with yellow advertising.

"Hurry up!" Bobby called to Edgar. "Give Whitey here a bone, if ya know vhat's gudt for ya, or he'll teach ya a lesson ya soon won't forget."

"Oh, I almost forgot," Edgar said, quickly grabbing a dog biscuit from the back of the truck. A large white German shepherd sauntered over to us. "Don't reach out to him," Edgar warned me. "He can bite, but as long as I pop him a bone, he'll let us alone." With that Edgar shoved a biscuit in the dog's mouth, and Whitey did an abrupt turn and headed back down the driveway, his legs hitting the ground in rhythm to Bobby's laughter.

Bobby carried himself rather stiffly, assertively, as though someone had just taken him over to the air pump and blown his chest up like a tire. Yet his demeanor was not at all overblown or pompous. In fact, if anything, I liked him at once, especially his grand smile that pushed his large face out into many hills and crevasses, just like a cabbage patch doll. His face, in fact, looked quilted, the result of the puckering and wrinkling from all those laugh lines.

Bobby's face was well marked with laugh cracks: at the corners of the eyes, under the eyes, from the nose to the corners of his mouth, along his forehead. Days, weeks, months, and years of laughing and smiling had formed permanent fissures on his face. When his face relaxed, the cracks still remained, though the skin in between didn't puff up in pillows.

Bobby was glad to see Edgar, not just because Edgar was there to castrate the lambs, but because he honestly liked my husband.

"Hey, Doc," he said in his Dutchy accent. "Haven't seen ya since last year, isn't thadt right?" He pumped Edgar's hand up and down.

"Yeah, guess it's been awhile," Edgar said, smiling almost as broadly as Bobby.

"See you have an assistant with ya today now-a," Bobby said, nodding and grabbing my hand, too.

"Well, sort of. You remember my wife, Gay," Edgar said. "She helped us a while back—a few years ago one time."

"How are you, Mr. Miller?" I said, smiling.

"Naw, chust call me Boppy," he said, smiling. "Oh, yeah—naw I sort of remember. But, cheez, she doessn't haf to help us today. We godt plenty of gudt, strong help," he said, pointing to the young man. "Evil, here, can't wait to help you castrate dem lambs."

"Evil?" Edgar repeated. He looked at the man in the gray coveralls standing next to Bobby. "Who's Evil? And why's he evil?"

"I'm Evil," the shorter man said proudly, raising his right hand. "Well, dat iss, I'm not really evil, but I'm Evil."

"Yeah—okay, fine," Edgar said, grinning. "A not-so-evil Evel."

"Dat's me," Evil asserted, his hands thrust deeply into his denim pockets.

At that remark Bobby started to snort. Then he began to laugh in full force. Evil just stood by soaking it all up, happy to be the cause of so much amusement.

"I'll have to tell you guys the story about Evil sometime, Doc. It's a riot! Let's do the lambs first, though." Then Bobby let out a banshee laugh that resounded from the depths of his lungs. It was hard resisting Bobby's contagious laugh. A person who allowed himself to roar in such complete abandon was surely an honest sort—a kind man. To be sure, he was not a dimwit, a feeble person who didn't know any better than to laugh an idiot's laugh. His farm, I'd learn later, was the epitome of organization and discipline.

Di and Bobby outside Miller's Country Store at Fairyland Farm

Bobby, however, had no appearances to keep up, no impressions to make. He was a happy sort and wasn't afraid to show it. So many people are so self-conscious about laughing, not wanting to appear out of control or overreactive. Or they think it's uncool to let themselves loose and cackle freely. It was a pleasure to listen to his mirth; it made me want to stand there and hoot out my guts, too. In fact, I found myself jiggling back and forth in a prelude to a laughing fit, laughing for laughing's sake at the laughing man who held nothing back—merely howling and snorting from the bottom of his lungs.

Edgar and I gathered up the health certificates, stethoscope, and castrating tools from the back of the truck. Bobby introduced me to his daughter, Di, a slender, petite thing, who looked as though, despite her size, she could wrestle a kimodo dragon. Though tiny, she looked strong, her arm muscles pumped up from years of work on the farm. Alongside her stood Evil, looking anything but.

On the way to the sheep barn, Bobby questioned Edgar about all that'd been happening with his veterinary practice since he had seen him last year. Edgar explained that he had hired another associate and that things had been pretty busy, especially this spring when the horse breeding work was heavy.

"And haw's that Scotch Highlander of yours," Bobby yelled with a huge smile.

"Huh? The Highlander?" Edgar said, puzzled.

"That big brute of yours with the long red hairdo and the bik horns," Bobby roared.

"O-o-oh, the Scotch Highland steer—Scotty? He's fine—still knocking down the fence whenever he gets the chance, though."

Bobby chuckled and held onto Edgar's words.

I added, "Yeah, and he is still licking out his nostrils with his tongue."

Bobby slapped his knees. "Ya, ya, that's a bik pastime with steers and bulls, now isn't it? Vell, they can't wery well pick their noses, naw can dey?" Then came the shrieking laugh, the high-pitched squeal not unlike Lowell when he was upset. But Bobby wasn't upset; he was just happy.

We all walked into the large sheep barn, but at first all I saw were two black pigs in a pen and a bunch of chickens walking around.

Bobby and Di and Evil marched down the aisleway toward the flock of sheep. A few of them needed health certificates for a show.

Di and Bobby climbed the wooden fence into the sheep pen. I was surprised how lithe Bobby was for his age and heft. He merely hopped the partitions and landed on his heels like a fairy sprite. Maybe that's why they called the place Fairyland, I thought with amusement.

The sheep ran en masse to the far end of the pen. Four of them wore baling twine "bow ties" around their necks—the ones going to the show. Di and Evil began herding them back toward Edgar and Bobby so that they could catch them and work on them.

"So, what kind of show are you going to?" Edgar asked as he readied the ear tags. Just as the flock ran past him, Edgar reached out and snagged a bow-tied sheep and pushed its back end into the corner of the pen. "Got one!" Edgar yelled, and Bobby hurried to his side to help hold the animal. Then Edgar took his stethoscope out of his pocket and put the disk to the animal's side. He listened for a few seconds, reached for his thermometer and inserted it. While they waited for the temperature to register, Bobby answered Edgar's question.

"Vhy, ve're goin' inta the carcass class at the Farm Show awt in Harrisburg next week. Haf ya ever been to a carcass class?" he said.

"No, can't say as I have," Edgar said. I was beginning to get a pretty good idea of just what it entailed, and I really didn't like the sound of it.

"How do they judge those classes?" Edgar said.

Bobby took a deep breath. The whole matter was obviously very important to him, for his face went abruptly serious. This was his livelihood we were discussing, after all. The success of his lamb operation probably depended in part on his being able to walk away with a few awards from carcass classes. "First, ya must take your lamb inta the showring and be judged 'on the hoof.' If you doan't show 'em in the ring at the end of a lead, dey disqualify ya. Then, after dey make the preliminary judging, dey load up all the sheep and take 'em to the butcher. Once the lambs are skinned, the judges go to the slaughter-house (he pronounced it "slawterhaus") and judge the carcasses."

I shuddered to think that by this time next week the four lambs that wore baling-twine bow ties today would be dead.

I was learning ever so slowly that the animal and human family thing would never be accomplished anytime soon. Families' livelihoods depended on exploiting animals for food, which didn't make it right or moral, but that was how it was. In thousands of years, perhaps, things might be different. People may be vegetarians. But then there was another problem: Who could convince the animals not to hunt and eat each other? The situation was problematic—a mingled yarn if I ever saw one.

Though I refused to eat pork, veal, and lamb for personal and ethical reasons, I still ate fish, poultry, and beef. I was basically a walking contradiction. Because of that it was hard for me to pass judgment on people like the Millers who were hard-working, honest folks. Raising lambs for the supper table was this family's livelihood. They had as much right to it as any other farmer or breeder of livestock.

Edgar felt along the backbone of one of the bow-tied lambs. He pressed and poked and said, "Feels pretty nice to me—not too much fat, not too skinny. Well, I hope you do well out there next week."

"Yop, I do too-a," Bobby said. "This von here-a looks like it's the best, but it's Di's lamb. What a shame for me!" Then he laughed like hell.

Di said, "Well, last year you beat me, Dad. This year it's my turn." She turned to Edgar and said, "And I think I'm going to do it, too."

Di, Evil, and Bobby wrestled the three other bow-tied lambs. Edgar listened to them, took their temperatures, inspected their feet, their nostrils, their eyes. Then he put a tag in each one's ear. "They're just fine," he said, crawling over the fence and back into the aisleway. The Millers and Evil followed.

"Now what's this story about Evil?" Edgar asked, nodding to the young man by my side.

Bobby took a deep breath. A smile cracked and sent his face into a hill of moguls. I stifled a giggle.

Bobby looked like he was going to explode with the telling. "Vell, Evil's real name iss Brian, and Brian, who iss our neighbor, grew up on our farm. He was one of Di's elementary school friends. Von day in Nowember vhen ve vere vorking aroundt here and Brian vas abawt nine or ten years oldt, he brought his motorized minibike up here to try awt." Bobby started to laugh, holding his guts below his belt with his right hand even before he got to the punch line. "Anyvay, he vant-ed to see if he could chump overtop the manure pit with his cycle. Ve all varned him not to try it, but he vouldn't listen—ten years oldt and all—a real know-it-all. So, he revs hiss engine, started back about a hundred feet, and then he let 'er fly. Up the ramp to the manure pit he flew. But guess what! He didn't clear it! He and the bike went right into the shit pile!"

Bobby roared with the memory, at the same time holding his guts together so that they wouldn't blow all over the barn. I could just imagine the young man at my side entertaining the troops at Fairyland with his motorcycle mishap. Evil seemed to be getting as much of a kick out of the whole incident as was everyone else. In fact, he actually looked proud. I started giggling, and Edgar was chuckling, too.

"From that day on we called him Evil—ya know, from Evil Knievel." Bobby bent over, holding his intestines, and Evil wore a fuschia color on his cheeks.

Bobby continued, "And, Di, do ya remember when Evil and us vere at our grocery store. Dis voman chust left with some sveet corn, and I happened to call to Evil. I said, 'Evil, come here voncet.' Do you remember vhat she saidt to her husbandt? She saidt, 'Issn't that awful. Did you hear what they call that boy? They called that poor boy, evil.' Oh, cheez, I thought I'dt bust, I laughed so hardt. Di, haw long didt it take us to pry him outta dat manure pit? I doan't know, naw, but it shore vas funny, vasn't it? Do ya remember? We vorked wit da shovels for abawt half a day naw-a, didn't ve? Oh, vhat a mess he vas. But, ya know, I doan't really think he minded much at all being in that shit pile."

Edgar and I laughed. Di and Evil did, too.

"Doc, ya can fill awt the papers later back at the store. Let's get this castration thing over vit."

"Okay, Bobby, if you say so. Here, Gay, carry the health papers back to the truck and put my stethoscope and thermometer back where they belong. We'll get started castrating these lambs. Just come back in the barn then. We may need your help."

It only took me about ten minutes to put things away and tidy up the truck. Then I slid open the doors to the big barn and proceeded down the aisle where the castration was already underway. I could see Bobby and Di holding the back end of a sheep at a handy angle to Edgar's scalpel.

As I reached the lamb pen, I noticed Evil standing off to the side. Something was wrong. He was white as an old bone and was leaning heavily on his elbows into the corner. He was about to get sick or faint.

I had seen that color and staggering stance many times before. I was about to open my mouth and alert the group, but Evil beat me to it. Just as Edgar touched the scalpel to the testicle, the lamb yelled, and Evil took off at a run, making his erratic, zigzagging escape to the far side of the pen. In his drunken, blood-fearing rampage, he tripped in the straw, did a complete somersault, and landed face and hands first in a pile of sheep manure.

Bobby looked at Evil prostrate in the straw, and suddenly his face broke out in mounds and pillows all over again. "Ah, *NO!*" Bobby roared, his laughter interrupting his words. "Evil can't standt the sight of bludt, say not!" he hiccuped. Di and Edgar laughed, and Edgar smiled as he made the last incision and pulled the testicle from the lamb's body.

"Hey, Evil," Edgar yelled. "Ya all right?"

There was no answer. Evil was out cold.

The castration complete, they let the lamb back into the flock after marking its back with a pink chalk line. Bobby grabbed another lamb around the neck and positioned it just so. Meanwhile Di and I grabbed Evil by the arms and propped him into a sitting position in a corner of the pen. His face full of manure, he sat with his chin on his chest until almost all the castrating was complete. Then he woke up.

After it was all over, Evil had regained some of his natural color, but Bobby hadn't regained his composure. Every time he looked over his shoulder at Evil, he started to laugh. Evil, too, was snickering to himself, but he certainly wasn't laughing the way Bobby was. Bobby's was so loud, so intoxicating, that the only recourse one had was to join in the laughter oneself.

Which I did, with as much self-abandon.

By the time Edgar and I had cleaned up and gathered the castrating equipment, Evil was on his feet looking quite fresh. Di had scraped the remains of the sheep shit from his upper lip, and Bobby was still chuckling—flashbacks of Evil in the manure pile perhaps. He accompanied us back to the truck while Di and Bobby observed the newly castrated lambs, who appeared not to be feeling a thing.

A few minutes later Di and Evil appeared from the barn. Bobby took one look at Evil and grabbed for his belly. Evil broke into a wide smile, an appreciative smile, proud of his own rare ability as a "sit-down" comic.

* * *

Whenever Edgar and I go to the Miller farm, we are treated as part of their family. How do I know that? They put us to work. No one would put a stranger to work on his place. And how else am I sure I'm one of them? They joke with us, tease us, and offer us goodies. And they have our Dutch accent. I am flattered to be a part of their family, for these people are good, hard-working souls. Their enjoyment of each other, their animals, and us is wholly evident.

And Bobby's laughter is intoxicating.

Fancy

"I DON'T KNOW WHAT TO DO EITHER," Edgar said, wiping his eyes with a hand. I had already lost my own attempt at self-control and was trembling openly. I had several balled-up Kleenexes in my coat pockets and had snatched a paper towel from a dispenser near Fancy's hospital stall—one of four horse stalls in a separate barn only feet away from the large animal hospital bay. There, two days ago, Dr. Randy Bimes, an equine surgeon at Quakertown Vet Clinic, and Edgar had straightened out Fancy's small intestine after it had somehow become twisted out on pasture.

"I can't stand this—knowing she is suffering so badly. And we still don't have any guarantee that she will make it, even though the surgery was a success," I said dabbing at my nose. Edgar sighed heavily. He looked worn out from worry and vigilance. Neither of us had had much sleep in the last 48 hours, especially Edgar. We had made several runs to Quakertown, an hour's drive from home, plus Edgar had had his regular patients to take care of.

"No, unfortunately there's never any guarantees after a colic surgery. If only we knew whether she would be improving in a day or so, it would be a little easier to tolerate seeing her in pain this way. But

Fancy and Edgar

this is tough. I sure would hate to see her endure misery like this only to die in two or three days anyway. If only we could be sure." Edgar looked through the bars of the hospital stall where Fancy leaned deliriously into the corner. "What do you think?"

I mulled over the options for several minutes. "Well, I know it's serious that her guts still are not moving. They should be by now, according to Randy. He says we just have to be patient and wait for them to start again. But he also said they may not start up at *all*, in which case, all her pain is for nothing. But what else can we do but wait for things to turn a corner?"

I dabbed my eyes with a hanky and went on. "If we put her to sleep now, she'll be out of her misery, but what if she would have lived? What if her intestines would have begun moving tomorrow or the next day? I don't want to put her to sleep prematurely. I could never live with myself. If she does turn around, she could have ten or more years with us—nice long summer days in the pasture. Considering that, this suffering would have been worth the second chance at life."

Edgar nodded. Neither of us was ready to give up on her. "I don't think I can do it. Putting her down may be the humane thing to do, but in this case I don't know if it's the best choice. We just don't know."

Edgar gripped the stall bars. There was silence except for Fancy's repeated stomping the floor—a reaction to pain. Seeing her so distressed was torturous: she was usually so happy and feisty.

Minutes passed before Edgar said, "Okay, then, let's give her two more days. If she is not improving at all by then—still painful—and they are still pumping gallons and gallons of fluid off her stomach every two hours, then we'll just have to be strong enough and unselfish enough to put her to sleep. But you're right. We've got to give her more time for her insides to start healing and working. It's just that we all expected them to have started by now. And neither Randy nor I can figure out why they haven't begun to move yet."

It had been approximately two and a half days since we had discovered Fancy with a bellyache one evening at five o'clock. As usual, I had put her oats in front of her in her wooden bunk. But this time, instead of plunging her muzzle into the mound of grain, she turned her face away in disgust. Then she displayed the characteristic behavior of a horse with colic: the flehmin, a reaching out with the upper lip, as if she were reaching up to pluck an apple from a high branch.

I ran to the house to tell Edgar, who immediately gathered equipment from his truck: a stethoscope to hear if her intestines were moving, measure her heart rate, and count her respiration; Banamine, a pain killer; a rectal sleeve to cover his arm when checking for an intestinal blockage, or, heaven forbid, a twist in her guts; and a thermometer, in case it wasn't a colic but a comparatively harmless flu instead. I held Fancy's halter while he listened to her belly.

"Decreased gut sounds," he said, and then he moved to her other side to listen there—same thing. She had had no raised temperature, so influenza wasn't likely. Too bad—a flu would've been a walk in the park compared to colic. Everything else was okay—the color of her gums, her heart rate and respiration. Hopefully it was just a simple colic, he had said. He gave her an injection of Banamine, and in ten minutes her head was bent over her manger, and she was nibbling grain.

But she wasn't voracious for it, not like a normal horse would be.

That evening Edgar rechecked her around eight o'clock. All the other horses nickered a greeting when he entered the barn. Fancy wasn't even visible. He ran to the side of her stall where she lay on her side in the sawdust. He coaxed her to get up and examined her again. She was not sweating, which would have been usual for a horse with a bellyache, but when he took the stethoscope to her side again, he heard nothing—not a squeak, not a grunt, not a rumble. Nothing. Her guts were dead calm like a stagnant lagoon.

That wasn't good.

Edgar knew how upset I get when one of our animals is sick. To spare me the worry, he didn't want to tell me about Fancy's relapse. Besides, some colics were a little more stubborn to fix, and maybe that was the case with Fancy's. So, by himself and without telling me, he tied Fancy to the corner of her stall and did a rectal to check again for any abnormalities. He found none, he told me, when he came in from the barn. As he watched her standing quietly in her stall, not sweating, not stomping her feet in any kind of severe pain, he administered more Banamine and dipyrone, the wonder drug against colic pain in horses. He decided to check her again in an hour.

When he came back to the house, he avoided telling me about Fancy's worsening condition. I had no reason to suspect any problem, so I fell asleep in front of the TV. When I finally woke to go upstairs to bed, Edgar was looming over me.

"It's Fancy," he said. I blinked, groggy, but I knew something was amiss by the look on his face.

"What's wrong?" I blurted, throwing off the covers. "I thought she was okay after dinner. What time is it?"

"Eleven o'clock. She's not better. She hasn't been quite right since I checked her at eight, and now my drugs aren't holding the pain. She's much more painful than when I found her down in the stall at eight, and . . ."

"She was *down!* Why didn't you tell me?"

"I didn't want you to worry."

"Then why are you telling me now?" I sputtered.

"Because I think we may have to take her for surgery, and I need you to . . ."

"Surgery! My Fancy! No, it can't be!" I yelled, running for my shoes. "What could be wrong with her? Do you feel anything twisted? Is she blocked? For Christ's sake, what are we doing wrong around here that we have so many colics with our horses?" My tears began to well, and I ran upstairs to pull on street clothes.

I scrambled to pull on a pair of shorts and a T-shirt. Why? Why? I kept asking myself. I knew Edgar wasn't overreacting to the situation because it wasn't in his nature to be a worrywart. Fancy's condition was probably very serious. And why did we have so many colics in our barn? With only six horses, this would be our fourth colic surgery: one for Nicky a few years ago when the stones and dirt he unknowingly slurped up with his hay became blocked inside him, and two surgeries for Lucy, our pinto saddlebred, who had twisted her guts twice. Now Fancy! I raced to dress and plummeted downstairs and out the door.

I saw our truck's taillights disappearing down the driveway. Edgar was going to hitch up the horse trailer so that we could haul Fancy to Quakertown Vet Clinic, an hour's drive away, where she would be readied for surgery. I peered into Fancy's stall. She stood anxiously, her eye wrinkled. I went to her side, talking calmly to her, and she stamped her foot, only once but in an angry manner, as though she were trying to beat out the pain in her belly. I took her by the halter and stroked her ear, whispering to her not to worry.

I couldn't stand it. My own Fancy—my showboat. "We won't let anything happen to you, girl," I assured her.

I continued to stroke her ear as she lay her face against my chest. My first show horse leaned heavily against me. We had gone through so much together: training, practicing an hour every day through bitter cold and sweltering heat, riding the cornfields and dirt roads in our leisure time. She couldn't die—it wouldn't be fair to me or, especially, to her.

Soon our truck's headlights were racing up the driveway, and behind the truck, the orange lights of the horse trailer. Quickly I put the leg wraps around Fancy's lower legs. I attached a lead to her halter and led her out the barn. It was a balmy June evening. The stars were clear, and the air was still. I stood with Fancy waiting for Edgar to line up the trailer. I heard a whinny from the barn: the horses were puzzled. They wondered what was happening that one of their family was being led from the barn in the middle of the night.

Edgar backed the trailer around, stopped, pulled down the ramp, and waited for me to lead her into the compartment. I led Fancy up the ramp, and she followed obediently, not evidencing much pain at all. I almost suggested that we wait awhile, that indeed she looked a little better. But I didn't. Fancy's life was too precious for us to delay. If she did need surgery, time was of the essence. The earlier a colic surgery is performed, the better the animal's chances of surviving.

We pulled into Quakertown's parking lot about 12:30 that night. Crickets chirped sporadically as we led Fancy into the examining room for large animals. The place was dead except for this end of the clinic which was lit up for our arrival. A technician came in and said Dr. Bimes would be with us in a few minutes.

I put Fancy into the horse stocks. Her pain was increasing. I could do nothing to soothe her anxiety. She stood pawing and stomping the rubber mat. I could only steady her head so that she wouldn't hurt herself against the heavy metal stocks.

In fifteen minutes that seemed like an hour, Randy appeared, stethoscope around his neck. I'm sure he could see the glassy look in my eyes that anticipated my horse's imminent death. But he nodded, smiled, and immediately went to work on her. He listened to her gut sounds, pausing for several minutes to listen to each side. Then he reached for a rectal sleeve while Edgar updated him on the medications he had administered since the beginning of the colic episode.

"And then I gave her a shot of dipyrone," I heard Edgar say. "The rectal at ten o'clock was normal. But looking at her now, I'd say she appears a bit bloated on her right side. Let's see what you feel on the rectal."

Randy covered his arm with the clear sleeve, pulled a few bits of manure from Fancy's rectum and inserted his arm. He leaned up against her back end up to his armpit, trying to feel for a twist or abnormal placement of intestine. His brow knitted as he mentally compared Fancy's guts to the thousands of guts he had felt in other horses with colic.

"Large bowel is fine," he said.

I sighed in relief and held Fancy's head while he completed the uncomfortable rectal examination.

"Huh," Randy grunted. "I don't like this." He twisted his arm around inside her to get a better feel.

I swallowed hard.

"I feel distention in the small bowel."

I looked to Edgar to see what that meant. His eyes were tightly closed. "Small intestine? You sure?" Edgar repeated.

"Yeah, unfortunately," Randy said, withdrawing his arm and whipping the sleeve off into a trash can. "I'm pretty sure we have a displacement of the small bowel. The trouble is, I can't reach far enough, so it's a bit hard to say for certain."

"The rectal I did was normal at home," Edgar added. "Of course, I guess that could have changed in an hour."

"Yeah," Randy said. "We're going to do a tap, just to be sure she hasn't ruptured her gut. If she has, there's no use even opening her up." I winced. He looked around to Fancy's head and asked a few more questions about when she began showing pain and the different analgesics Edgar had given her. Then, looking thoughtful, he said, "I just don't like the way she looks. I'd almost like to see her in more pain. More pain would indicate a large bowel problem, which is fairly correctable. But this is showing all the signs of a small bowel twist, which, as you know, is much more serious than if we had to do surgery on the colon."

I held Fancy's head, and she closed her eyes against my chest. I squeezed my eyes and held my breath.

"What do you think we should do?" Edgar said.

"Well, I'll tell you, Ed—I'd like to watch her through the night. She's a fairly old horse now, around twenty, right?"

Edgar nodded.

"I don't want to do surgery on her unless it's absolutely necessary. You know—older horse—more of a surgical risk and all that. . . ."

"Yes, she might not be able to handle the anesthesia," Edgar concurred.

I couldn't stand it any longer. "Please don't consider the anesthetic risk," I said, my voice quaking. "She is my dearest horse. She taught me to ride, and we owe it to her to get her through this—no matter the cost, no matter the risk. So, if you think surgery is the only way, please, don't wait to operate. If she needs surgery, then by all means do it. Besides, if you don't do surgery, she'll probably die anyway—surgery risk or no surgery risk."

Randy looked for agreement to Edgar. Edgar thought and finally said, "I agree. Absolutely, Randy, our only concern is that Fancy have every advantage. She's our favorite. There's a lot of history standing there. It'd be awful if we lost her."

"Okay, then," Randy said. "But I'm still not going to go in right away since her pain isn't all that bad. I'm going to put her on fluids—rehydrate her—and analgesics. With a little luck she just might get over this without our having to open her up. I'll have the techs watch her, and if the pain gets so bad that we can't control it anymore, we'll go in. Go back home, and try not to worry about her. If I feel we need to do surgery, I'll give you a call, Ed. I assume you'd want to assist?"

"Yes, definitely," Edgar said. "Just give me a call." With that I kissed Fancy on her forehead, and Edgar patted her flank, "See ya, girl. Get better for us."

"'Bye, Fancy," I said wiping my tears madly. But Fancy was less concerned with being left in a strange place than she was with the consistently dull pain in her belly. The last thing I heard as we got back into the truck was her hoof striking the rubber mat in an angry *thud, thud, thud* against the pain.

We drove home mostly in silence, slicing the damp, heavy summer air before us. Edgar knew I was worried. "Might not have to operate at all," he said cheerfully. "She might get better on her own." It was rationalization at its finest. I knew he was only trying to boost me up.

"What is the likelihood of that happening," I moaned, the eternal pessimist. "You heard him say there was something out of whack with her small bowel. After all this time, and all the drugs you've given her, why has she only gotten worse? Any other colic would have come around by now."

"I don't know. We just have to wait it out. The techs will watch her through the night. If they see she's getting a lot worse, then they'll tell Randy, and he'll call us. All we can do is wait for his telephone call."

"I won't sleep a wink waiting for that phone to ring," I said, and my fingers flew to my mouth. "My poor Fancy. She doesn't deserve this. She's too good, too kind a horse to die."

"I know, but colic happens to the good horses, too."

"This will be the longest night ever," I said.

"Yeah. Well, let's hope she won't need surgery after all. Think positively."

In an hour we were pulling into our driveway. It was two in the morning, and we both climbed the woody mountain to bed. Sleep eluded us for a while. I did manage to sleep fitfully until the phone jarred us awake at four o'clock.

"She is?" I heard Edgar ask. "You are?" There was a pause. "Okay, I'll be right there."

My heart tightened; I felt sick. Fancy was worse, and Randy had no choice but to operate.

"Yep, we'll be operating on her in about an hour," Edgar told me as I jolted upright in bed. He headed toward the bathroom where he pulled on some clothes. The last I heard was his truck leaving the garage and speeding into the night.

Consumed by worry, I couldn't sleep. Would an older horse like Fancy be able to survive the anesthesia, let alone the surgery itself? Maybe we were putting her through needless suffering. Maybe the vengeful Fates were ganging up on us. Perhaps Fancy's time had come. Would we only be delaying the inevitable? But just yesterday she was fine and eating like a horse. All kinds of questions and concerns clouded my thoughts. I went downstairs and sat staring at the blank television screen.

Although I had not turned on the TV, all kinds of pictures—pictures of Fancy and me and Fancy and Edgar rolled before my eyes as though they possessed the screen. The TV seemed to glow with a ghostly image of Edgar leading a yearling Fancy, full of wild life and spirit, through the woods around our house. One day Fancy had decided it was so much more fun to lead than be led, so without warning she had taken off at a gallop with Edgar clinging helplessly to the end of the lead rope. She dragged him at a run through the woods, over dead branches, across flat rocks, over groundhog holes and every other obstacle in sight. Edgar ran as fast as he could to keep up. Out of pride alone he would never let a recalcitrant horse go, so he galloped himself, clasping the rope, jumping and skipping over obstacles like a deer.

Unfortunately he hadn't seen one large fallen branch.

Fancy had raced through the woods, hell bent for the pasture, and Edgar was determined to hang on. Unknown to him a snake lay in the grass—a wooden snake—that would decide to coil evilly around his ankle. Suddenly the camouflaged branch leaped up and struck Edgar from below, curling around his ankles and throwing him to the ground like a lassoed steer. His face hit the mud, and the rest of him hit the dirt in domino effect. The lead rope *zizz-zz-zzed* out of his hand, and he lay in a tangle as Fancy skipped merrily away, her tail waving like a victory flag.

The image on the television faded slowly away and another took its place as my fingers flew to my mouth with another worry pang. On the screen before me was Fancy and me the day of our first riding lesson.

When I started to ride her, she was only about three years old. Even though I was an adult, my riding age, by comparison, was about that of a six-year-old. We taught each other many lessons in those horse-showing years; we trained each other. I watched Fancy and me gliding around the imaginary scene. What a precarious rider I used to be. The memories made me smile.

In those days nobody had ever told me I was a good rider, not even my mother. Any bit of safe riding I had done before riding Fancy was accomplished only by luck and with the good graces of the Fates, who viewed my first horse-riding attempts with laughter and ridicule. The mythological giantesses probably pitied my ineptness too much to seriously conjure a disaster. For a while, anyway, they ignored me.

Just the same—privately, I would've given anything to be known as an equestrienne.

I hadn't realized how badly I rode a horse until one evening when Edgar paused from his veterinary journal and said out of the clear blue, "Why don't you start taking riding lessons?"

"What?" I said, jumping from the sofa, a cat hurtling off my lap. I clasped my chest in disbelief, "Me, take lessons?" Silence followed. "Why?" I challenged, hands on hips, foot tapping. "I already *can* ride!"

"Just a suggestion," Edgar said, turning back to his journal.

But the suggestion stuck like a knife. "I'm perfectly capable on horseback. I do *all right!*" I stalked across the room. He might as well have said I was a terrible teacher, or worse, yet, a lousy lover.

He looked up, placed his journal in his lap, and said with sincerity, "I'm just afraid you'll get hurt."

Arms falling limply to my side, I said, "I'm really that bad . . . you think I may hurt myself?" I faltered, wringing my hands.

I really wanted him to say, "No, I'm only kidding. You remind me of the girl in *National Velvet*." But instead he looked sorry.

His pronouncement was all the more devastating because he rarely exaggerated; Edgar was always honest and straightforward. He would never say anything to deliberately upset or tease me. He was telling me the awful truth.

"All right," I said, my own words stinging in my mouth. "I'll call someone tomorrow for lessons."

My eyes glazed over in front of the "possessed" TV as the screen switched to a scene in which my newly-trained horse and I awaited my riding instructor for my first riding lesson.

I had expected thunder thighs—a woman the size of Godzilla's first born. After all, I figured, a person uses a lot of *leg* when riding, and after all her years of experience in the saddle (which, to my figuring, made her about retirement age), her trotters must rival those of a Sumo wrestler. I pictured a steely gray-haired old lady who carried her fleshy saddle with her wherever she went. I would dare her to teach me anything.

But when the little brown sports car skidded to a stop in our drive-way, I wished I wouldn't have worn my T-shirt that said I CAN'T BELIEVE I ATE THE WHOLE THING. I peeked from the barn door and sauntered out to the car, my chest thrust forward. Catching sight of a perky blonde ponytail, I stopped dead, and my confident grin fizzled at the sight of a pretty, petite face encircled by curls.

The young woman alighted from the car. From her docksiders to her jeans and Izod shirt, she was everything I had ever hoped to look like. My instinctive jealousy of other attractive women erupted primitively. I would've fought this opponent for my man, ripping her ponytail right out of her head. She was a picture. She was disgustingly lanky—a Modigliani without the distortion. Her natural blonde tresses were pulled hurriedly through a tortoise-shell hairclip and curled in quiet disarray around her head—the Dr. Pepper look, that messy, windblown picture of loveliness—a California girl.

The California beach nymph perspired sexily and while the sand glistened on her skin like granulated sugar on a vanilla cookie, I could only rival a lump of unbaked dough. I sweated like a container of cold tunafish salad on a humid day and developed embarrassing water stains under my sleeves. Sand never glistened like crystals on my skin. It just sandblasted the remains of any make-up and caused a rash down my thighs. No, I never could look disheveled with any degree of class.

"Hi, my name's Gale—as in the wind," she said, brushing a stray hair from her face.

"Hi, I'm Gay," I said. I heard a disbelieving giggle. "Well, I'm Gay, but not gay. . . Not that there's anything wrong with it. . . ."

"I see you have the horse ready to go. This is the first time you've ridden her since she came home from training, right?" She eyed Fancy, sizing up her conformation as I strapped on an old, beat-up English hard hat. She turned, saw the moth-eaten thing perched atop my head and said, "Why are you wearing that?"

As the elastic chinstrap bit into my cheeks (I felt like a fat baby in an Easter bonnet), I said grandly, "Better to be safe than sorry—that's my motto." She looked amused, and there was a long silence.

I swallowed the lump of hot pride, "I guess I'm not a very experienced rider; my husband's afraid I'll hurt myself."

Smiling weakly, I climbed into the saddle. Only I knew I was wearing that hat because I couldn't stand the sight of my own blood. But the pride welled up again, stronger this time. "Yes, he's such a worry wart," I said, patting the hard hat onto my head. The dust puffed out around it. "He's so silly—thinks I can't ride." A nervous laugh shot from my mouth.

We walked to the middle of the outdoor ring. "We'll see in a few minutes, won't we?" Gale said. "Head her on out and circle to the left around the outside of the ring. Try to find her center of balance."

Fancy and I followed the path along the fence.

"That's it: take it easy at a walk, and keep her together between your hands and legs," she shouted. "Drive that back end underneath you;

we're looking for a bit of collection here. Good riding is the ability to ride a balanced seat on a balanced animal." And so came the barrage of knowledge, filling my well of concentration.

As "balanced seat," "collection," and "drive from behind" swam dizzily in my head, I heard a loud bugle-like sound issue from below. Tossing her head and snorting, Fancy suddenly stepped into a high-headed prance. I felt my blood turn to glass as my seat went out from under me. All of a sudden I abandoned my steed for a white-water canoe. First the front end pitched, then it came up, and I lurched atop it, loose, like a ragdoll, my legs flying in the stirrups, my hands clinging to the mane.

Fancy was "hot," as horsemen say. Such behavior did not phase a professional who could ride out a sudden spurt of energy. But I froze in my stirrups, fearing for my life. Edgar was right. Fancy was a fiery three-year-old, only broke to ride six short months ago. Suddenly I was scared to death.

I realized that before this I had probably been lucky with riding my old horse, Nicky, and others at local hack stables. They took care of me, flattering me into thinking I was an adequate rider. After carrying me through the woods and along the country roads, they made sure I had always arrived safely back at the barn.

But Fancy in her youth was different. At the trainer's we'd been confined to a circular path in the indoor arena. Here I was outside on two acres of hills and ditches with their scary shadows, wind, and darting cats. At the trainer's, Fancy hadn't been distracted by even a tree or any other animals.

In vain I prayed for Fancy to act sensibly and protect me. "*SIT UP STRAIGHT!* Bring her down into a walk and collect your thoughts and your balance," Gale called.

"I want to see a canter—*NOW!*" Gale yelled from the center of the ring. "Collect her first; ride the back end, and cue her for the canter."

This is it, I said to myself. I can't canter. I'm going to hurt myself. I clenched the reins and prayed for a nose-bleed.

"Let's go! Cue her for that canter!" Gale cried. Then, not even thinking that I should just stop the horse and get off, apologize meekly and admit I couldn't ride a toilet seat, let alone a horse, I cued Fancy for the canter.

Like a spring bursting from a broken toy, she leaped into the air. Instead of gripping harder, my body reacted by shutting itself down.

My guts sank, loosening from the body wall, and lay in a heap next to my bladder while my arms and legs loosened and hung from their joints—the white flag of surrender. Worst of all, my eyes involuntarily closed, pitching me into darkness.

"Gay, don't fall apart!" Gale commanded. "Stay with her and look where you're going! Don't go forward! Sit up straight—don't grab her neck!"

My heart heaved, and my guts liquified as I grabbed for her ears—an albatross around her neck. I was a dead weight, clasping her gullet in a death grip. But I could not let go despite Fancy's strangulated snorts. The white-water canoe mutated into a runaway go-cart, to whose wheel I helplessly clung. Finally, I opened my eyes—only to see my nemesis, the beckoning ground.

Fancy plummeted around that pasture and banked into the turns. Her head was stretched out straight from the shoulder, and there was no way to stop her in her frenzied flight. I could only pitch and heave aboard her, my arms clinging around her neck.

"*STOP HER! PULL BACK ON THE REINS!*" I heard a voice from the sky boom. "*GET OFF HER NECK! SIT UP STRAIGHT OR YOU'LL. . . .*"

CRUNCH! I hit the ground. The world went black.

I opened my eyes. Fancy was staring at me, blue sky enhaloing her head.

"Do you hear me, Gay? Get back on your horse. You're all right. Just knocked the wind out of you." It was Gale.

A stone was digging me in the middle of my back. "I'm alive," I moaned in a weak voice. My back creaked into place. "Nothing really hurts, only a little stiff," I said twisting my head from side to side.

"You're just fine. Get up. The reason you went off is because all your weight was on her front end. I couldn't get you to stop her; she was out of control, but you should've leaned back when you stopped. Now get back on, and we'll go around a few times at a walk."

I stepped stiffly into the saddle. Fancy seemed calm enough now.

"When she stopped on a dime, you took a swan dive over her left shoulder, landing first on your side, then your back. It wasn't a bad fall, and you didn't fall very far. Actually, you were already halfway to the ground, hanging down around her neck. It's a bit strange," she said, contemplating the skyline. "It almost seemed as though you wanted to fall off. Of course, that's absolutely silly, isn't it. Nobody ever wants to fall off a horse." She shot me a side glance.

Might it be that a person's subconscious, expecting something to happen, could cause it to occur? Had so many people told me horses were dangerous and I wasn't such a great rider that I actually, subconsciously, fulfilled their predictions by falling off? Did I hope to erase all their hauntings if, psychologically, I'd just give in and get it over with?

Fancy and I walked around the pasture, and I dismounted. I had made a fool of myself.

Leading Fancy back to the barn, I listened to Gale's analysis," You've got a long way to go if you want to learn to ride a horse."

"Well, I didn't feel very good today anyway. My sinuses are acting up, and I can't see clearly." I could rationalize with the best of them. "Besides, when I rode Fancy at the trainer's, she had only one little spot in which to run. She had no room to act up. Here she has fourteen acres! It's just not fair. Everybody else can ride a horse without falling off."

Dead silence. Gale was smiling.

She began, "First of all, you don't sound stuffed up at all. Besides, I didn't know sinus problems could cause incoordination. And you also weren't riding in fourteen acres, but only in about two. You are not the only one to fall off a horse, so don't expect any pity from me. Plain and simple, you need to *learn* how to ride properly, that's all. No one has ever taught you to ride. Once you understand and master the basics, you'll be able to ride with the best of them, but not before then."

I lowered my head, embarrassed.

When I looked up, Gale's visage had disappeared from the TV screen and was replaced by another. It was Fancy—my hard-working companion, a family member—standing shivering in pain in the stocks at Quakertown Veterinary Clinic.

Gradually the rest of the living room came into focus, and I glanced down at my watch. It was six in the morning. I wondered if Fancy was still alive and, if she was, whether they had found anything blocking her insides. Were they able to correct the problem? How long would she be in the recovery room? I knew Edgar would call as soon as he got out of surgery. She must still be under, then, or he would've called.

I had bitten my nails down to little nubs by seven o'clock when the phone rang. I snatched it from the receiver, "Yeah?"

"It's me. So far, so good. The operation's over. It took so long because we had to run through all her small intestine to find the problem. We started at the duodenum and examined every inch of bowel for a blockage. . . ."

"So, what did you find?" I said, chewing my lower lip.

"We didn't find a blockage but did find an area that was swollen and red. There may have been a partial twist in that area, but then it must have untwisted as we started examining the gut. So we stripped the gas out of the whole small intestine and into the large bowel. We had to do that because it's easier for the guts to start moving again, post-surgery, if there's no gas in there. That alone took an hour. After that, we put everything back inside and closed her up."

"So how's she doing now?" I said.

"Okay. She's holding her own. I stayed with her until she got up, and the first time she tried to stand, she lost her balance and fell back down. She hit her nose and cut her lip open pretty bad. But that'll heal eventually."

"Oh, my poor Fancy." But I was relieved. At least she was alive. "Now it's only a matter of time, right—until she's recuperated?"

"Well, it's a little more than that. This wasn't a routine colic surgery because it involved the small bowel. The large bowel is much easier to operate on, and it's also speedier to recover from a surgery. The most critical thing now is that her guts must start moving. Once they're traumatized by surgery, they shut down. Most start back up in a few hours, or it can even take a few days. Because Fancy's case was so serious, I have no idea how long it'll take for her to get going again—if she ever does."

I flinched.

"Anyway," he said, "now it's a waiting game. I'm going to recheck Fancy now that she's in the recovery stall, and then I'm heading home. Maybe later this afternoon we'll drive down here to visit her. Do you want to?"

"Of course," I said. "Eggie, do you think she'll make it?'

"I hope so, but I don't know for sure. Let's give her a few hours and check her again. I'll be home in about an hour."

"Okay, Hon. Thanks for saving Fancy."

"I wish I could tell you I think she's saved. But I just don't know that yet. See you in a little bit."

Later that afternoon we drove to Quakertown to visit Fancy in the hospital. I expected her to look a bit bleak, like a person does after surgery, but I wasn't prepared for what I saw, and neither was Edgar.

When we checked in at the hospital, we were told that Fancy was

still in the recovery area—a full six hours after the surgery. I was
alarmed and rushed to where I found Fancy standing in the horse
stocks. Horses are put into stocks so that they didn't injure people or
themselves. Why was it necessary in this case? I went to her side, but
she hardly seemed to recognize me, so preoccupied by pain was she. At
first sight of her, my eyes became glassy. I looked to Edgar for comfort,
but he was struggling with his own pain at seeing her in so much misery. Fancy stood pawing the rubber floor mat. She was bathed in a slick
sweat, rivulets of perspiration streaming from her brow down her long
face and dripping onto the floor. Her neck was foamy with sweat. Her
mane was wet-heavy and hung like a limp rag. Taped to the outside of
her left nostril was the end of a stomach tube the size of a garden hose.
The other end lay inside her stomach.

I swallowed a lump and said, "Fancy?" I could only detect a very small
movement of recognition beneath her closed eyelids—frozen in pain.
"Fancy? You're my girl. You'll just feel really bad for a few hours until your
guts start moving again. But I want you to hang in there, Fancy."

No response.

"And then we'll bring you home to the other guys." I wiped the
water beneath her forelock onto my sweatpants. "We love you, Fancy."

I looked at Edgar, who listened intently to her side with his stethoscope.
His expression was grim. I could tell he wasn't hearing anything moving. I
bit my lip as Fancy suddenly slammed a foot onto the rubber mat.

"I don't know, Gay. She looks a lot worse than when I left her this
morning." He blinked back tears. "I can't figure out why she's so
painful. She shouldn't be *this* bad. Maybe it's time for her shot of
painkiller."

As if in agreement, Fancy stomped her foot again, and her eyeball
rolled beneath its lid.

Edgar wrapped the stethoscope around his neck. He said, his
mouth in a grimace, "I just don't like the way she looks—too painful."

"Gut sounds?" I said, straightening Fancy's soaked forelock.

"I hear nothing," Edgar said. "Absolute silence. I can't stand to see her
in so much pain, and I can't figure out *why* she's so painful."

Just then Randy burst through the swinging door. I mustered a smile,
thanking him for trying to save Fancy. The tall, young equine surgeon of
impeccable reputation and expertise eyed Fancy thoughtfully.

"Why all this pain?" Edgar asked. "I expected to see some improvement—not regression—at this point. It is almost ten hours after surgery. She's pawing, puffing; her respiration is elevated. What's going on?"

"Goes that way sometimes," Randy said matter-of-factly. He didn't take his eyes from Fancy, evaluating every twitch and breath. "You're right; she's in a lot of pain, but she's not due for another injection of Banamine for. . . ." he consulted the medical log, "for another hour. I don't want to give her too much because of the risk of developing ulcers."

"Why all the sweating?" I stammered, my eyes welling. "She's in absolute misery. Do you think she could have retwisted something while she was in recovery?"

"Unlikely," said Randy taking a stethoscope to Fancy's side. "The sweating is a pain response. She's probably very depressed, too; after all, that stomach tube is not comfortable, but it's got to stay there." He consulted the chart again. "Already this afternoon we've expelled ten gallons of fluid off her stomach. She's due for another treatment in an hour, too."

"Why?" I blurted.

"Well, after a hard surgery like this, the guts shut down, as you know—mainly because we handled them. That's a natural response—an ileus. People go through the same thing with intestinal surgery. In a few days the naso-gastric tube is removed, but only after the guts have started moving again. Hers obviously haven't started up yet. It may take several days. And sometimes they don't start up again ever, or the post-op care becomes so expensive that an owner will opt to put their animal to sleep. Until then, we're pumping the fluids into her tissues at a tremendous rate. But, by the same token, a lot of them pool in the stomach, causing distention. If that distention is not relieved every few hours, then her stomach could rupture, and that's the end. Also, an enlarged stomach is antithetical to getting the guts moving again. That's why we must keep the tube in and drain off gallons of fluid every two hours. There's a lot of aftercare with something of this nature. I won't beat around the bush; she's in very serious condition."

"I can't stand to see her in this much pain," I said, stroking Fancy's damp forehead. Her eyes were slits.

Edgar said, "Yes, is that much pain normal for this situation?"

"Well," said Randy, removing his stethoscope from Fancy's side, "some of that could be pain from the injection we gave to stimulate her gut." Then he flung the stethoscope around his neck, crossed his arms on his chest and backed up against a medicine chest. "We use erythromycin and dipyrone to jump-start the guts. And each one of them tends to irritate the digestive system. That's the whole idea, in fact. We try to irritate and thereby stimulate the gut into moving."

Edgar said, "That's odd. You use erythromycin to stimulate the gut. That's an antibiotic."

"Yeah, and it's also tough on the digestive system. Lots of people don't feel good when they take erythro. It upsets their whole bowel situation even while it's fighting a disease. So Fancy not only has post-op pain but also discomfort in the stomach from the erythro. It's a nasty scenario, but we have to get the guts going again, or she'll die."

I shuddered and held Fancy close.

Randy continued, "And we're going to keep the naso-gastric tube in her until she stops refluxing—pooling fluid in her stomach. I can't see putting the tube in and out every two hours, so we'll just keep it in there. It's easier on her and us." He looked at his watch. "In fact, Ed, she's almost due to be emptied again. We need to drain off about another eight gallons of fluid from her stomach. You can get some idea of how many gallons of fluid we've been going through and how many we'll go through in the next few days. You can see we have the drip on full. The IV fluids aren't really 'dripping' into her; they're 'pouring' into her."

I looked at the huge bag of fluids hanging high above Fancy's head, and I could see the stream running through the tube down to the catheter in her vein. It was running full blast. Randy said, "We need to get her rehydrated again; her blood work shows her total protein is up. We've got to get her total solids down, and until then we've got to keep pumping the fluids to her and then draining them off her stomach. Let's reflux her now, Ed, while you're here." He turned to gather the stomach pump and a stainless steel bucket.

I didn't know if I wanted to stick around for such an awful job, but I had to stay to calm Fancy. Surely if she could tolerate all the pain and discomfort of the stomach tube, I could have the courage to watch and attend. So I stayed. After Randy attached the pump and got a suction going inside her stomach, he took the end of the hose off the pump and directed the hose from her nostril into the bucket.

Almost immediately a thick stream of greenish water burst through the hose, hitting the bucket with full force. I swallowed hard and turned away. Fancy stood calmly as I stroked her neck, and I tried not to look or listen to the gross sounds reverberating off the walls of the stark large animal recovery room. When that bucket was full, Edgar quickly replaced it with another empty one which the stomach tube filled nearly to its brim, too. Then, finally, when only a few drops ran from the hose, Randy taped the end of it back onto her halter where it would stay tied for days.

"There," Randy said, dumping the second bucketful of stomach juices down a drain hole in the floor. "That's done for another two hours."

"For how long will you have to do that?" I asked.

"Every two hours until the amount we get out each time lessens. Then we can try to get away with every three hours, then every four, et cetera, until her guts finally start up and begin to get rid of the excess fluid by themselves. Once her guts start drawing the fluid out of the stomach, we're basically out of the woods. Day by day we should be getting fewer gallons from her. The day we only get a half a gallon or so, and I actually hear peristalsis, is when we'll be able to take the naso-gastric tube out. Then we'll know her guts are working. It could be a few days, though, before that happens. Fancy is looking at a rough time ahead of her."

"A few days of this?" I said, my mouth agape.

"At least two days, maybe three," he affirmed.

The next day when we visited Fancy, the situation had not changed. She had been moved to a more comfortable stall with a window and nice clean sawdust; however, since she could dislodge the stomach tube in her nose, she was tied to a post in the corner so that she couldn't rub against it and possibly remove it. She was forced to stand with her head in a corner, and she could not eat or drink a thing because that would add to the volume of fluids already pooling inside her stomach from the IV. We consulted her medical chart hanging on her stall door, and, sure enough, she had had her stomach contents emptied every two hours. Like clockwork, the vet technicians were removing eight gallons every two hours. There was no improvement: no less an amount of fluid being drained, and she was still very uncomfortable.

That was the day Edgar and I discussed euthanasia. Finally we decided that any suffering would be worth the second chance at life, so we determined to give her another two days to turn a corner. We only needed slight improvement, perhaps a gallon less of reflux or just hearing one squeak or gurgle through the stethoscope, to continue with the critical care. But if at any time her condition began to deteriorate, we had to call it quits, for her sake alone—to end her suffering.

In two more days, the veterinary technicians were still pumping nearly the same amount of fluid off Fancy's stomach, and her gut sounds were still stone still. When Edgar and I made our daily visit, we had the inevitable euthanasia conversation with Randy. Fancy still moped in the corner, her eyes slits, the awful hose still protruding from her nose and tied alongside her halter. When she swallowed or snorted, a loud, gurgling sound erupted from the end of the tube, and every once in a while, especially when she lowered her head, a thin drool of fluid leaked out onto the floor.

"Not just yet," Randy said to our question about putting her to sleep.

I was relieved, and so was Edgar.

Randy continued, "She has no pain anymore—just discomfort. She's definitely not happy with that tube in her nose. It's beginning to chafe her, and I know she's thirsty as hell. She'd love to sip some water, but she is hydrated enough. We just can't add to the volume in her stomach. She's gone through twenty cases of fluids so far—a thousand dollars worth, at least—and we had to order another dozen cases because we're running low." He took the stethoscope to her side, listening intently. Then he pulled it out of his ears. "Nothing yet, but I'm not giving up. We all have already invested a lot in this mare—the surgery, her getting through the pain of recovery, the endless times we've pumped out her stomach. Let's just wait awhile before we make any decision to euthanize. I know her guts should have started by now, but some of these tough cases take almost a week to begin working. Sometimes they seem to take forever to come around."

"What are her odds of surviving this?" I asked.

"I'd say fifty-fifty—only because her guts haven't started up yet. But she doesn't have any infection. Her heart rate is good, and so is her color. Her vital signs are good. It's just her guts that are being stubborn. Let's give her a few more days."

"Okay, Randy," Edgar said, looking at Fancy, who barely seemed to notice us. She stood in the corner with her head hanging, clearly depressed. "We'll be here again tomorrow to check her."

The next day we arrived earlier. Edgar wanted to do a thorough exam before Randy got there for our update. We walked into the stall, and this time Fancy acknowledged us. She turned toward us and nickered, the sound gurgling grotesquely through the end of her stomach tube.

"Oh, Fancy," I said, cradling her head.

Edgar whipped the stethoscope from around his head and held the disk to her flank. I held my breath and steadied Fancy's head so as not to make any noise.

"I hear something!" Edgar said, smiling broadly as he redirected the stethoscope's disk a little higher on her side. "A gurgle—peristaltic movement, for sure. I hear her guts moving, just a little, though. I think she's turning around." I felt near to bursting with hope. Then Edgar walked around the horse to listen to the other side. "It's a lot louder on the right side," he said, slipping the stethoscope from his ears as he walked out of the stall.

I stroked Fancy's forehead, straightening her tangled mane with my fingers, and whispered, "You're gonna make it, Fance, my showboat."

"She's not out of the woods yet," Edgar said, returning with her chart in his hands. Then he flipped to the current page and yelled, "Great! The last time they drained any fluid off her was early this morning. That proves her guts are beginning to move. That was eight hours ago. They used to be getting five to eight gallons every two hours. Now it looks as though it's five gallons every eight hours."

"I can't believe it," I said, biting my lip. I patted Fancy's neck and looked over Edgar's shoulder at her medical chart. "She must finally be coming around, then. Do you really think so?"

"Yes, it appears so."

Just then Randy walked into the barn. He saw us with the chart and smiled broadly. "Congratulations, folks. She's doing better. Haven't had to drain fluids for quite a while. That means the fluids we're dripping into her are going somewhere by some means. She's urinating well, and her total protein, the last time we took blood work, was down to almost normal. I think in another couple days she'll be out of the woods. We're past the infectious stage. That would've occurred between three and five days, so it's no longer an issue. All we have to do is see a little manure being produced and see that reflux reduced to almost nothing.

"Gay, why don't you take her out of the stall for a little walk around the parking lot," Randy suggested. "She'd probably like a change of scene for awhile; it would cheer her up. Being in a stall all the time when she's used to being on pasture all day is tough on her, no doubt."

"Great," I said, grabbing a lead rope. I went into Fancy's stall and snapped the lead to her halter. She looked at me curiously. I turned her slowly away from the corner and out the door. She perked up immediately. I led her out the barn, and we began to walk a large circle around the parking lot, past cars and trucks, past the vet clinic, and down into an extra parking area. The whole time, she walked with me as if discovering the outdoors for the first time. She smelled the air, lowered her head to check out her moving feet, nuzzled my armpit, and even whinnied to anyone who cared to hear. After a few minutes and several laps around the parking lot, she picked up her pace.

People taking their cats and dogs to the hospital stared as Fancy and I walked past. No doubt they were wondering what had happened to this horse with the wide strip of adhesive tape around her neck, a catheter sticking up from it and a hose poking from the end of her nose. She looked alien.

It was a matter of relativity. A large animal such as a horse is a bigger, and, therefore, stranger hospital patient than a human or a cat or dog. There are not many secrets or much subtlety to administering to a larger animal because the doctors don't use many tiny instruments on these animals. Everything is blatantly visual—"in your face."

Likewise, the illnesses and treatments seem more dramatic—more shocking. The largeness is the thing. Because everything associated with the physicality of larger animals is more Brobdingnagian, the effect is also experienced out of normal proportions. Suffering seems greater because the pain is so violent, loud and visually arresting— horses pawing, kicking, rolling in torture. Surgery seems riskier because of the relative smallness of the surgeon's hands and tools in comparison with the giant organs to be operated on. Post-op treatments seem more brutal, more barbarian, again because of the huge equipment and their visual effects.

Fancy and I were getting looks from the small animal pet owners sashaying in and out of the office. In comparison, their problems occurred on a relative minuscule scale: anything from the microscopic flea to a barely-there worm could pose a problem. Certainly there were numerous other diseases that small animals were prone to, but the treatments, being on a smaller scale, usually seemed more discreet, less invasive. Even if a cat was made to endure a naso-gastric tube, it didn't send shivers through one's spine because it was only a tiny tube in a tiny nostril, not a giant tube the size of an industrial garden hose.

Fancy and I made three more passes through the parking lots while Edgar and Randy watched. They discussed the next stages of her recovery and the possibility of her coming home within a week. Then I led her back to her stall where, unfortunately, I had to tie her up again to the post so that she wouldn't dislodge the hose. Despite being tied, her spirits seemed better. She had hope for life. The walk around the lot had reminded her that she was capable of walking and feeling like a normal horse again. It buoyed her attitude as no pile of alfalfa hay ever could.

Gradually, as the days passed, Fancy stopped refluxing altogether. One day Randy took the tube out of her nose, and she savored her first drink of water and her first bite of hay. She was given only small amounts at first, and she immediately began making manure, though it resembled cow flops more than horse balls. Her guts were still not right, but she was markedly improved.

In a few days, after Randy felt her condition had stabilized and she was eating somewhat normally, we were able to take her home. When we sped up the driveway, Fancy in tow, our other horses ran down the side of the pasture to greet her. Unfortunately, she could not be allowed out to pasture with them for four weeks. She needed stall rest until the incision healed properly.

The rest of Fancy's recuperation was fairly uneventful. Part of her incision split open, and she was left with a hernia that later Randy said wasn't worth fixing because of the surgical risk. Today she walks around with a soft spot the size of my fist in the bottom of her belly where Randy made the incision. She also developed ulcers because of the high doses of the painkiller Banamine. So, we put her on Tagamet for several months until her appetite improved. In six months she was as good as new.

The operation cost us thousands of dollars and countless moments of worry and dread, but as we look back on it now, it was our only recourse. Fancy was a part of the family—we could have done no less. Saving her was something we have never regretted.

In all the years I've owned Fancy, she has given me far more than thousands of dollars worth of medical care. She had taught me to ride and given me the self-esteem and confidence I gained through showing her. She has birthed in me a new dimension of self that I would have lacked without her. We owed her a new chance at life. Edgar, too, felt something special for the older mare, who, as a filly, had dragged him through the mud at the end of a lead rope. It was Fancy who, every night, whickered "good night" to him after he did his barn check, and it was Fancy who nuzzled his face and breathed her hot breath against him when he gave her a hug.

She was a part of us.

And thanks to Dr. Bimes's care and the care of his staff, our animal family remained intact. Altogether, over the years, the Quakertown Veterinary Hospital's staff had saved three of our horses and Thumbelina. And Dr. Wilbers, who was an associate vet there, helped Lowell with his septic arthritis. The kind of concern the veterinarians felt toward our animals was just the tip of the iceberg of dedication. I'm sure all animal and human families receive the same kind of caring treatment there—just as we had. The interaction going on at Quakertown Vet Hospital between human and animal on a daily basis was nothing short of astounding.

Pig Immersion

WITH OUR FANCY ALIVE AND WELL, I was up for an extreme sort of celebration for my forty-somethingth birthday.

"Anything you want to do," Edgar beamed.

"Anything?"

"Yep—except New York City. I don't want to go to New York," he said, eyes slitted.

"Okay. Let's see." I paused, thinking. "I get to do anything I want on my birthday?"

"You got it."

"All right, then. I want to immerse myself in pigs," I declared. "I want to visit Susan Armstrong's pot-bellied pig farm."

We pulled up into Ross Mill Farm's driveway two hours later. Susan rushed from her 18th-century stone farmhouse to greet us as Edgar was hauling bags of apples from the back of the car.

"Happy Birthday, Gay!" Susan shouted, throwing her arms around me. "I was so excited when you called this morning wanting to visit. What brings you here?"

"This," I said grandly, my arms outstretched, "is my birthday present."

Susan looked puzzled. Just then a sporty-looking pig danced from around the side of the house. I recognized him immediately—Ink. He trotted up to me, stopped, sat solidly on his haunches, and with an open-mouth, smiled up at me—a happy birthday greeting.

"All this is my gift," I repeated mysteriously. "And Ink, too. I can't think of another place I'd rather be on my birthday than conversing with you and your pigs." I hugged myself dramatically and spun around. "I want to be surrounded by pigs. I want to schmooze with pigs. I want to be immersed in hogdom."

"Okay," she said, laughing with mild trepidation. "Go right ahead and drown yourself or whatever in my animals. Knock yourself out. Maybe when you're all pigged out, we'll go into town for lunch. How about it?"

"Sure," Edgar said, hoisting his last sack of apples from the car. "At least I'll get something out of the deal then."

Susan saw the ten bags of apples and went into the house for a knife.

"Okay," I directed Edgar. "Would you quarter each apple and load the pieces into these two plastic bags for me? When you get one bag full, I'll take it over to the pigpens. And when I have run out of apples, I'll trade you the empty bag for another full one. Okay?"

"Anything you say, birthday girl," he smiled.

Absolutely in my glory, I went from one pigpen to another popping apples into gaping, smiling piggy mouths. Ordinarily Susan wouldn't let people feed loads of fruit to her animals because she likes to keep her pigs sleek. And some pigs get so excited by the treats that they lose their manners and get pushy. But I wasn't afraid of a fresh pig. Once scolded for rude behavior, even the most rambunctious ones behave themselves. Many of the pigs on Susan's farm are there as boarders to lose weight. She'd only allow me to give those pigs one quarter of an apple. (When she wasn't looking, I slipped them another one. Apples weren't that fattening, after all.)

Edgar was busy cutting apples while I traipsed around the farm doling out treats to Rambo, Jake, Punkin, Bessie, April, Dixie, Dolly, Homer, Gilly, Grady, Millie, Pita, Miss Minnie, Lucy, Lillie, Junior, Jill, Isaac, Slag, Snapple, Tillie, Olive, Uncle Milton, Winston, Rosie, Paulie, Susie, Phoebe, Mama Jo, Zonka, Georgia Lea, Hamlet, Charles, Lawrence, Amos, Bess, Porgy, Henry, Petey, Angie, Bridges,

Mildred, Gordy, PJ, Jessie, Louise, Ralph, Alice, Norton, Pig-achoo, Pigasus, Spike, Lulabelle, Corky, Kokie Roberts, Emmett Smith, Milo, Bethany, Dudley, Decoy, Elvis, Gidget, Hopi, Huey, and Bromley.

I was in love with pig enthusiasm, pig smiles, pig gratitude, pig politeness, pig energy, and pig synergy.

I was halfway through the last bag of apples when Edgar sneaked up behind with the last batch. Jake saw his heavy-laden bag and abandoned me and my surrounding porcine crowd for Edgar. Jake stood before Edgar, his mouth wide open. Edgar marveled that he could see all the way down Jake's throat. He offered Jake a slice of fruit. Jake, like all the other pigs, relished the taste of apple, as was obvious by the smacking of the lips, the snorting, and the hopping in place.

"Hey," Edgar yelled as he and Jake turned down a dirt lane. "There are more pigpens way back here, Gay."

"Where?" I called. All I could see was woods; Susan wouldn't have kept any pigs that far from the house, way out in the woods.

"Right here!" Edgar's voice was distant.

I ran, a gaggle of pigs behind me. They knew a good thing when they met her.

There, perhaps 500 feet from the farmhouse, was a pen with six large pigs. Edgar was already doling out their treats from his bag. "Look at these guys! They're huge!"

I grabbed some apple slices from his bag, and a white sow with a hanging, wrinkly belly put her front feet up on the second rung of the hog panel. Sniffing and snorting, she smiled and opened her mouth.

"Yes," I told the white pig. "I know that's where I have to put the apple. I know food goes into a mouth."

She hopped with her front feet on the fence, and I threw an apple into the opening as I would a beanbag into a hole. The mouth clamped shut and started to chew. She was tasting, chewing, and smiling all at the same time. And I could see the food being pulverized in her mouth cavity before she swallowed it.

Beside her stood a black and white, terribly wrinkly pig. He was intent on Edgar and the bag of apples, too. He was not so excited that he was standing on the hog panel, but he was turning circles and huffing. Each pig begs in his or her own way. This one was more reserved in his mooching. Finally, Edgar showed him a slice of apple, and he tilted his head up and opened his mouth wide. Edgar dropped the apple in, and in a microsecond it was devoured.

"Oh, this is great!" I said, hopping up and down. "Thanks so much for bringing me here. All Susan's pigs are so happy, so pleasant, and so appreciative—like we couldn't give them anything better."

"They certainly are that," Edgar agreed, flipping another apple in the frantic white one's mouth. In seconds the other four were lined up along the inside of the fence, their mouths opened as if to say, "See— here's where you put that food. Right here—see the big opening?"

Now Edgar likes pigs, but he is not the aficionado I am. As the more practical and technical of us, he made it his job to see that each pig got equal shares of the apple slices. "Here," he said with a deter- mined look. "That one over there didn't get a third piece. Here ya go, Piggy." With that he lobbed the apple into the gaping pink mouth.

Soon the bag was empty, and I could see disappointment written all over the six big pigs' faces. They didn't pout or cry as some human kids do when they don't get their way. Though they weren't being fed any more, they were as equally grateful to having their faces rubbed. I crouched down beside the fence, and the white one came nose-to-nose with me. She knew that we had run out of apples and wasn't expecting any more. She just wanted to say hello. With opened mouth she huffed a greeting, and I huffed back—friendship cemented.

"Okay," Edgar said, stuffing his empty plastic sack into his jacket pocket. "Are you ready to go to the house yet?"

I was still crouched down next to the white one. She was sniffing my bangs, and I could feel her hot breath on my cheek. "Huh?" I poked my hand through the hog panel, and she pushed her pink wet nose into my palm. "Oh, yeah, sure. Yeah, we're all out of apples. I sup- pose we can go." I paused. "Ya know, this one really likes me."

"Yeah, yeah. All the pigs like you. They like anyone who feeds them apples."

"It's more than that. I can tell. They really like me."

"Sure. Let's go have lunch."

I patted the white one on the head and said "'bye" to the other very large ones in that pen so remote from the rest of the pig farm.

At lunch I said, "Susan, what about those really huge pigs way out on the outside of your farm. What's up with them?"

"Oh, them," Susan laughed. "I call that pen The Land of the Gentle Giants. They're such good, gentle souls. When I feed them, they're so polite with me and with each other. I never have to worry about them knocking me over in a feeding frenzy or anything."

I smiled. "And they *sure* could knock you over if they wanted to. They're not particularly fat, but they're so-o-o-o big," I said as if telling her something new. I paused. "They'll never get homes, will they?"

"Oh, no," Susan said with absolute assurance. "They're way too tall and long for most people. Folks want to adopt pot-bellies that are small, like a medium-sized poodle. They aren't really attracted to such big ones. No, I'm afraid those guys will be here until they die."

On the way home that afternoon I was silent—those gentle giants weighing heavily on my mind. Sure, they had a wooden shelter with Susan, but they didn't have pasture or heat in their house. All my pigs had heated pens, and on the coldest days I invited them into the house for snacks and naps. Our place was a haven for hogs. But, sadly, those pigs would never even have the opportunity of being adopted out to finer accommodations. Susan had relegated them to the farthest reaches of the farm. As long as they were kept there, those pigs were out of adoptees' sight and, therefore, out of mind.

The drive home was scenic, though long. At lunch I remembered Susan worrying about the huge number of pigs she had. She said she was overrun with hogs—had 142 of them. She even had some in crates in the living room. Adopting pigs out, even with the help of the Internet, wasn't easy. And it sure wasn't easy adopting out really long, tall ones like those in The Land of the Gentle Giants.

"Edgar," I said, staring straight ahead at the road before us. "Do you think we could adopt those gentle giants?" I stopped, waiting for the excruciating moan I knew would follow. "That way I could sort of do my part helping Susan adopt out pigs. She is so overrun with pigs right now, I feel I should do my part to help out."

There was silence.

There was silence for a good, long time.

"Ya know. . . . " he said, looking straight ahead.

I just knew it would be like that. He didn't want any part of having any more animals and wouldn't go for the idea.

He glanced over at me. "Ya know, you take good care of all our animals. If you want those pigs, you can have them."

"Get awt!" I shouted, craning my neck. "I can really have them?"

"Yep—providing I don't have to do any work for them."

"Oh, I can't wait to get home to call Susan and tell her. Never would she think those pigs would get as nice a home as they will have with us. Oh, you're the greatest."

He smiled. "Where are we going to put them?"

"Well, I don't want them in with Lowell, Lucille, Ivy, and Annie because I don't want fighting, which is what will happen if I introduce them to strange pigs. They'll be vying for top pig, and then there'll be bloodshed. That wouldn't be good." I thought a while. "Since they all already know each other, they shouldn't fight for dominance. That they've already worked out, I'm sure, at Susan's. How about that old three-sided shack out in the middle of the horse pastures—the one the horses never use anyway. We could just fix it up a little, and that would be as good a house as what they're used to at Susan's. But with us they'd have a huge pasture. Grass—they'd be in heaven!"

"Wonder what it'd take to fix up that old shack," Edgar thought. "We'll have to look at it tomorrow and see what to do with it."

The next morning I called Susan with the good news. She was ecstatic. "Oh, my God! You've absolutely made my day. Those pigs will just love it at your place. They'll have pasture, and you'll feed them goodies all the time. They're just such good pigs. You and they deserve each other. Oh, Gay—I'm so happy."

"I'm happy too," I said, beaming on the end of the telephone line. "This morning Edgar and I are going out to the old shack to see how we can fix it up for the pigs. We already have a hydrant out there, so water's no problem. We should just have to do a few things, and then we can pick up the gentle giants and bring them to the Balliets' Land of Oz." I laughed.

"Oh, it's terrific. Call me when you're ready. I'm going out to the gentle giants right now and tell them the great news."

"Oh," I said, "before you hang up—what are their names?"

"Miss Piggy, Grunt, Big Will, Wilber, Ashley, and Sally."

"Tell me which one is the white one."

"That's Sally. She's really old, but she is a really good pig. I've had her about nine years. She doesn't see too well. Oh, yeah—Wilber's sort of, well—he's sort of blind."

"Blind?" I said, alarmed.

"He'll be fine. He sees a little bit. You have to talk to him as you approach him so he knows you're there. Otherwise, he gets startled easily."

"And Miss Piggy? That's not the Miss Piggy I had written about in my *Lowell* book, is it?"

"That's the same Miss Piggy."

"The one whose owner died of asthma?"

"That's Miss Piggy."

"Wow," I said. "How weird is it that I'd end up adopting a pig I wrote about more than a year ago?"

"I'd say it's pretty weird," Susan admitted. "You were destined to have her."

That morning Edgar and I walked out to the horse pastures where sat the raggedy old three-sided shack meant to protect the horses in case they were ever caught in a thunderstorm. The horses never went into that shelter, and the few times they had been caught in a storm, they just put their butts to the wind and rode it out.

"Well," Edgar said, striding up to the shack. A couple of boards were missing from one side, and the corrugated roof had big chunks out of it. "Let's see what we have here." He pushed against the corner post, and the thing gave way beneath his weight. "Wow! This is no good." He pushed at the other end, and the whole building teetered as though it were about to fall over. "Posts are rotted off. I'm surprised this thing is standing at all."

"Just great," I moaned. "Now what?"

"Well," he said with minor irritation. "I suppose I'll have to build them another shack. Just like this one."

I cringed.

"I don't suppose it will be a major deal—drill into the same post-holes we had before. I have some lumber left over from other projects that we ought to be able to use. Won't take much."

"Okay," I said in a sheepish voice. I couldn't push Edgar because his being absolved of work for the pigs was one of the conditions for my adopting them in the first place. If he thought for a minute that he'd have to put a whole lot of his own time, energy, and money into it, he'd nix the whole thing.

"Let's see how this works," he said, walking over to the old hydrant. He pulled on the handle. It didn't budge. *"UH!"* he grunted, putting all his weight into it. "Rusted shut—gotta get a new hydrant. Damn—thought we could use the shack and the hydrant, but neither one of them is usable."

"Maybe we shouldn't get the pigs then. It'll cost too much," I said in a defeated voice. Reverse psychology was my only recourse.

"No—I said you could have them. I don't care so much about the cost as I do having to do the work. I don't have time to build something for them."

"How about one of those prefabricated tool sheds we always see by the side of the road? They're not real expensive, are they?"

"Don't think so. Yeah, that's a good idea. I'll check into it. We'll only have to pick one out and have it delivered, and *voila!* The pigs have their house. But we must replace the hydrant, and to do that, we have to hire someone to dig it out. I know someone who'll probably do it."

Acquiring the gentle giants was another one of our projects that was destined to snowball. But it turned into more of an avalanche. We bought the shed—easy enough—but had to make a foundation of level stone to set it on. When it was finally set in place, amid much complaining and sweating by Edgar, we decided that if we were going to put heat in it, which, of course, I insisted on, it needed to be insulated. Not wanting to irritate Edgar further, I insulated it myself.

But pigs love to chew on insulation. The inside of the house had to be lined with plywood, and I was afraid of the circular saw. "Please," I whined to Edgar. "I'd rather have you do the cutting. Just do this one other thing for me, and that'll be the end of it. I promise. Of course, I can help hammer the panels in place, but please do the cutting."

"All right!" Edgar barked.

So, while we paneled the inside, Edgar arranged for a new water hydrant to be installed. We needed electricity to the house from the barn, which was approximately 300 feet away. The costs on the Pig Palace were beginning to add up, so, instead of hiring someone to do the work, Edgar rented a ditch witch to dig the trench for the 220 line. It was one of those machines a person had to walk behind, but for a person of Edgar's rather slight stature, it was more like being "blutsed" behind, as the Dutchmen say. For 300 some feet the behemoth of a machine jerked and wrangled Edgar through the rocky underbrush of the woods and then blutsed him through some of the hardest, driest hardpan on the property. Poor Edgar wasn't the same for a week. His bones ached, and he had a headache from the rattling his brain suffered in its skull-box.

After the ditch witch fiasco, Edgar decided to hire an electrician. "I'm not getting electrocuted over a bunch of pigs," he declared one afternoon. So, an electrician hooked up the little house in the middle of the pasture for lights and a fan.

"You want a cabana fan in here, too?" the electrician said after he had hooked up the heater. "For pigs? This *is* a house for pigs, not humans?"

"That's right," I said. "They'll need heat in the winter and a fan in the summer. There're no trees way out here for any shade, so the fan is essential."

"Fine, lady. Whatever."

Another day, in preparation for my pigs' arrival, we went to the Quakertown Farm and Country Store and bought several rolls of box-wire fencing, just in case the pigs decided the Pig Palace wasn't palatial enough for them. The split-rail fencing for the horses could allow a smaller pig to scoot underneath the bottom rung, but even a bigger pig, given enough ingenuity, might wriggle itself through the space.

After Edgar and I nailed the fencing to the bottom of the split-rail, we stood looking at the accomplishment. The little cedar hut sparkled in its newness, as did the fancy water hydrant. Edgar and I both laughed at the cabana fan, and he threatened to move into the house if I got any more brainstorms. "I thought I wasn't going to have to do any work for these pigs," he scowled.

I laughed. "Well, I did as much of the work as I could. Ya know, I'm only a gi-r-r-rl."

"Yeah, right. Looks as though we're ready to go pick up the pigs. When do you want to get them?"

"Well, I would like just one more thing."

"What!" he blurted. "The place is already a friggin' castle! The pigs will live better than we do."

"That's a bit of an exaggeration," I admonished. "Just one more thing, Hon. There's no shade out here, and pigs, as you know, are very sensitive to heat. I'd like a small addition built onto the east side of the shed for a shady area."

"Now I've got to build an addition!" he roared. "Nope—won't do it. You can get Randy to do it, but I won't."

"Well, I can't see paying your sister's husband to do something if we can do it ourselves."

"There you go again with that 'we' shit. They're *your* pigs! You call Randy if you want a shady area. This is starting to get ridiculous." Edgar trudged off toward the house.

In a few days Randy was at work. In another week I had my addition, and Randy had a little extra change in his pocket.

It amazed me what a kick the workers, contractors, and interested relatives got out of my Pig Palace, which soon came to be known as the Pig Complex, because that is what the simple idea had become. Proudly Edgar and I showed off the new center for our soon-to-be adopted pig-kids. People's reactions were a mixture of awe and disbelief.

"For pigs?" they sputtered, laughed, and coughed. "This is nice enough for people to live in. Indoor-outdoor carpeting, fan, lights, heater—it's the friggin' Taj Mahal, for Christ's sake." They laughed until the tears came.

I guess it was amusing to a non-animal person. But these pigs were going to become family, and no way would I be comfortable in my own house if I knew my pigs were sweltering or freezing in theirs. My pigs would have living conditions nearly equivalent to humans'.

No one would believe that a few months after the pigs came to live with us we'd put another addition onto the west side of the cedar hut—to block the winter wind if the pigs wanted to bask in the sun. It's true.

Edgar was at his wit's end.

That July Fourth, less than two months after I had first met them, the pigs arrived.

What a celebration the six gentle giants had when they came home to live with us. We opened the gate to their pasture and drove inside carrying four of the pigs behind us in the horse trailer. Susan followed with the other two in her van. We stopped, opened the horse trailer door, and watched as the pigs came tumbling out into the pasture. Wherever they stepped out onto the grass is where each one stayed because when they saw the lush pasture at their feet, they immediately began to feast. They had no reason to move. All they wanted was right there.

"I know how they feel," I told Edgar. "It's as if I were let out into a field of French fries."

"Or potato chips," Edgar said, smiling. "Or a field of pierogies, or even steak sandwiches, or maybe even. . . ."

"Okay. Enough."

The pigs and I watched as Edgar and Susan pulled their vehicles out of the pasture. I had seldom seen such a beautiful sight: those black and white pigs standing out in bas-relief against the bright green grass. They looked lovely standing snout-deep in the field.

Susan ran toward me. "They absolutely love it here. They're not one bit afraid."

We stayed with the pigs all afternoon. I learned each one's name. Ashley I'd remember because she had white anklets above her feet,

Miss Piggy, Sally, and Grunt

looking as though she were wearing white patent leather shoes. Sally, the white one who had been so friendly the first time I saw the giants at Susan's farm, was old, and her little belly was saggy and wrinkly. Miss Piggy was the biggest of the bunch, round and fully packed, while Grunt, her bosom buddy and the handsomest of the group, resembled the typical piggy bank. Wilber, the blind one, was quite large, too, but I was able to distinguish him from Miss Piggy by the blonde highlights atop his back hairs. And Big Will was the most remarkable. He was the skinniest and, with his wrinkles, he looked more like a shar-pei than a pig.

"I love 'em already," I said later that day when Susan was almost ready to leave. "See how comfortable they look here? Like they've been here all their lives."

"They sure do," Susan agreed.

After Susan left, I called the pigs into their complex where they sniffed and prodded the blankets I had bought on special at K-mart. Four bucks each—Edgar had been thrilled. Then I fed them their evening meal—girls inside and boys outside. They were all very polite. I showed them their water dishes and then propped open the door for the night. Already Sally was prodding her blanket into sleepy submission.

I left so full of satisfaction that giving gives that I was nearly bursting.

In the next few weeks the gentle giants gradually cozied up to me. Grunt was exceptionally shy, and Wilber was a bit hard to tame because he couldn't see very well. I had to yell at him as I approached so he knew I was coming, and then he couldn't see my hand when I reached down to pet him. Perhaps he thought a bird was swooping down on him.

Right from the beginning Miss Piggy and Sally accepted me as one of their own. When I went out to the pasture and lay, legs splayed apart, in the grass, Miss Piggy grunted and slowly came toward me. On my belly in the pasture, I raised my head, and Miss Piggy sniffed my arm and face and turned so that her butt was parallel my head and her head across from my feet. Then she simply lay down next to me. It was how pigs lie against each other. To Miss Piggy I was a sister. That is the highest compliment a pig can pay another being—accepting it as one of its own kind. Thrilled, I rubbed her belly, and she lay back on her side, luxuriating in my touch.

Sally, too, jostled for position beside me.

Any time I stepped into the acre pasture, the pigs immediately came toward me, grunting a greeting. Each lay beside me, across my head, on either side of me, or at my feet. If there were already pigs on all sides of my body, the leftover pigs lay down close by, soaking up the warm summer sun and their human and pig companions.

Perhaps animals and humans would not become family in my lifetime, but I was sure it would happen sometime. As Miss Piggy grunted alongside me, her body rocking against mine, I was certain, too, that the first efforts would come from the animal world. They would be the initiators. Animals were so accepting of humans, so forgiving, so non-judgmental—many times more so than humans are with each other. If an animal had the assurance he would not be hurt, then he would make the first step toward familiarizing himself with the human species.

Left to the animals, if humans abandoned their predatory behavior, we would simply be another species on Earth, not one to fear but one to live with and beside, to live in peace with, in cooperation with, and in mutual respect with. Animals and humans could live synergistically.

Though humans are far different from animals, our needs are the same, our fears similar. Rather than setting us apart from each other, those differences only make us more similar to each other.

It may take thousands of years. Even then, depending on the human species, it may never happen at all. But seeing the cosmic family becoming reality in the hard work of our veterinary friends and clients, the caring of the circus people, zookeepers, those involved in animal exhibits worldwide, and the media promoting the naturalization of animals and people, not to mention my own close family of animals, I have every confidence that this reality can be realized on a wider scale.

The animals are receptive, so must we be.

Television Pigsonas

A FEW WEEKS AFTER THE GENTLE GIANTS CAME to live with us, Susan called asking me to take her place on two television shows featuring pot-bellied pigs. The TV stations requested Susan's appearance for Pet Week, but she was already committed with her own animals at other functions. She was as excited about my having the chance to appear on television as I was, at first, reluctant.

"Go ahead. Do it," Susan coaxed. She had appeared with several of her pigs on TV before. "You'll have a great time. Besides, pigs need the publicity, and you're a good one to do it. One show is with a small station in Lancaster, Pennsylvania, called *12:30 Live* and the other one is two days later on Fox's *Good Day, Philadelphia.*"

"I don't know," I said, gritting my teeth. I gripped the receiver with a tight fist. "I've never been on television before—a little intimidating."

"You won't have any problem. You teach, remember? That's why I'm asking you. You'll be a fine representative for all of us pig people, and so will your pigs."

"Okay," I said at last. "I'll do it."

Despite my reticence, I was thrilled to have a chance at television fame. Since I was a little girl, I had faithfully perused the fashion and TV tabloid magazines, vicariously living the glamorous life of a star. This would probably be my only chance for that one second—well, maybe two minutes—worth of fame that everyone at some point in his or her life yearns for. I yearned for fame, all right. I was as hungry for the exposure as Lowell was for a crate of watermelons.

"We're gonna be on friggin' TV!" I yelled to Edgar when he pulled into the driveway that afternoon. "Do you believe it? We're taking Susan's place for Pet Week."

"*Us?*" Edgar asked suspiciously as he stepped down from the truck.

"Yes—Lowell and me," I said.

"Good," he smiled, relieved. "I don't want any part of this TV stuff, though I think it's terrific you are able to help Susan out. Just don't drag me into it. You can soak up the limelight. I'll take you there, but I *don't* want to be on TV." He grabbed a handful of vet forms and walked into the garage. Before he went inside, he said, "Pretty neat, Hon. This could be your and Lowell's big break."

I followed Edgar into the house, still overflowing with excitement at the possible kudos I could accumulate—this country girl whose previous bid for attention amounted to winning a few blue ribbons at the local horse shows. Finally, I mused, my chance to make it big. The possibilities were endless: Would I be recognized in Northampton's finest restaurants and at local clambakes? Would anyone at our town's Food Fair be impressed as, innocent of my celebrity status, I picked through the pile of mushrooms in the produce department?

I could envision it all: "Oh, look," a young blonde woman with a perky nose would gasp enviously to her friend, "There's that Gay Balliet. I saw her on television the other day with her pot-bellied pig. Oh, look. She must like mushrooms. I think I'll get some, too, even though I hate them. Look at her sniffing each one like a real mushroom connoisseur. How heady! Do you think she would give us her autograph?"

Volcanic with pride and possibility, I followed Edgar into the den where he sat down and began sifting through the mail. He looked up at me over his reading spectacles and said with a broad smile, "So, when are you going to make your debut?"

"Next Monday and Wednesday," I blurted. "You will drive us down, won't you?"

"With bells on," he said. "Just as long as I don't have to be on TV. Which pig are you taking?"

"Lowell, of course," I responded.

"Lowell?"

"Yeah, Lowell. Why? What's the matter with taking Lowell?"

He stood up and stared solidly at me over his glasses. "Just how do you propose to get a two-hundred-pound pig to Lancaster and Philadelphia?"

I thought and thought, then stammered, "I hadn't thought about that. I'm just basking in my glory right now. You'll find a way, I'm sure."

"Don't hang that albatross around my neck. This is *your* project, and you better work out a way to get Lowell there. He won't use a ramp, like Ivy Mae used to when she was little, so how do you expect to get him into the back of the truck? At his weight, we can't very well lift him under his belly. Then, you have to think about whether he'll behave himself at the studios or not. He can be testy at times, you know. Seems to me you have an awful lot of planning to do. If I were you, I wouldn't just float around here on your TV laurels. I'd get going devising a plan of attack so that these TV stints come off smoothly, with as little hassle for us and Lowell as possible."

"Boy, nothing like raining on my parade," I said glumly. "Okay, I'll get on it right away. I'll figure out how to get Lowell to TV land."

I sat at my desk and tried imagining the scene: first, we would have to load Lowell into our SUV at home. Then, once we arrived at the TV station, we would need to extract the pig from the vehicle. We would then have to get him inside the building in such a way as to guarantee he could not run into traffic or hurt himself in any way. Once in the studio he would probably be fine on his harness and leash. Then, after the show was over, we'd have to get him back to the vehicle, lift him up and inside, drive home, and lift him down from the truck. *Voila! Fait accompli!*

The first thing was to find a crate large enough for a 200-pound pig. I called Susan back. "You'll need the Giant Vari-Kennel that you can get at any pet store. The giant size—that's the 700 series—might have to be ordered, so you better go hunting for one soon. Then once you're at the station, you'll need a cart of some kind to wheel him from the car to the building. That should do it."

I thanked Susan, and before I even hung up the phone, I looked up the number of the local pet shop. I was in luck: they had a Giant Vari-Kennel in stock. With our old black pickup I brought home the Vari-Kennel. The kennel was a beast designed to contain a beast—not even a mini-rhino could blast through its tough gray plastic walls and sturdy door. Even without a pig, it took two clerks and me to load it into the truck bed. I couldn't imagine how heavy it would be with my pig celebrity inside.

No sooner had I brought it home than I introduced it to Lowell. He sidled up to it, eyeing it suspiciously, and then gave it the sniff test. To his surprise it issued a wonderful aroma of—surprise—peanuts and grapes. Yes, there to his delight on the floor of the kennel were a slew of goodies for noshing. I stood back and waited, biting my lip. Not too many minutes passed before Lowell put one foot and then another through the door. Soon his whole body was inside.

I squealed with victory as Lowell gobbled up the last of the peanuts in the kennel. He was not upset or claustrophobic in the least, but when I asked him to back out of the crate, he hooked a foot on the doorsill and then flatly refused—his existential personality exerting itself. Beside catching his foot in the door, he didn't like backing where he couldn't see, and the floor's surface was slippery. Finally, with much coaxing, he did back out, but he didn't like it at all, whining and complaining the entire time.

We rehearsed time and again with the goodies. Inside he went, but moving in reverse thwarted his sense of style. He hated it. I had an idea, though, to eliminate the backing problem. A few more practice sessions and for sure he would march courageously inside the crate on the morning of the TV shows.

That afternoon when Edgar pulled into the driveway, he saw the huge four-foot-long by three-foot-wide and high kennel sitting in the grass. I was anxious to discuss my plan with him.

"A couple of necessary adjustments to the kennel?" Edgar said with a doubtful eye. "Like what? You're never happy with the way things are. I can see it already—just like with the Giants—the snowball's starting to form. What's wrong with it the way it is?"

I stood, hands on hips, "You said I was to handle this, and I am. The only thing I'm asking you to do is make a few repairs to it, so that it's more comfortable for Lowell. The side windows at the top of the kennel are in the wrong place for a pig. They should be placed lower so that Lowell can see out and look at the scenery as we travel. So I've turned it upside down—better for a pig's-eye view. The kennel was made for a large dog, like a Saint Bernard, that can see out the top window. But Lowell wouldn't have been able to see anything. Now he can. And I've taken old carpet and glue-gunned it to the floor for better footing. Now all I need is for you to put a door on the other end. He doesn't like backing out of the crate."

"Well, rooty-toot," Edgar said in a haughty voice. "Who does he think he is? I'm not putting another door in it. That's silly. It's fine the way it is."

"Please," I begged. "Lowell would feel much better about the whole thing if he could just walk right out through a front door."

"Have him turn around inside the crate. Then he doesn't have to back out."

I frowned. "He can't turn around inside it. He's too fat. I've tried to get him around inside, and there's just not enough room. His nose gets caught on the side walls."

Edgar looked very annoyed. He hadn't wanted to get involved in this project from the start. All he had bargained for was driving us to the TV stations. The rest was my ball of wax. "No, I don't want to. I won't."

By the end of the next day, Lowell had his newly renovated transportation crate—with doors at both ends. My father and Edgar both went to work on the kennel, installing an old metal door from a dog cage. That afternoon we showed the newly renovated cage to Lowell, His Royal Highness, to see if it met with his approval. Lowell stepped inside the back door and into the kennel, scarfed up all the grapes and peanuts, and when we opened the door at his head, he stepped outside as if he had done it a hundred times before. Despite Edgar's initial stubbornness, he was happy to see Lowell comfortably moving in and out the crate.

"Okay," I said, as we watched Lowell exit through the homemade door for the eleventh time, "there's only one more thing to do."

"What!" Edgar wailed.

"Well, we'll need to get Lowell from the vehicle to the building. We can't carry him all the way in because he's too heavy. So, we need a dollie or handcart or something."

Edgar rolled his eyes. "Oh, come on," he moaned. "You're gettin' ridiculous."

"Well, how else do you think we can get him from the SUV into the station? He can't walk because we don't know how he'll react to traffic, strange people, and surroundings. Sure, he'll be wearing his harness. But what if he should panic and take off at a run? Neither you nor I could stop a barrel-assing two-hundred-pound animal. No way—I'm not taking any chances. I don't want anything to happen to Lowell just because I'm making him be on TV."

"All right, all right. I know what'll work."

By the next afternoon we were equipped with the hot setup: one inverted, carpeted Giant Vari-Kennel with an extra, removable front door and one large wagon, its sides removed and the bottom enlarged to fit the kennel. Edgar demonstrated the efficiency of the arrangement; he plopped the kennel atop the wagon and wheeled it around the driveway. I smiled. It was perfect.

In a few minutes and with much grunting (from us, not the pig) we managed to hoist Lowell inside his crate and onto the wagon. We pulled him around the yard to see how he would react. He wasn't crazy about it, especially the way the cats stared and made funny faces at him as he rolled cumbersomely by. And who knows what the other pigs thought when they saw their 200-pound brother doing wheelies in the driveway.

"The only other problem is how we're going to lift him into and out of the SUV," Edgar said. "I suppose I could call my brother to help us here at home. But when we get to the stations, who will help us there?"

"I'm sure once we're there we can muster up a couple of brutes to help us unload him and then load him again. All they have to do is lift him off the back of the SUV. Then we wheel him into the station. It's a piece of cake," I said.

The logistics of transporting a 200-pound pig were well conceptualized. All I needed to do before the big days was to bone up on pig facts and think briefly about an outfit for myself, one that would magically subtract the ten pounds the TV was said to pack onto a person. And I asked my good friend, Karen Schell, if she wouldn't mind helping us and taking a few pictures and maybe a video.

"Absolutely!" she said with as much enthusiasm as I felt. "I wouldn't miss it! You'll need all the hands you can get, what with brushing Lowell off before his big moment and fixing yourself up a little. I can help carry things, and I'll definitely capture all the action on film. I can't wait."

The morning of the Lancaster show, Karen raced into the driveway around nine o'clock. The customized Vari-Kennel awaited in the back yard.

"Okay," she called. "Let's get this show on the road. We're gonna be famous today."

I had put on a pair of black pants and a plain hot-pink top—my TV outfit, as I called it. But I was not nearly so concerned with myself as I was for Lowell's comfort and safety. Though ordinarily I would have agonized over what to wear and how to style my hair, this time I gave them only mild consideration. I just wanted a smooth "go."

The wagon was waiting alongside the kennel, as was an egg crate filled with necessaries: paper towels, peanuts, grapes, tissues, a baggy with Gatorade powder to quench Lowell's thirst later, a bowl for him to drink from, pig facts I needed to refamiliarize myself with on the way down, directions, still camera, and video camera—oh, and a rectal sleeve for cleaning up any Lowell turds. All I'd need to do if Lowell made a mess in his kennel was to don the sleeve, grab the manure, turn the sleeve inside out over my hand, and chuck it into the nearest garbage can.

Edgar came out of the house. "Ready? Let's get going. We've got a two-hour ride ahead of us. I'll call Bruce to come down and help load the crate."

With that I coaxed Lowell from his cozy pen and opened the door to the kennel. I shook in a half cup of peanuts. Within minutes Lowell walked inside. We backed the Rover around toward the crate, both doors of which were locked, with Lowell inside. We opened the back door, and Bruce, Edgar, Karen, and I hoisted Lowell's crate into the air. A grunt sounded from the kennel. We pushed its bottom edge onto the floor of the SUV. Then we tipped the front edge forward, but it lodged in the opening.

"It's too damn big!" Edgar yelled, his face a blistery red. "Everybody push!"

We pushed.

"Won't fit," Bruce said. "Let's try it again. Wiggle it a little."

We did, but it was no use. The kennel was too big for the back of the SUV. It was the one thing I hadn't thought of—that the kennel might not fit inside the SUV.

"Gay, didn't you measure this thing to see that it would fit?" Edgar grunted. "Okay, everybody, let's put it back down on the ground."

We slowly set Lowell back on the grass. I felt defeated. After days of planning, here we were, grounded because I didn't think to measure the crate. What would we do now?

"Daddy's Tahoe!" I exclaimed. I ran for the phone and dialed my parents' number. "Oh, can we? That would be great. Do you think it'll fit? Okay, we'll come get it right away."

Within fifteen minutes we had crammed Lowell in his giant kennel, the folded wagon, and the egg crate into my father's Tahoe. There was barely enough room for us three passengers, but that was all right. My dream of being on TV was materializing at last. What a snug crew we were—as bugs, and with no room to spare.

Throughout the ride to Lancaster I pleaded with Lowell to lie down and enjoy the scenery, but he refused. He obviously didn't like the motion of the truck and felt more stable on his own four feet. I tried to calm him, pointing out the cows, talking gently to him when the tractor trailers passed on the left. I poked a few grapes inside the grating for him to snack on.

My attempts were futile. He just didn't enjoy riding in the car. The trip seemed endless to me and, no doubt, to Lowell, who never took his weight off his hind legs for the entire two hours. Such torture he never endured at home where the most he hiked in a day was to the house and back out to the barn again. He wasn't used to exercise or staying on his feet for a long time.

The ride was uneventful, except that Lowell was uptight the whole time—so nervous that we had to stop and use the rectal sleeve. Finally we arrived at the station. We were in plenty of time, and a slew of big guys volunteered to help lift Lowell from the back of the Tahoe. In minutes he was on the ground. Then we took out the wagon, unfolded it, and put Lowell on top. Karen grabbed the egg crate, and I began to wheel the Lowell mobile into the station through the service entrance.

Once inside the studio area amongst the cameras, lights, and other equipment, the men lowered Lowell's cage to the floor. I opened the jury-rigged door. Very calmly Lowell marched out while I slipped his harness over his head and shoulders and buckled it. Then I attached a horse lead rope.

We were ready.

I walked Lowell up the handicapped ramp to the stage dressed up with a fake fireplace and two overstuffed chairs. Already a blanket awaited Lowell near my chair. Lowell, who was very tired from his long ride, was happy to rest on it. His feet were probably killing him.

The set next to ours was prepared for a cooking show. I could smell some delicious aromas coming from the little kitchen, and I'm sure Lowell noticed them, too.

Once I had Lowell settled on his blanket, the show producer introduced himself and the interviewer to me. Steve, the producer, instructed me as to the format of the show and how everything would be happening. He asked me to fill out a form, just standard procedure, and everybody took their places. We had five minutes until showtime.

I took my place in the stuffed chair on the set and reviewed my pig facts one last time. I wiped my brow and looked out at the cameras. The lights were intensely bright and hot. In a minute I would have big perspiration rings under my armpits. I squinted against them, and Steve sauntered over to me. "Do you think you could get Lowell to face the cameras?" he said.

I looked down.

There beside me on his blanket was Lowell with his big round butt facing the cameras. "Get up, Lowell," I urged, pulling on his harness. "Hurry up. You've got to face the cameras. Come on; get up now." I stood up, rearranged the microphone that had been attached to my blouse, and tried to steer Lowell in the opposite direction.

"Whree—whree—whree!" Lowell complained. He stood up.

I managed to move him 180 degrees, but when the harsh light struck his eyes, he turned around, his backside to the cameras.

"Four minutes!" I heard someone yell. Karen rushed up to me, a comb in hand. She raked my hair off my shoulders. The interviewer sat down beside me

I tugged on Lowell's leash, "Please face the cameras, Lowell."

Lowell whined, pulling away from me, wanting to spin away. I was starting to feel flustered with only three minutes until the show aired live. I pulled Lowell toward me. "Come on, big guy—do Mommy a favor and face the cameras."

But it was no use. The existentialist in him rebelled. Just as I managed to turn him toward the cameras, he balked at the hot, glaring lights and turned right around again. The lights hurt his eyes, and he would not face them—not for me or my need for fame.

"Ten seconds," someone called. "Ten, nine, eight. . . . "

The interviewer began, "Welcome to *12:30 Live*. Today we have a very special guest with us . . . ."

It was happening. I smiled gratefully, answered the interviewer's questions as entertainingly and informatively as possible. I was a natural, it seemed to me—the biggest "ham" on stage, to be sure. I had no sense of being nervous or shy. Instead of withdrawing into a shell, I blossomed, my pig by my side. I was on a mission to benefit the future of pigs, and I was loving it.

Lowell, on the other hand, defied the cameras and stardom. From time to time a grunt erupted from him, but aside from that little bit of conversation, Lowell refused to cooperate. He was by no means a behavior problem, neither leaping off the stage nor farting defiantly at the cameras, but he did little more than tolerate the entire expedition. He simply pointed his behind at the audience as if to say, like Alex in *A Clockwork Orange*, "Kiss my sharries."

The interview over, we had two minutes while they played commercials to usher Lowell from the studio. It was a team effort with Edgar, Karen, and I hurrying my disgruntled (no pun intended) pig

Gay, Lowell, and Edgar on the set of WGAL, Lancaster, Pennsylvania

out the doors. We escorted him outside where several curious people from the station came to pet him and ask questions about pot-bellies in general. Then we lured him back into his kennel, lifted him into the Tahoe with the assist of the six big guys, and headed for home

"It was super!" Karen said, turning around in her seat. "You guys were great! I'm amazed that you weren't scared to death."

I poked a grape through the grating of Lowell's window. "Geez, I really didn't have time to think about being nervous. I guess I was so preoccupied with Lowell and his sticking his butt to the audience that I forgot all about myself. Huh, it never occurred to me to be nervous. All my energy was focused on PR for pigs, I guess."

"Lowell looked pretty good, anyway," Edgar said, turning the SUV onto the main highway home. "Too bad about his butt, but he was well-behaved, seemed to like meeting all the people, and he was quiet. He didn't have a hissy fit or anything. I thought it went rather well. I'm a proud TV dad. Yes, I am."

We drove for about an hour, Lowell standing the entire time, and then stopped at a Kentucky Fried Chicken for some chicken strips, of which Lowell heartedly approved. He, Karen, Edgar, and I dined on tasty chicken strips before hitting the road for the second hour. Still Lowell refused to sit down.

The first television show was deemed a success, though Lowell exerted all his existential rights not to "ham it up" for the audience's sake. If he had to be on TV at all, he probably thought, he would do it in his style and no one else's.

I wonder what the viewers at home thought about Lowell's butt crack staring at them. If they were at all like me, they probably got a real hoot out of it. It would have been nice for Lowell to project his face toward the cameras, but what was my existential pig if he could not make his own personal refusal? What a perfect way for him to demonstrate that a pig acts according to the imperatives of the self than by humans' needs. Television wasn't special to Lowell, just because it was special to us. No, siree—TV didn't impress him at all.

"I am a pig; therefore, I rebel," is Lowell's maxim. The day after the Lancaster show Lowell flatly refused to walk into his giant kennel. I had wanted to practice loading and unloading him, but he refused to budge.

"Lowell, I'm begging you. All we have to do is get through one more TV show, and then you can sit out by the pool every day and lounge until you're blue in the face. Just get into the damn kennel, please."

Nope. He wasn't going to do it.

I tried everything I knew of in my "conditioning bible" to get Lowell into the crate. I even tried luring him inside with strawberries. Nothing worked. Lowell was in revolutionary mode. He had evidently hated standing during the ride down and back from Lancaster so much that he was not going to do anything to encourage it to happen again. He was no dummy; that I already knew. He was not going to be on TV again—not if he didn't want to.

I tried conditioning for two hours. By the end of that time, Lowell's belly was near to bursting with strawberries, peanuts, and grapes, but he was no closer to getting into the crate. I had to think quickly. What was I going to do? The star refused to appear. What would the nice folks at *Good Day, Philadelphia* think? What would Susan think if I bungled this publicity opportunity for pigs?

Luckily I had the phone number for the scheduling manager of the Fox station. I called him and explained the situation from my existential pig's point of view. I said, "Would you mind if I brought another of my pigs instead?" To be sure, it was no problem, he said.

I hung up the phone and went to work. I only had half an afternoon to train Lucille to board the animal taxi. Within minutes I was at work with her. I was amazed. She was an even quicker learner than Lowell. In a matter of only seven minutes, I had her hopping into and out of the kennel like Br'er Rabbit out of the tar pit. She loved the kennel and all the goodies it offered. The rest of the afternoon, I brushed and slicked Lucille to a shine. I knew she would be well-behaved at the Philly studio because her former owner had taken her on numerous excursions to Gracedale, the local nursing home. There she visited with the old folks, poking her muzzle into their hands and accepting treats from them. She would be fine for TV.

By a quarter to six in the morning, Karen was flying into the driveway. We had to be in Philly by 8 AM, and it would take a good hour and a half. This time Edgar, Karen, and I lifted the pig crate into the Tahoe by ourselves. Lucille was a good deal lighter than Lowell—probably maxing out at 150 pounds. We slid the wagon in beside her, along with the egg crates and blankets. Then we took off.

It wasn't ten minutes into the ride before Lucille lay down in the kennel. "That's great, Lucille. You just relax and enjoy the view. I'll give you a grape every once in a while, and before you know it, we'll be in Philadelphia," I promised.

She grunted contentedly.

"You're gonna be a star, Lucille," Karen said. Edgar smiled, and Karen snapped off a couple of pictures for my scrapbook.

An hour and a half later we pulled up in front of the Fox Network building on Market Street. We surveyed the area—center city—we three and a large pig. Okay, where do we go from here?

"I'll go inside and ask where we should bring her in," Karen volunteered. We waited in the Tahoe until, moments later, Karen appeared at my SUV window. "We have to take her up these five stairs," she said, pointing to the concrete steps leading to the building. "Someone inside will direct us from there."

So the three of us, with some difficulty and much grunting and moaning, hoisted Lucille and her kennel from the back of the Tahoe. We slid the wagon out onto the pavement and lifted her onto it, then wheeled her about fifty feet to the steps, and we lifted her over them. At the top her wagon awaited.

Lucille was such a tractable animal. Lowell had been agreeable, too, considering all the fuss, but Lucille put her full trust in us. She knew we would take care of her.

At the top of the stairs we situated Lucille on the wagon again and pulled her through the glass doors where a hostess ushered us into an elevator and downstairs to the studio. The basement certainly wasn't the glamorous setting I had expected. It was like any high school or college basement—concrete block walls, linoleum floors, piping in the ceiling—nothing special.

In the dungeon we lifted Lucille from the wagon and onto the linoleum floor where we opened the kennel door. She stepped out, and we were informed that we would not be allowed into the studio until the station break. We could make ourselves at home in the hallway. The producer wanted to know if Lucille would be quiet when they took us inside, and I assured them she would be quite the young lady.

A few important-looking people passed by as we three and Lucille sat in the bare hall atop a pile of pig blankets. Then the lit sign, ON THE

AIR, went dark, and a studio attendant came through the swinging doors. "All right. Are you folks ready?" he asked. "We'll get you and the pig all set up in there, and then," he looked at his watch, "we'll be ready to roll in about three minutes."

I was excited, not nervous, just revved up like a gyroscope. We stood up, scooped up the blankets, and ushered Lucille through the door to the studio. We stepped carefully over the camera wires, and the producer pointed to a large empty area beneath the GOOD DAY, PHILADELPHIA sign. "Would you like to make yourself comfortable underneath the billboard?" he said in a low voice.

"Will do," I whispered and led Lucille to the spot. Karen and Edgar dropped the blankets on the floor and spread them out. I sat down, my legs tucked underneath, and with a contented groan Lucille lay down beside me. Then Karen and Edgar retreated behind the cameras to watch the action—the guy in the audio room who was monitoring computers behind large window panes, the camera technicians, the expeditors organizing the morning's schedule. Behind their desk the two news commentators bantered while the camera crew showed a film clip for the traffic report. Then the producer silenced them with an authoritative finger, and Dana, the co-anchor, prepared the audience for our segment.

Lucille was perfect, facing into the camera instead of away from it. But she had an advantage that Lowell hadn't. The *Good Day, Philadelphia* lights were more ambient, not the harsh, torturous things that had bitten into Lowell's eyes. I stroked her back as she stretched out beside me just as she does at home. "Great," I thought, "This is terrific! She's going to put on her sun-bathing routine, spreading out as if luxuriating on a tropical beach." It was a very appealing look for a pig woman such as herself. I sighed with relief. This was going to be fun.

The producer counted down the seconds until our segment; finally he pointed his finger toward us. We were on the air. The two anchors, Mike and Dana, introduced us, and I listened as they read information about Lucille from the teleprompter.

The cameras turned toward Lucille and me sitting on the blankets. I smiled, looking fondly at my blanket-side partner, who was behaving herself in such a regal manner. "Hi, Mike. Hi, Dana," I said as though they were old alumni friends. "Thanks for having me here today."

I felt disembodied. My voice did not sound as if it belonged to me.

Don't say anything stupid, for heaven's sake, I told myself as I grinned appreciatively into the cameras. Don't move, or Lucille might get up out of her couch-potato position and ruin everything. Straighten your shoulders. Where's that bra strap that was hanging out of your sleeve earlier? Does Lucille look all right? And so the worries flooded my mind.

Dana couldn't have been more flattering of Lucille. She bent down, straightened her skirt around her knees and patted Lucille on her flank. Lucille grunted proudly. Dana called Mike over to join her.

"So Lucille is Lowell's sister. Why didn't Lowell come here today?" Mike said in his best TV voice.

Grinning and stroking Lucille, I said, "He flatly refused—always the true existentialist. He simply refused to get into the crate. But Lucille said she would gladly take his place, so here she is."

Dana chimed in, "Gay, you told me during the station break that Lucille was evicted from her home in Allentown, right?"

"Yes," I said. "Unfortunately for Lucille and her former owner, Lucille was considered livestock and was unwelcome within the city limits."

"That's something that people need to be aware of when they're thinking of adopting a pot-belly pig, correct?" Dana said.

I smiled into the camera. "Definitely. People should always check their zoning laws, or they could suffer a very big disappointment later."

As Dana and I were discussing pigs and pig behavior, Mike crouched low to the ground toward Lucille. He wasn't quite sure what to expect from a pig. Was she friendly? Would she bite? Would she leap to her feet and pin him helplessly to the floor? He was clearly hesitant to touch her.

But as part of his job, he had to survive a two-minute pig segment. I watched Mike squatting next to Lucille; he reached toward her, but snatched his hand away whenever she moved her head or grunted. The cameras were right on top of him. I'm sure the audience was enjoying his squeamishness. Meanwhile as Dana questioned me on the special nature of pot-bellies, I noticed some small thing sail through the air and land in front of Lucille.

Lucille whined.

I rubbed her back. Don't get up now, Lucille, I thought. Not yet. We only have another minute and a half to go.

Another morsel flew past. What *was* that?

"Pigs, many people don't realize, are natured very much like humans," I heard myself say. I saw another object hit the ground in front of Lucille.

She grunted. Then she stood up.

I tried to keep my attention focused on Dana's question. "They can be eccentric, moody, and defiant. Likewise, they are very affectionate animals; they're good-hearted and mix well at human parties. Most of all, they are existential beings who . . ."

I was interrupted by another flying object passing through my side-view vision. I needed to look, but I finished my sentence first. ". . . follow their own needs, not necessarily the needs of their owners."

It was an M&M.

From several feet away Mike was bribing Lucille with M&Ms. Because he was a little wary of her, instead of handing them nicely to her, he was throwing them at her. Lucille didn't care one iota about how she was getting them, just as long as she was getting them. With

Gay, Lucille, and the hosts of Good Day Philadelphia

each toss, she reached with her nose and lapped the treat into her mouth.

Another round yellow candy flew past. Mike saw me look and said, "I hope it's all right to be feeding her these. What would your vet husband say about that?"

"Well, pigs really shouldn't have a whole lot of chocolate, but . . . "

"Oh," he blurted like a naughty child, "I'll stop then. I'll stop." He put the rest of the bag in his jacket pocket.

Patting Lucille on the head, Dana said, "Gay, you have another pig named Lowell. Do he and Lucille get along, or is there sibling rivalry and all that?"

"Lowell and Lucille get along just. . . ."

"Little do you know," Mike said in a sing-song voice, "that Lowell and Lucille get along famously—you know, a little hanky panky in the barn."

"Oh, no," I assured the audience. "They're both 'fixed.'"

Ignoring my remark, Mike quipped, smiling into the camera, "Really making that barn rock and roll, I'll bet. Hey, hey! They're probably out there makin' bacon."

I put my hands on my hips and, feigning indignation, said, "No bacon jokes!"

Mike looked contrite. "Sorry about that, Lucille." She was standing up, sniffing his pockets for more M&Ms. She was kind enough to keep her distance from Mike, and I'm glad she did because he was still not too sure of her.

"Nice piggy," he said, reaching out to touch her head. "nice piggy."

Suddenly Lucille let out a sharp bark.

"WHOA!" Mike yelled, jumping back. He clasped his hand protectively to his chest. The sudden movement startled Lucille who turned to me for comfort and buried her head in my arms.

"Don't be afraid of Lucille, Mike," Dana giggled, demonstrating how gentle she knew Lucille to be. She stroked her back, using a touch that was not tentative like Mike's. "She won't hurt you, Mike."

He said with some degree of exasperation, "Oh, I'm not afraid. I don't *know* pigs, is all." To prove to his audience that he was as brave as Dana, he got on his knees, bent his head down, and looked Lucille right in the eye.

She looked back.

"Wow," he said in a low voice, "She has such neat eyes. She's looking at me."

"Of course she's looking at you," Dana laughed. "You're in her face!"

"It's really neat down here on her level," he said, not two feet from her. I had a good hard grip on Lucille's lead rope just in case she should decide to taste his nose. "Hey," he said inching closer, braver with every second, "you ought to come over to where I am, Dana. She's really neat from a basement point of view."

"Jeez, Mike, you look as if you want to kiss the pig."

He was embarrassed. "No, by God, I don't want to kiss the pig."

Then the fun started, with Mike the butt of the joke. The entire camera crew and whoever else was in the background began to chant, "Kiss . . . kiss. . . kiss . . . kiss . . . kiss. . . ."

"No, no, no, no," Mike sang back, playing the good sport.

"Come on," I chimed in. I bent over and gave Lucille a peck on the cheek. She grunted affectionately. Lucille loves kisses. "See—nothing to it. And she seems to like you. Pigs love people. They consider us one of them."

This, I thought, was a really important moment to let thousands of people see how people and animals can not only co-exist but thrive in each other's company.

It was some kid's dare-me game. Everyone in the studio had picked up on Mike's tentativeness with Lucille, and they were badgering him into a display of bravery before the entire Philadelphia viewing audience. Finally, he caved in.

"All right. I'll kiss the pig." And with the announcement came the deed. Indeed, the once skittish Mike leaned over and air-kissed Lucille's nose.

Everyone exploded with hoots and applause for a job bravely done.

"Yech!" he screeched, jumping to his feet. "Bad breath!" He fanned the air before him, putting on a real act, as though the sewage of Hades surrounded him.

I laughed, and again Lucille put her nose lovingly in my armpit.

With that dramatic finale, Dana reminded the audience that it was Pet Week and to be especially kind to animals, then thanked Lucille and me for visiting.

I thanked them both for having us on their show, and then the cameras switched to a live weather report from the Philly Skycam.

Quickly Lucille and I walked from the studio. Karen and Edgar gathered up the blankets, thanked the crew, and sped out behind us. We loaded Lucille into her crate, lifted her onto her wagon, pulled her into the elevator, and rode to the first floor. When the elevator doors opened, we rolled her out, lifted her down the five outside steps, and rolled her to the back of the Tahoe.

A passerby with a knapsack was kind enough to help hoist Lucille into the Tahoe. In minutes we were on the road and making our way back home. We had done it and done it well. The event would be earmarked in our history book, my scrapbook. And perhaps, just perhaps, a few people's perspectives on animals had been changed for the better.

"It was awesome," Karen said as Edgar pulled away from the parking space. "Really cool."

"Yeah," Edgar added. "Mike was really afraid of Lucille at first. He didn't want to touch her. Instead of petting her, he threw her a couple of M&Ms. Too much."

"Lucille didn't seem to mind him at all. And she just loved his candy," Karen added.

"Yeah," Edgar said, pulling onto the turnpike. "She was a real ham!"

With a groan, Lucille settled back into her carrier for a nice nap.

The television exposure had been good for both my pigs and me. Of course, I never received an Emmy for my performance, but I was able to pass on valuable information to the public about pot-bellied pigs and pigs in general. My pigs had behaved themselves admirably; they had become more sophisticated, more social through the exposure, too. And I discovered an untapped dimension in myself. I found I had a talent for entertaining before a camera. When it came to explaining the phenomena of pigs and their relationship to the human species, I could root out a story with the best of them.

Lovey

ONE UNSEASONABLY CHILLY SPRING DAY as we were anxiously driving to Assante's for lunch, the car phone blasted its insistent horn. Edgar pushed the speaker phone, and Lori's voice explained about an emergency that had just occurred over in New Tripoli. "One of Silas Warner's mares just ran into a door head-on, and she's bleeding badly from the nose. Silas is pretty upset about her and would like you to have a look."

"Tell him I'll be right there," Edgar said, and he snapped the phone button off. He turned right at the next intersection, and we headed back in the direction we had come.

"So long, spinach sauté and chicken fingers," I said regretfully.

"Yeah, well, par for the course," he said.

"So, what are the Warner's like?" I asked as, heading toward Slatington, we sped through Cementon. From Slatington the northern route would be mostly back roads. "Do you think it's likely to be a real emergency, or are the people just super careful—you know, the type to call at the drop of a hat."

"Definitely a 'drop'," he said. "They're kind of nerdy when it comes to their animals—if their horses even look cross-eyed, they call us. It's

understandable, though. Sue and Silas have had a disaster or two in the
past, so I'm sure they're gun-shy. They're very particular about their
horses' care. They do everything just so, fussing, and doting on them.
The animals are their kids, kind of—like ours are."

"Nothing wrong with that." I thought about my theory of animals
and family. Definitely nothing was wrong with that.

"No doubt the horse's nose is bleeding, but knowing them and how
overly concerned they've been in the past, it's probably just a little drip,
not anything like a faucet running full out."

"Yeah, but we really don't know for sure, do we. It just may be
something serious," I said.

"Yep," he nodded. "Got to check it out."

While we raced along the country roads toward New Tripoli, I
thought about the different-natured clients whose animals we tended.
Some like Mrs. Dreck, with her newborn foal that hadn't nursed and
had trouble standing on buckled legs, were ignorant of and indifferent
to their horses' comfort and health. Her animals had already passed
their survival test, just living with her lackadaisical attitude, her dangerous fencing, and the absence of veterinary care. Thanks to the concern of Edgar and Sally—and a little luck—her foal had somehow
managed to live. We believed Mrs. Dreck probably hadn't learned her
lesson. Sometimes people just don't get it the first time around.
Sometimes they actually have to neglect and destroy a number of lives
in order to reap any spiritual benefit. I hoped that Mrs. Dreck's lesson
would be one of her last and that she wouldn't wreak any more damage on her animals. I still had a burning desire to anonymously mail
her a copy of *The Complete Guide to Practical Horse Care*.

"Speaking of over-protective horse owners. . . ." I mused.

"Were we?"

"No, actually, we weren't. I was just thinking about something related. I was thinking about how some people seem to dote on their horses
while others, like Mrs. Dreck, are negligent. Remember her two other
mares that were in foal. How did those foals make out? Are they okay?"

"One died. The other lived," he said, swinging the steering wheel
hard to the right up a gravel road.

"One died!" I said. "How?"

"Again, the woman thought it was nursing, and it hadn't been.

Then the foal developed diarrhea, but by the time Mrs. Dreck noticed it had the runs and called us, the foal was very dehydrated. When I got there, I started giving it fluids right away, but it was too far gone. It died right there as I was administering the solution." He shook his head, sick at the remembrance.

"Some people have to destroy a bunch of lives before they are enlightened, huh?" I said. "I wonder how many more foals she's going to have to kill before she either gives up horse breeding or educates herself about their care?"

"Yeah, I wonder, too" Edgar said, his teeth set. "And guess what? I heard she bred all her mares back again this year."

Goosebumps broke out on the back of my neck. "No way!" I snorted. "She's breeding them again—the woman who is afraid of horses and doesn't know a thing about breeding them? She almost killed one with neglect, and she did manage to kill another. The whole thing is nothing short of abuse. How can you stop someone like that?"

He shrugged his shoulders, "You can't. There's nothing anyone can do. All I hope is that she calls a vet for vaccinations. If she calls our office, at least we can make sure the mares get all their injections. We can keep an eye on the horses and advise her about what she needs to do as their pregnancies progress. But that's about all we can do. One doesn't need a license to breed animals recklessly."

"Those poor things," I said, grabbing the door handle as we plummeted up the next road.

How did the Fates decide which animals procured an abundant, loving home and which endured misery from the first moments of birth? I was kidding myself, I knew, if I expected any answer to fall magically out of the sky. I guess it was just luck, the same luck that visited humans. Some of us have it good; some of us don't. But people have so many more advantages than animals do in finding aid. For instance, myriad agencies assist children in need, but for animals, there are only a few shelters where people are concerned. The final solution for overpopulation, neglect, and abuse in those places is the euthanasia needle, and that does no animal any good.

Unlike abandoned or abused animals, we humans can pretty much fend for ourselves once we are adults. We are able to make choices, good or bad; we choose spouses, careers, the places we live. We are fairly self-determined, barring a natural disaster or some such unlucky thing. But animals aren't that lucky. Many depend on humans for survival.

How did Mrs. Dreck's foals come to be stuck with her? An animal, a pet, can hardly choose its owner. Our pigs were lucky enough to have stepped into our path littered with pig treats, comfortable beds, heated stalls, and offers to visit with us inside our house, but many animals are not that fortunate. For all those who have wonderful, coddled lives, there are as many others that live out their lives in misery or mediocrity. Some walk away from their food dishes with as nearly empty bellies as when they approached. Some endure the winter's hoar and frost with inadequate shelters. Others do not see a veterinarian their entire lives.

I can think of several instances of neglect that were not even perceived as neglect by the human perpetrators, such as the many barn cats whose owners don't feed them, asserting that the animals get by on mice they catch. Then there're the horse owners who provide no shelters, not even three-sided shacks, for their animals to get out of the winter's wind. And there are other people who have collected so many animals that they can't afford to give each one a decent life with adequate veterinary care.

Edgar swung the wheel, and we headed up the steep gravelly incline that was the Warners' driveway. A sign that read LOVEY'S LANE greeted us as we wound our way toward the small barn perched on the hilltop.

We finally made it onto the top of the mountain where a slim, middle-aged man in a light jacket, jeans, and mucker boots raised a hand. Edgar shut off the engine, and we both headed toward the barn, shielding our faces against the wind with our jacket collars. I wondered how in the world the guy stayed warm in such a skimpy coat. The wind atop his hill was blowing furiously—hard enough to penetrate the threads of any coat.

Silas directed us to the first stall, in which his wife stood holding their bay mare's head. The animal had already smelled the veterinarian's approach and was breathing nervously. At first glance she seemed fine to me—not much out of the ordinary, except for a little swelling just above the nostrils and a small blood clot hanging from her left nostril. The mare was standing; her eyes looked steady and clear. And she was visibly concerned that Edgar the veterinarian had come to see her. She was entirely coherent and aware. In fact, in order to avoid him, she bolted backward into the corner of the stall.

"Now, now, Lovey. Settle down," Sue whispered. The horse cowered in the corner, and Sue gently urged her back to the stall door opening. Mrs. Warner held a blood-splattered rag against the mare's nose, and underneath it she held one of those ice packs companies use to keep products cold during shipment.

"We're real worried, here, Doc," Silas said, nervously rubbing his ice-blue hands. Sue's expression reflected Silas's. This was one unhappy couple. They looked worse than the horse did.

"Tell Doc what happened, Silas," Sue said, rearranging the blood-besotted rag and ice pack on Lovey's nose.

Edgar checked beneath the left nostril from which the clot hung. He looked for lacerations around the nose and switched on a mini-flashlight to peer into the nose, stretching the nostril skin wide so that he could see up and into the long cave. Lovey's eyes grew wide as Edgar peered up her nozzle.

"Seems to have stopped bleeding now," Edgar muttered with satisfaction.

Sue eyebrows were knitted, and Silas continued to wring his hands.

"What happened?" Edgar asked Silas. Edgar continued his head trauma exam as Silas explained the accident in detail.

"I witnessed it, I sure did, Doc. You see, Lovey doesn't get along well with this new horse we just brought into the barn. She's been real skittish lately because of the newcomer. She's a real nervous Nelly. Anyway, I was going through my normal routine, bringing the horses in from the pasture so that they could have their afternoon snack. Lovey, though, was still upset because of this new horse, and somehow she got away from me and ran into the same stall with Cupid here." He pointed to a white Arab in the box stall across from Lovey.

"Well, Lovey got Cupid upset, so Cupid ran back out of the stall and down the aisle heading straight for that people door," he said, pointing. "I had left it open by mistake. But that door, as you can see, is not nearly tall enough to allow a horse through. Cupid saw the opening, ducked, and ran through, and Lovey was right behind. The only problem was that Lovey was following Cupid so close behind that she didn't see the dropped header."

Silas winced, and so did Sue at his telling of the accident, "It was just awful. I can still see how it happened; I'll probably have nightmares about it. Cupid ran out, and Lovey followed close on her heels, her head up, her neck stretched the way horses do when they get full of themselves. I could see it coming, but there was nothing I could do. Then I heard the *CRACK!*

"Lovey had forgotten to duck. Anyway, after Cupid ran through, Lovey ran right into the header with the front of her face. But even that didn't stop her. She just blasted right through that tiny opening. But I sure heard her head hit. It sounded just like a branch breaking off a tree. I thought for sure she'd broken her neck or punched her skull right down into her brain. I expected that she would drop over dead right in front of me. All I could do was pray she wouldn't. Amazingly enough, she didn't. I quick got her back into the barn, and that's when I noticed all the blood."

Sue interrupted, "Yes, Silas came running into the house yelling for me. When I saw Lovey's bloody nose, all I could think about was our other horse, the one we'd treated so long for that nasal tumor. I was so worried she wouldn't be able to breathe, just like that mare had trouble breathing."

"Yeah, that was a real sad case," Edgar said, thinking back to the mare that he'd eventually had to euthanize because of a nose tumor blocking the air flow. We did everything we knew to do with that thing, and it just kept growing and growing. Not fun."

Edgar continued to probe the surface of Lovey's face as Silas described the accident. He pushed on her frontal sinus and then the temporal lobe. Lovey showed no pain response. Then he pushed and prodded all along the front of her face. Finally, when he reached the left eye socket, she threw her head backward in obvious pain.

"Easy, Lovey baby," Sue said, taking the rag and ice pack from her face. "We just want to see where it hurts."

"She definitely feels it there," Edgar said, and he continued to palpate Lovey's entire face toward the nose. The mare flinched as Edgar probed all the way down the left side of her face. "Yes, she's beginning to swell up pretty good. But I can't feel anything broken in there. You see," he explained, showing the Warners the areas on the face, "this is all cartilage in here—all around the nostril area itself. So it's not really any big deal if she hit nose-first because it's more flexible than bone and would be far less likely to break. Now farther up," he pressed the bony growth halfway between the end of the nose and the eye, "there's bone and behind it a large, humongous sinus. That's also all right—I feel nothing broken. I've seen cases in which horses' heads are all caved in like soup bowls. Lovey doesn't have that. If Lovey *had* broken her skull, there'd really be nothing much I could do about it. Since there's a big space behind it, we would just let it heal that way. The animal would just have to live with a concave face."

Edgar pressed farther up where Lovey first showed signs of pain, and then he said, "Here is where it's really starting to swell, and she is painful on it. But the eye socket is fine—unbroken—as far as I can tell. I don't have my X-ray machine with me right now, but I'm fairly certain nothing at all is broken in Lovey's head."

"What about the brain?" Silas asked, his knitted brow beginning to relax.

"Oh, that's no problem. The brain is way back here, behind the ears," he indicated with a finger. "By the description of the accident, the brain wouldn't have been involved at all. She hit more with the broad front of her face."

"Geez, Doc," Silas said, his cheeks puffed out. "I'm all worked up over this. We do the best we can around here for our animals with our meager funds. Little by little we improve things as we can afford them. We're always so meticulous about everything around here, and we give our horses the best care we can. But I feel so guilty because Sue has been after me for a while to make that human door into a horse door, just so that something like this would never happen." He smiled tightly. "Guess I should've fixed it when she first mentioned it."

Sue looked firmly at him, but there was no anger in her eyes, just keen appreciation for his guilt.

"That will be my next project. That's for sure," Silas said.

"I'm going for my ophthalmoscope to check her eyes," Edgar said. "I don't see any nystagmus, but I want to make sure."

"You'll be all right, girl," he assured Lovey with a smile, then went to his truck for the instrument.

"Oh, it was such a horrendous sound," Silas repeated to me as I leaned against a stall wall. "I thought for sure she would drop over dead right afterward."

"These animals can fool ya sometimes," I said to lighten the atmosphere. I could tell Lovey was going to be just fine, except for a bad headache and stiff neck for a few days—and I wasn't the vet. "Their heads are pretty hard. Takes a lot to split 'em open."

Suddenly Sue yelled, *"I see no steam!"*

I spun around. She was looking at Lovey's nose. "No steam?" I said, curiously. "What do you m . . ."

Lovey stood calmly.

"From her left nostril!" Sue yelled. "She can't breathe! I see steam coming from the right one, but not the left. I don't think she can breathe out of her left nostril! You better get Doc back in here right away!"

"She's fine, Mrs. Warner," I said. "Watch," I said. I closed off the right nostril lightly with my hand, and then Sue could see the thin trail of vapor being exhaled from the left side.

"Oh, yeah. *There's* the steam! Thank God." She breathed a heavy sigh. "I see it now. Whew! There for a minute I thought she couldn't breathe out of her left side."

Soon Edgar came back into the box stall. He shined the ophthalmoscope's light in each of Lovey's eyes. "Looks just fine—-no bleeding, no nystagmus. Eyes look clear as can be. She's fine."

"Are you sure?" Sue said. "She couldn't have broken anything or damaged her brain?"

"No, Sue," Edgar assured her. "I really don't feel anything broken, and for sure her brain is all right. Then Edgar pulled three syringes from his shirt pocket. "Gay, come inside the stall here and hold these syringes. Give them to me when I'm ready."

I moved into the stall alongside Sue, Edgar, and Lovey.

Edgar explained the treatment, "I'm going to give her some Solu-Delta-Cortef, a powerful steroid that should reduce any swelling. It's important we keep the swelling in the nose down as best we can. The other shot is acepromazine, a relaxing agent to help her stay as calm as possible so that the bleeding stops completely, though it looks like it has pretty much stopped already. Then the final shot is Banamine, which will help with pain. All in all, though, she's in real good shape. She could have done a lot more damage to herself. I've certainly seen a lot worse head trauma cases than this. She's very lucky—no pushed-in face, no broken bones. Good deal.

"I want you to keep her quiet for the next day. Feed her just a tiny bit of oats tonight. I don't want her chewing and getting that sinus area all riled up. It could start bleeding again. But when you hay the others, give her a little bit, too; otherwise, she might get all upset that the others are eating when she can't. After twenty-four hours of rest, she can go outside again as normal."

"Will you check her legs, too, just to make sure she didn't catch anything there?" Silas said, his brow knit.

"Okay, sure." Edgar bent down and palpated each leg, smoothing the hair along the bone, looking for possible fractures or lacerations. "They look clean as a whistle. That's good. We're in pretty good shape here, actually."

"Yeah, well, we didn't know what you'd find, Doc. So," Silas said, smiling, "I got the horse trailer all ready and hooked up to take her to Quakertown if you thought she needed surgery. At least we won't have that expense."

"Did you call work, Silas?" Sue said, suddenly remembering their second-shift work schedule.

"Yeah, after I called Doc, I called us both off work." Then he looked at Edgar. "We don't want to leave her alone, just in case something should happen."

"Oh, you would've been all right to go to work. She's really quite fine. But being extra careful won't hurt, I guess," Edgar said. "Check her every once in a while, but she really should be okay."

"Thanks so much for coming right away," Sue said, rearranging the ice pack on Lovey's face. "We'll take turns holding the ice pack to her face this afternoon. We were so worried when it happened. Ya know, Silas wouldn't have been bringing in the horses in the middle of the afternoon if it weren't for the fact that we changed their feeding schedule after Cupid colicked on us that time. Remember?"

"Yes, I remember. She got over that incident with little problem, right?"

"Yeah, but we decided perhaps the horses wouldn't get so gassy if we fed them three times a day instead of two. And I really believe it helps. After all, horses out on the range rarely get colic. I think it's because they're grazing all day and are always pushing things through. Anyway, it seems to be working out fairly well—we haven't had a colic in a while. But, then, this had to happen."

"Well, when you have animals, weird things can always happen. It comes with the territory," Edgar said, putting the three empty syringes back in his shirt pocket. "We have our own problems with our animals, too. Don't we, Gay?"

"Yep, sure do. Always something happening. It seems no matter how much you try to reduce your chances, bad things still happen. Still, sometimes you can help reduce the probability by keeping a nice, clean, safe place and developing good feeding habits."

"Okay," Edgar finished, "we're all set here then. You'll follow up tonight with Azium powder for swelling and Promazine granules to keep her calm. We should keep her quiet so that the bleeding doesn't start up again. You'll be fine, Lovey," Edgar said, patting her head as he left the stall. "I won't pet you on your face 'cause I know it hurts."

Edgar walked to the truck, and I started to follow. Sue remarked to Silas about cleaning up the blood that Lovey had smeared along the side of the stall.

"Oh, sure," Silas said, hurrying to the storage cabinet. He opened one side of the huge thing, and inside were all kinds of medicines, bandages, cottons, and ointments. He grabbed a rag and rushed back to Lovey's stall. As Sue continued to hold the ice pack to Lovey's face, she directed Silas toward the bloody stains.

"Silas, there's one you missed," Sue said, pointing to a blood smear on the stall's side. He turned, scouring the area furiously while Sue pointed out other stained areas.

"Oh," exclaimed Sue. Then she looked at me. "Could you call Dr. Balliet back? I wanted to ask him to check Cupid's throat. When she eats grain, she always raises her head so funny as if she needs gravity's help to get things down."

Sue demonstrated Cupid's peculiar eating habits. She craned her neck straight into the air as if sniffing the atmosphere for a hidden scent. "That's how she goes," Sue repeated, straining her neck skyward again. "Like this," she demonstrated again. "It's really weird, and I was worried she wasn't able to eat right or something."

Edgar just happened to have walked in on Sue's demonstration. "What's the matter with Cupid?" he asked.

Finished wiping down Lovey's stall, Silas stood by Sue's side, his bloody rag lowered, his brows knitted tightly again. Everything was so serious here. Sue and Silas were nice enough people, but they seemed a bit overly concerned about their horses' health. They almost seemed to be looking for trouble. Of course, that was eons better than being negligent. "Yes, Doctor, we think Cupid might be having trouble swallowing. We had Carlin out here to check her, but she couldn't find anything wrong. Would you watch her eat her grain?"

"Sure. Throw some in her feedbin," Edgar said.

Silas put a cupful of sweet feed in Cupid's grain dish. Cupid went voraciously to it, gobbling half the scoopful at one time.

"Now watch," Silas said with a serious, dire expression that said, *We may not be veterinarians, but this head-raising business is surely something serious.*

Nothing. Cupid chewed her grain, swallowed it with the head and neck in the usual position for horses eating grain, and went to the dish for another mouthful. Again she chewed and swallowed at the normal horse-eating level.

"She's not doing it now," Sue said with consternation. "Doc, stand back away from her stall a little bit. She's probably self-conscious. She'll do it if you don't crowd her."

Edgar snickered and backed obediently away.

Still Cupid continued to eat her grain the way all horses eat it.

"She's making liars of us. How about that, Silas," Sue marveled. "I can't believe she's not putting her nose in the air."

Silas shook his head, the worried look engraved on his face. "Yeah, I can hardly believe it either. She always puts her head in the air." Then he looked at Edgar, who was dutifully observing the eating horse. "Always—like she can't swallow."

"Well, she looks perfectly fine to me—good mastication. Doesn't seem to be anything wrong with her ability to swallow," Edgar said.

I offered a solution. "Maybe by throwing her head, she could be warning other people or horses to let her alone while she eats. She might be protecting her food, so to speak."

Silas and Sue looked at me thoughtfully. Sue said, "Well, we really thought she had trouble getting her food down."

"Does she do it just with the grain or with hay, too?" Edgar asked, trying to get at the root of the problem.

"Only with grain," Silas claimed.

"Well, I can't see anything wrong with her. I guess we could scope her sometime if you're still worried about it, but I think it's largely unnecessary. Okay, Gay, let's get going."

Silas and Sue followed us closely to the truck. On the way Sue showed me the new outdoor ring they were putting in and the extra pasture area for the horses. The fencing looked relatively new; it was made of white vinyl bands, the safest horse fencing to be bought. Vinyl fencing was virtually indestructible—wouldn't rot or need repainting. It also didn't have any sharp surfaces on which to cut an animal.

"Yes, and we plan to build a bigger barn next year, too," Sue said proudly. "We're saving our pennies."

"Oh, that'll be very nice for the horses," I said, curling my coat collar up against my neck. The wind was clawing at us as we cleaned up the back of Edgar's truck. I didn't know how Silas withstood the wind through that skinny jacket.

"Yes, I can't wait," Sue said, pulling her hood over her head. "Lovey just loves to be outside, and more pasture area will be better so that the horses won't colic."

"Yes, that's probably true," I agreed. "Colic can be a problem sometimes. We've had our share of colic surgeries, that's for sure. It's a nasty business."

"Let's go, Gay," Edgar called. "It's going to take us a good forty minutes to get home, and our own guys are probably anxious to get in and eat."

In minutes we were heading down the Warner's driveway. At the end we smiled at the sign that read LOVEY'S LANE.

I said, "Lovey's Lane, huh? A horse named Lovey. And Cupid? This place is, indeed, a heaven for animals. They're almost as nerdy about their animals as I am."

"Yeah, and that's saying a lot."

"And how. Those animals are lucky to have found the Warners. If you ever throw me out of the house, I think I'll come here to live," I laughed. "Of course, I could just move in with the Giants."

Edgar laughed too and pulled out onto the gravel road, the long trail that would eventually lead us back home. Then, just as I always do when I am riding along with Edgar, I began to think about other things. I was not one to keep up a running conversation, and I am sure Edgar appreciated that. We drove much of the time in complete silence. My thoughts were often my own entertainment.

I thought of the Warners' place and their attitude toward their animals, and then I thought of Mrs. Dreck and her sad brood. What a difference a little luck would have meant for the Drecks' foals. Had Mrs. Dreck's first foal been born in the Warner's barn, her crooked legs and inability to nurse would have been discovered within the first few moments because the Warners would have camped out in the barn for their mare's birthing. The Warners would have never left a mare ready to foal to indulge themselves in sleep until the next morning. They certainly would have made sure the mare was up-to-date on all her vaccinations. And the Warners would certainly have been in that straw-lined stall helping Edgar tend to the foal.

I sighed heavily. The Warners would make good spokespeople for my cosmic family theory. No doubt they would agree with me that people need to stop exploiting animals and learn to live side-by-side with them.

Perhaps sometime I'll tell them my theory.

Pedro

FOR MUCH OF THE SUMMER I entertained the pigs poolside and played with my horses and cats. Edgar kept me abreast of his clients and his daily routine, and I promised him I would accompany him on his rounds. To this day I wish I had assisted him the day he first drove up to the Mirkovics' place.

When Edgar pulled the truck through the intimidating iron gate, he didn't know quite what to expect. All he knew was that he was checking a goat for mastitis. As he slowly came to a stop in the drive-way, he wondered what kind of people lived there—not your usual kind, certainly. He was surrounded by twenty-odd buildings: duck sheds, doghouses, henhouses, goathouses, pigpens, horse sheds—many miniature homes fit for dolls. Each house was delicate, as small as if it were made for a child, and painted in a rainbow-colored, gingerbread house style. Later, when I visited, the Mirkovics' place would remind me of my favorite childhood game, Candyland.

Not only was their haven a fantasyland, but it was designed for practicality and utility as well. Each of the mini-mansions was situated within a grassy or gravel yard which was also enclosed by wire or board fencing. Water troughs were plentiful and food bins accessible. Each pen was protected from the sun by well-placed shade trees. These pets had a better life than Riley.

These folks collected animals the way some people collect keychains, and they took excellent care of them all.

For several minutes Edgar surveyed the animal compound. He was astounded by the variety of critters milling about: goats, both mini and standard-sized, shared an enclosure with sheep; mini-horses were in another pen, and regular-sized horses in a large barnyard. Variegated water fowl shared two ponds. Fancy chickens, exotic pheasants, and two pot-bellied pigs occupied another mini-house. Connecting the animal pens was a winding, macadam path just wide enough to allow two people to pass. Edgar later found that it also served as a mini-highway for the golf cart on which the Mirkovics made their daily rounds. In addition, the place was framed by a seven-foot gray fence. It was a miniature Dickensian village—for animals.

Edgar shut off the truck's engine. Over the cackling of geese and chattering of chickens, Edgar detected a human voice. Jon was calling from one of the pens, so he set off in that direction.

"Looks like a good case of mastitis," Edgar said, palpating the goat's udder. "It's pretty red, and there's even some swelling on the left side. You'll have to strip her out every couple of hours, and we'll put her on antibiotics. I'll put some Hetacin K ointment into each teat, too, and it should come around in a few days. You can also try hot compacts."

"Okay, Doc. We appreciate your coming out here for Sarah. She's one of our nicest goats."

That was the first time Edgar treated an animal at Mirkovics' Melange of Miniatures, as he and I jokingly referred to it after that. When he came home and told me about the place, I resolved to attend the next time. I wanted to experience it for myself. With that many animals to take care of, it wasn't too long before Sue Mirkovic phoned again. This time it was for a behavioral problem with one of the standard-sized horses: it was scary and shied away from the silliest things—pitchforks, shovels, barn doors, hay bales. She thought for sure it was a medical, not psychological, problem. She also wanted Edgar to check a mini donkey that had turned up lame overnight.

So that day Edgar and I headed to Marshall's Creek, a town about

fifty minutes north of home. Just as Edgar had before, we entered the
Mirkovics' property through the stern iron gate that belied a Heidi-like village housing a kindly menagerie. Here was my Candyland game come to
life—paths winding from one colorful child-size house to another. The animal shelters were cozy enough for children to play house while dreaming of
festive-colored lollipops and pastel bonbons. I was tempted to stay and play.

Edgar gave me the grand tour as we drove through Imagination-
land. To our immediate left was a small, sky-blue summer house that
Jon and Sue only opened up to guests or relatives in for a visit. Just
beyond that and to the right was their own red brick ranch, the front
yard of which was loaded with assorted squabbling white, yellow, and
speckled exotic ducks. A clutch of daffodil-colored chicks paraded
behind their mother unaware of our oncoming truck, and Edgar
braked to let them pass. We turned onto the left arm of the driveway
where lived the two pot-bellied pigs, Sonny and Cher.

As a proud owner and afficionado of ten pot-bellied pigs, I resolved
to visit Sonny and Cher immediately after we treated our patients.

Edgar pointed to the right of the pig house. Across from the pigs'
pastel-colored cottage stood a three-foot chain-link fence with a building for the larger goats and various and assorted poultry squatters: fancy
chickens, snowy geese, and bantam roosters. Behind that yard lived the
pigmy goats in their own Lilliputian pen and shed. Outside the pen was
a small feed house where the food for all the animals was stored and a
brown and white pigmy goat, Muffin, had taken up residence.

To the left and even farther away from the goat pens was the
fenced-in field for the miniature horses, Lucky and Millie, and the
mini-donkey, Pedro, the one to be checked for lameness. They grazed
in a lush pasture complete with shade trees and a three-sided shed for
protection against the weather.

To the right side of the compound, alongside the people house, was
a large pond with a fountain where variegated waterfowl splashed and
quacked. They certainly were a noisy crowd, arguing and harrassing
each other. Across from the pond was a barn for the full-sized horses,
Charlie and Chance, the one that feared everything. Next to them was
yet another smaller pond where more fowl played and squabbled and
hunted for spilled grain.

"Wow," I said, looking around, "I thought we had a lot of animals.

This is quite some operation—all these tiny houses are so meticulously kept and carefully laid out. This is like a little zoo. Can the public come to see the animals?"

"Oh, no," Edgar said. "These animals are strictly pets. Jon and Sue don't want any hassles with people noseying around their property— note the iron gate and high fence. Intruders of the human species are not welcome here, but animals are, as you can see. These guys are their buddies, their kids. They dote on them."

"Oh, look," I yelled as the pot-bellied pigs rolled out of their tiny house and down the ramp into their outside pen. "Aren't they cute." I jumped from the truck and ran to the side of the pen.

"That's Sonny and Cher," Edgar called. Sonny and Cher were really *big* pot-bellies, even bigger than Lowell.

"Gads, I thought *ours* were big—these guys are as big as the Giants! Why are these pigs so large when they're obviously confined to this pen?"

"Well, Sue says her husband thinks they're always hungry, so he makes sure they always have lots of food in front of them. He doesn't quite understand that pigs always have appetites, no matter how much you feed them. Sue tries to feed them less, but Jon always worries they're starving and slips them goodies on the sly. Personally, I think he has sympathetic hunger pangs."

That must have been the case, considering their loaded food dish. Feed blossomed over the rim of the dish and flowed down the side. The pigs were evidently so full that they had *no* desire to eat—a strange phenomenon for *any* pig.

Edgar crouched down to the pigs' own level. "Yep, one of these days I must trim their tusks. They're starting to get pretty long." Sonny and Cher eyed him suspiciously.

"Another fun job, huh?" I laughed. "I think I'll go along to help you with that. Su-mo! Su-mo!" I sang.

A voice rang out from behind. "Hi, Doc! See you brought your better half with you today," Sue called. A short, round, middle-aged woman, she sported bib overalls over a blue-striped polo shirt.

I said with a grin, "Yes, he did! Hi. I'm Gay—but not really. Not that there's anything wrong with that. Quite a place you have here. I thought we had a lot of animals, but we look like a couple of amateurs compared to you guys. What do you do with them all?"

"Nothing. Look at them, pet them, feed them, take care of them—feed them, and feed them some more," she laughed. "I sometimes feel like the house mother at a frat house."

A gaggle of geese waddled by, complaining in high voices at the strangers in their territory. I nodded toward the pigs, "I have a couple of pot-bellies myself. And I don't feel so bad about my really heavy one now. He's a Tinkerbell compared to your two."

"Well, my husband sympathizes with anything that has an insatiable appetite—reminds him of himself," she laughed. "He can't stand the sight of a hungry animal. I tell him not to feed them so much, but he still loads up their dishes. Just look at all that wasted food," she said pointing to the overflowing pig bowl. "They're always full; that's why they're so fat."

Then she turned from the pigs and motioned Edgar to follow, "First, let's take a look at my horse Chance. She's been shying a lot lately. Afraid of the silliest things: large weeds, water buckets, and sometimes she even spooks at her pasture mate, Charlie."

We entered the large horse pen and closed the gate. Standing next to the barn was a bay mare. There was no mistaking our patient, for when she turned towards us, her left eye glowed eerily, like a blue, cloudy marble—an alien thing. Beside her stood Charlie, an old, arthritic-looking chestnut gelding. Edgar walked toward Chance's good side so that the horse could see him with her good eye. Then he took her by the halter and turned her bad left eye toward him. Turning on his ophthalmoscope, he directed the tiny thin beam into the horse's opaque orb.

In less than a minute he had his diagnosis: a cataract that was so bad it had left the animal blind in that eye. "A textbook cataract, all right," Edgar said, checking the eye again. He flashed his hand in front of it, looking for a flinch, but Chance showed no reaction. "Can't see a thing out of it," Edgar said. "That's why she's been shying a lot. When a person or another animal approaches her on her left, it startles her cause she doesn't see it coming. She gets along all right here in her little corral, right? Horses, even totally blind ones, can adjust fairly well to having no sight, as long as no one rearranges the furniture, if you know what I mean."

"Yes," Sue said. "I hadn't noticed anything before except that when I took her out for a walk, she seemed scared of a lot of things that she shouldn't be. So, that's it, huh? She's absolutely blind in that eye?"

"Yeah. Now the animal hospital at the University of North Carolina can remove cataracts in horses, but I really don't recommend that since, on the whole, she seems to function all right. Considering her age and the fact that you don't ride her, she'll be fine as long as she doesn't develop one in the other eye." Edgar packed his ophthalmoscope back into its case and patted Chance on her back, and we all headed toward the gate and the miniature donkey pen.

"Now, what's the story with Pedro? He's the mini-donkey, right?" Edgar asked.

"Yes. He's been a bit lame since his accident a few days ago."

"What happened?" Edgar said as we parted a sea of chickens pecking the gravel walkway. We passed Sonny and Cher, sprawled out on their sides, their bellies pointing skyward as they enjoyed the late morning sun. Their food dish was still full of uneaten food pellets and scavanger blow flies.

"Well, I always feed the minis from hay nets so they don't pick up a lot of stones and gravel with their food. A few days ago I came out in the morning to feed, and Pedro was standing on three legs with his front foot caught in the hay bag. The net was all twisted and wrapped around his foot. In fact, it was so tight I had to cut it off with a hoof knife."

"How long was he caught like that?" Edgar asked with a raised eyebrow.

"Probably overnight, I'd have to guess. At least he was probably tangled in it for a good portion of the evening. The last time I did a barn check that night was nine o'clock. Conceivably, he could have gotten caught anywhere between nine and the next morning."

We entered the mini-horse pen. Pedro was resting against the tiny barn, his back warming in the sun. He stood on three legs with the fourth, the right front, resting on its toe. Edgar pushed on his left hindquarter to put his weight on the front right foot. Only very reluctantly did Pedro shift his weight onto that foot, then quickly back again to the other three feet.

"Gee, he wasn't this lame yesterday, Doc," Sue said. "He seems to mind it a lot more today. I'm glad we're checking it."

I leaned over to pet the shaggy grey Sicilian donkey. He looked at me with great sad eyes. "He looks uncomfortable," I volunteered.

"Yeah," Edgar said. "He's not happy. Let's see what we can do." With that Edgar bent over and palpated the leg, starting with the knee. He probed and pushed all the joints and tendons, but Pedro showed no pain response. So far, so good. Then Edgar bent over and lifted the leg, holding it by the cannon bone. He pressed around the coronet band with his thumbs, and with that Pedro yanked his leg from Edgar's grip in obvious discomfort. The donkey hopped sideways, only touching the tip of the hoof lightly to the ground to balance himself.

"I don't like the looks of that," Edgar said. "He is very sensitive at his coronet band. I hope getting that net caught around his foot didn't cut off all the circulation to the hoof. If it did, we could be in for some real trouble here. He could founder, or there could be worse problems."

Sue bit her lip.

"But we won't go looking for any trouble until it happens, right?"

Sue stared at Pedro. "I'm not even going to ask you what the worst could be," she said. "I don't think I want to know."

"I want you to keep a close eye on him for now. I'm going to give you analgesics for him to help with the pain. In a week or so we should know whether he's going to get better on his own or if we have to take heroic measures." Edgar led Pedro by the halter in a circle, and the little donkey followed reluctantly. "He's not walking too badly at this point, so he couldn't have broken anything. But if he starts not wanting to move at all or looks as though he's walking on eggs, I want you to call immediately. I'll give him some injectable bute now, and I'll give you bute for his grain. Then let's just keep our fingers crossed. All we can do is wait."

"I'll keep my fingers crossed, Doc."

I said good-bye to Sonny and Cher, and we were off to another call.

A week later the phone rang.

"He is?" I heard Edgar say in a serious tone. "I'll be up first thing this morning." He hung up and turned to me, "It's the Mirkovics—there's blood and fluid seeping from Pedro's coronet band. That's not good. I've got to check it out to be absolutely certain, but I think he may be sloughing his hoof."

I chewed my lower lip. The coronet band is the demarcation line between the bottom of a horse's or donkey's leg and the beginning of the hoof. If that line was oozing material, then something really traumatic was occurring inside the hoof. "It's a death sentence, isn't it?" I said.

"Sounds that way, I'm afraid. But let's not jump to conclusions. We'll head up there right away."

The iron gate was open when we turned into the Mirkovic's driveway. We pulled in right next to Pedro's pasture. Facing away from us, he leaned heavily against the barn, his bad foot resting on tiptoe.

Edgar grabbed the hoof testers from the back of the truck, and we headed toward the barn. The screen door slammed as Sue ran toward us. Geese and ducks protested noisily as we interrupted their breakfast.

"Yeah," Sue said. "I thought I better call you when I saw that stuff oozing from the coronet band. I don't like the looks of it."

"Let's just see before we get all worried about it," Edgar said as he reached for the gate. "It may be nothing."

Wishful thinking, I suspected—no different here than when dealing with human illness. One always hopes for the best until the final diagnosis. The victim, friends, and relatives pluck the straws and wish and hope and pray that the obvious won't end up becoming the reality. Unfortunately, it often adds up to wishful thinking spurred by quiet desperation. As far as I could tell, there was not much argument against a bleeding coronet band. It foretold disaster.

"Steady his back end, Gay," Edgar said. We managed to turn Pedro around so that when I leaned against his right hind hip, his left side had the support of the barn wall. With that Edgar was able to balance the donkey and lift up the front right leg, which he propped gently between his legs. Sue bent over and looked with him at the bottom of the hoof. Edgar would be on the lookout for founder, a condition in which the bones of the foot detach from the hoof wall and break through the bottom of the hard nail of the hoof. It's a very painful and sometimes irreversible condition, which sometimes requires euthanasia.

"How is it?" I said, unable to see while I balanced Pedro's back end between me and the barn wall.

Edgar pressed along the length of the coronet band which ran around the top edge of the hoof. Then I heard a strange POP! like a cork out of a wine bottle.

"Oh, my God!" Sue yelled, and she turned away, her hands cupping her face.

"What happened?" I said, straining to see around Edgar while still steadying Pedro. The donkey hadn't flinched at all, yet from Sue's exclamation it must have been awful.

"Sue, take Gay's place beside Pedro. Gay, run to the truck. I need bandaging material. This foot can't touch the ground, or everything'll get infected."

Sue ran to my side and put her weight into Pedro to keep him braced against the barn. Tears were streaming down her face. What could have happened? I ran to the truck and pulled out the canvas bag containing all the bandaging materials: gauze pads, cotton wraps, Vetwrap, adhesive tape, and scissors. Then I rushed back to where Edgar had Pedro's leg propped between his legs.

When I looked at it, I was stunned silent.

He was holding a bloody stump—a leg without a foot. Then, as if suddenly struck to consciousness by the horrific scene, I screeched, "WHERE'S THE HOOF?" I couldn't take my eyes off the spectacle. Never in all of Edgar's practicing veterinary medicine had I seen anything so uncanny, so disturbing.

Edgar didn't need to answer, for I could see the hoof lying on the ground next to him—a tiny casing for a tiny donkey foot—unattached to the animal it belonged to. It was surreal. What should have been a living body part, a covering for an appendage, was instead a separate, non-living object lying on the ground innocuously, like a bowl waiting to be filled with a few pansies, or like a discarded, reptilian body part, a snake skin or a severed leg that might magically grow back. But Pedro's hoof would probably never grow back again.

Edgar held the leg with its bloody bottom between his legs. He looked up at me pathetically and helplessly. "It just came off in my hand," he muttered weakly. He, too, stared at it as if it were some queer apparition, not quite of this world.

The bottom of the leg was a mass of blood clots, tendons, and tissue, and I thought I could even see pieces of bone protruding from the red mass. But Pedro didn't seem to mind that his foot had just fallen off. He was still standing calmly against the barn wall.

"All we can do at this time is treat it like another wound," Edgar said as he tore at once into the bandage bag. He immediately began to wrap gauze and then cotton wraps, loads of them, around the bloody bottom of the leg. He formed a thick mattress of padding around where Pedro's foot used to be, continued the wrap up the rest of the leg, then covered it all with Vetwrap and heavy-duty adhesive tape.

The atmosphere had become heavy with silence. Sue braced herself against Pedro, her eyes shut against the truth of the moment: her donkey was missing a foot. She was just toughing it out until Edgar was finished and she could get the entire prognosis.

When he was done, he lowered Pedro's leg to the ground. "Okay, Sue. Let's see if he puts any weight on that foot now," Edgar said, stepping away from the animal. Sue gently stood away, and the donkey's left hip came away from the barn wall.

Incredibly Pedro was standing on his own—on all four legs.

Edgar said, "He's not in pain at this point. The pain stage was probably a few days ago when the hoof wall started separating. After it finally did, he wasn't feeling much anymore. You saw that he didn't react when his hoof popped off in my hands."

"Yes, but now what? What does all this mean? Can he grow another hoof back? Will he be okay eventually?" Sue asked.

"It's very iffy," Edgar said. "Sometimes they can grow a little bit of nail back, but it doesn't happen often. All the nerves and circulation to that area have been destroyed by that hay net he was caught in. It's very unlikely he'll regrow another hoof, but there's always a chance."

"So, then," she said, blinking back tears, "the only other thing to do is put him to sleep, right?"

Edgar thought for awhile, and he stared at Pedro, who had reached down to lick a stray strand of hay. I bit my lip. As far as I knew, there wasn't much hope for a case like this. Even though Edgar had bandaged the stump, and the donkey was putting weight on it, the animal would eventually break through the bottom of the bandage and end up walking on the stump, grinding the bones of what remained of the foot and all its tissues, tendons, and nerves into the dirt. Pedro would need constant vigilance and bandage changing. And what about infection? Was there a possibility of the other three feet foundering from supporting the extra weight? It all seemed too overwhelmingly negative.

"Well, I'm certainly not going to put him to sleep right away. We'll see how he does with the bandage. I'll be up again in a few days to change it. We'll put him on antibiotics, of course, to keep away infection. We'll have to take this one day at a time."

"Pedro is my buddy," Sue said, stroking the donkey's mane and running her hand down the dark stripe along his spine. The animal looked up, snuffling her jacket, and she took a carrot from her pocket. "You know what my animals mean to me, Doc," Sue said with a smile. "I'll do anything for them. I'd appreciate any help you could give Pedro."

"I know what you are saying, and we'll do everything we can. But we must first see him through this event. If he shows no signs of infection, and if he bears weight on the leg, then we'll see what we can do." I had already rolled up the remains of the cotton wraps and stored them and the adhesive tape back in the canvas sack. Hoisting it over my shoulder, I turned toward the truck.

Edgar took the hoof testers and started to follow, then stopped, turned around, and picked up the alien hoof. He looked inside the bloody cavern and handed it to Sue. "Here, I know you always keep lost teeth, antlers, and other mementos from your animals. Pedro would want you to save his hoof, don't you think?"

"Oh, I had intended to save it, Doc. Don't worry. Ya know, Pedro's a pretty tough guy. Something tells me he's going to win this match."

"Let's hope so," Edgar said, and we headed for the truck.

In three days we arrived at the Mirkovics' to recheck Pedro. Sue flew out the door as Edgar pulled the truck to a stop. We glanced at Pedro from the truck. He was grazing in the pasture, his bandage still intact. "Something doesn't look right with the bandage," Edgar said, squinting at his subject. "Let's see what's going on." So, we stepped out of the truck and walked over to the donkey.

"The bandage seems to be slipping down his leg. See how it's all pancaked out at the bottom," Sue said, locking the gate behind us. "It's good you're here to put a new one on."

Edgar put his bandage sack down and went over to Pedro, who stopped munching his breakfast to inspect the person inspecting him. Pedro didn't move as Edgar squeezed up and down the leg. He just nuzzled the top of Edgar's head. "Not right," Edgar muttered. He stood up and took the leg between his own two legs, cutting open and unwrapping miles of bandage material. When he got down to the last layer before the gauze, he slowed and very carefully lifted the gauze from the tissue the separated hoof had left exposed.

Sue and I stood where we could easily see the unveiling. We didn't have long to await the verdict.

"No good," Edgar said in disgust. Now I could see what he was

concerned about. The bandage had not fallen down the leg and pancaked around the bottom because of gravity or other mysterious forces.
No—in the past three days the bones and tissues and tendons underneath the bandage had flattened out themselves without the bony covering of the hoof. Pedro, having no pain when he walked, had done
just that—he had walked around his pasture, and as he did, his weight
had flattened the bottom of his leg out to a good six inch pancake. He
was walking on a mass of smashed bones and tissue.

"This won't do," Edgar said.

"It's not time to put him to sleep, is it?" Sue said, her brow furrowed.

"No, not yet. But we have to design something so that he doesn't
wreck all the bones and tissue that were once protected by his hoof."

I set the bandage bag next to Edgar. He tore into it and began
rebandaging Pedro's leg. With his bare hands he tried to remodel the
squashed out part into something more tapered. With lots of pressure
on what had been encased by the hoof, he managed to reduce the pancaked area until it looked more normal.

"Now what do we do?" Sue asked as she stroked Pedro's mane.

"I'm going to have to cast the leg somehow," Edgar said, packing up the
bandage bag. "Don't let Pedro go just yet. I have to get some of that pressure off the leg. I'm going to try a light cast that'll go up to his knees. And
I'm going to fashion a little hoof-type thing on the end for him to walk on.
It'll be like giving him a cast with a heel. Maybe if I give him something to
walk on, he won't actually be walking on himself." Sue and I looked at each
other, amazed and hopeful that the innovative idea would work.

Sometimes in veterinary medicine the doctor needs to resort to ingenuity to help fix a problem. Even though small animal clinics are as
advanced as some human hospitals, or even more so, in treating their
patients, the large animal field veterinarian sometimes is at a loss for the
equipment and tools to treat a more demanding case. What he's trying
to accomplish he must do in the middle of a pasture, maybe in rain or
snow or swarms of flies, and certainly in less than sterile conditions. And
in many cases the aftercare just does not exist. It's very hard to convince
a large animal to keep still. One couldn't tell Pedro, for example, to stay
off his feet awhile until the foot healed and began to regrow a nail.

Pedro's case was particularly exasperating. Most veterinarians would
have put Pedro to sleep when the hoof slipped off in their hands. A

sloughed hoof is a dire prognosis. What help could be given Pedro was purely experimental, unproven. Edgar was doctoring the donkey on instinct and ingenuity, not on textbook diagnoses. But any treatment toward a workable end was better than putting Pedro to sleep without a fight, as long as the animal was reasonably comfortable. If Edgar could determine that Pedro's little pain was worth the gain of life, then he needed to act.

Head down, thinking, Edgar walked to the truck and gathered a boxful of casting material and a bucket of water. He came back to Pedro, whose bandaged leg I had been holding up and away from the ground, and went to work on Pedro's cast. Dipping each length of casting material—long, thin strips of fiberglass cloth—in the water, he molded the squashed foot bones into a tighter package, draping them with the soggy material. He built up the cast with layers and layers of fiberglass, waiting for each layer to set up and become hard before he applied another one. He continually checked the alignment of the leg to see that it was straight into the cast.

It was hard work, steadying the donkey, pulling on the casting material to tighten it around the leg, and preventing him from moving, but after half an hour, the cast was finished. We waited another ten minutes to be sure it had hardened well, and then Edgar lowered it to the ground. At first Pedro didn't want to move with the heavy, awkward thing weighing down his leg, but after a while the lure of the succulent grass coaxed him toward the pasture. We all watched, hoping he wouldn't go crazy feeling the ungainly cast on his leg. It would be the end, for sure, if he went into a rage, kicking, and throwing off the entire cast.

Fortunately, Pedro did nothing of the kind. He seemed to know that he needed to be careful. Step by careful step, he sauntered toward a patch of grass where he dropped his head to nibble.

Edgar smiled. "Good. He's tolerating that strange thing on his leg." He watched as the donkey moved quietly about the pasture. "I'll want to check that cast in a few days and make sure the leg isn't swelling up above it. I can't have it on too tight, either. Keep an eye on it, Sue, and if it seems to be working, we might try something else."

"So far, so good, Doc," Sue said. She stood with her hands on hips and smiled approvingly at her donkey. "Like I said before, he's a tough old bird."

In the next few weeks Edgar had made several trips to the

Mirkovic's place. Each time he cut off Pedro's cast, debrided dead tissue from the stump, and recast the animal's leg. Pedro appeared to be doing fine, marching around his field like an old soldier with a peg leg. He wasn't glum about his lack of mobility or depressed that he was walking on a stump supported by a cast instead of the hoof that nature had given him.

When Edgar had developed several weeks worth of X-rays of Pedro's foot, he discovered that the first two bones—those closest to the ground—had broken up. These bones are the equivalent of human finger bones, or phalanges. The bones had shattered from the pressure of the donkey's weight on the bottom of the cast, but the radiographs also showed that while the bones in the stump had disintegrated, the bottom of the leg was beginning to show signs of vital nail growth.

Pedro was beginning to grow a new foot.

Edgar, Pedro, and Jon and Sue Mirkovic

"Yep, looks now as if we have what we are going to have," Edgar told Sue one day when he came to change the cast. "Pedro appears to have grown a new hoof, but there's no bony support in it. His P3, P2, and half of P1 are completely gone. It means that in time his leg will begin to curve in."

Sue looked curious. "Well, now what do we do?"

"I read about this guy in Kentucky who makes prostheses for race-horses. In fact, I've already called him about Pedro. All he needs to make a device for Pedro is a mold, which I can do. A prosthesis will give support to the entire leg since he has none coming from his foot. It will be made of high density plastic and won't need to be replaced for two years, depending on how hard Pedro uses it. It comes with a rubber sole. But it's a bit pricey—about a thousand dollars. What do you think?"

"Order it," Sue said adamantly. "We didn't come all this way to just give up now. He's a good donkey, and I know Jon would want to get the prosthesis, too."

In a month Pedro was sporting his new, shiny white leg support. It fit him like a glove, and he walked his pasture and grazed happily alongside the mini horse and pony. He was a donkey with a new lease. Jon and Sue and Edgar and I were delighted.

Life's been fine for the Mirkovics, their menagerie, and Pedro. During the ordeal Pedro had lost weight, which was better for him and his problem. Today he weighs about 350 pounds and still walks his pasture with a prosthesis. He wore out the first one and is on his second. Miraculously the hoof has grown back entirely, though because he's lacking the foot bones, he still needs the prosthesis for support. He will never walk again without the prosthesis, but at least he can walk. The satisfaction the Mirkovics and we take away from Pedro's experience is nothing less than exhilarating. Admittedly, the undertaking was a gamble with less than lousy odds, but in the effort we beat it. It proves that people can accomplish the next to impossible with a combination of ingenuity, determination, and love.

All Earth's Animals

EDGAR SPUN THE STEERING WHEEL TO THE RIGHT and pressed the accelerator to the floor. We tumbled out onto a two-lane macadam road that would take us the back way toward Mirkovics' farm in the Poconos. It had been a while since we saw their pot-bellied pigs, Sonny and Cher, and the rest of their animal clan. At their place I could become immersed in all kinds of different animals, from ducks and chickens to horses, ponies, goats, and pigs. One was never lacking for company at the Mirkovics.

The sun rays filtered through the tree canopy overhead as we dipped and swayed over the road. I reached for my sunglasses and handed Edgar his. Edgar never took the shortest route to any of his calls—not the Thruway or Route 309—preferring instead to arrive at his destination after a scenic drive through the countryside. He didn't like bucking the heavy traffic of the Lehigh Valley, and he did not submit to aggressive driving and road rage as many harried drivers did, side-passing, cutting out, over, and around other vehicles on the road. He courted life in the slower, safer lane, the more scenic, saner lane. For Edgar, back roads were not only a route to a destination but also a source of aesthetics and a means for introspection. We could arrive at the next appointment—we hoped—with an altered mind state, refreshed by the beauty of the countryside, its primitive innocence, its transcendence, its natural lure. Driving through Pennsylvania's native woods and fields allowed both of us the time and the setting to reflect. Edgar most often thought about problem patients and their medical therapy, or else he was anticipating what course of veterinary care he would likely be providing at the next call. I, on the other hand, usually became engrossed in more philosophical or personal thoughts. I was a sentimentalist at heart, always looking for that sweet connection between myself and the world around me. And always I was reflecting on the majesty of nature and the wonder of her animals.

A warm breeze wafted through the truck cab as we bobbed along the uneven road that would take us into the tiny town of Aquashicola, which I pronounced "a-quash, a cola" just to make Edgar laugh. Aquashicola lay just outside Palmerton, a town whose many elderly inhabitants had grown up and worked in the neighboring zinc factory. The countryside was barren, the hills stripped of vegetation from years of pollution by the zinc company. The bald land at least provided a contrast to the lush flora we would experience farther north and east.

From Aquashicola we rolled along through another small town—Kunkletown. In five minutes we had passed through its famed covered bridge and its downtown area, which consisted of a mom and pop grocery store, Silar's dress factory, Roxy's bar, and a Shell gas station. Then we turned left off the Kunkletown Road to Route 715, where at McMichael's we headed east toward Marshall's Creek.

The drive from McMichael's through Reeder's, Tannersville, and Analomink was nothing short of luxuriant, lusher and thicker than the Lehigh Valley where we lived. It had an almost tropical feel, though of course the Poconos are hardly tropical. With the cooler temperatures and the rainfall, plant life exploded. Mountain laurel and rhododendron competed for space amongst the towering ash and oak trees, and vines of wild roses and grapes climbed into the canopies, beckoning toward the sunlight.

We swung along the winding road toward Marshall's Creek, the truck plunging in and out of the shadows, the moist smell of pine sifting through the windows. Every so often another car passed going in the other direction, but no one was in front of or behind us. We were on the road exclusively on a driving voyage that fostered personal freedom and caressed the imagination.

Each in our own world, we headed into the thick of the Poconos. Greenery engulfed us. Nature was a wonder.

We plummeted over a hill, and the road dropped us down the other side. To my right a thick forest stretched. What beasts lived, hunted, slept in that woods, I wondered. How many miles into the depth of the forest did a herd of hundreds of deer roam? What mother rabbit lay beneath that hemlock's apron with her batch of babies? I thought about the millions of insects that climbed the tree trunks, aphids that dined on leaves, spiders that sat atop grass blades, beetles that clung to slippery creek rocks, ticks that sucked the squirrels' blood. I smelled worms that were forced from their burrows in last night's downpour. Though I couldn't see any wildlife as we passed by the thick forest, I knew it was out there, the good, the bad, and the ugly, surrounding us.

The realization made me appreciative, safe, and at the same time a bit anxious. Though we were confined to the macadam road, I felt a part of the environment. We were no strangers to Mother Nature; we were one with her. The forest lapped the edge of our blacktopped path. She wrapped her moisture, her smells, her colors around us. She shared herself unselfishly with us, and I mentally opened myself up to her as well, even to the worms and snakes I knew lurked under her skirt.

Enfolded within the natural world, we drove on. The sensation of the woods and fields and all they harbored embraced me, and I slouched in the truck seat, my forehead resting against my passenger window. I contemplated the creatures that I knew lived and thrived beyond that window, and my eyes focused and unfocused on the trees sliding past in a sleepy haze.

My thoughts carried me back to Cayman where we had once gone on a scuba diving trip. Beneath the sea, the ocean clasping me, I sucked the air from my regulator, finned to keep my body stationary in the water, and looked up. I could see the sunlight filtering through the surface of the water. The rays glistened and rippled at the surface. A jellyfish floated past, and I held still to avoid its sting. Particles as small as insects floated in the water like peas in soup—plankton and shrimp and other creatures almost too small for the human eye to see.

In the distance I saw something dark mid-water. I craned to see, but all I could make out was a large mass that appeared to be spinning, turning in the water. I glanced to my left to check on Edgar, my diving buddy. He was focusing his video camera on a reef fish hiding in a coral crevice. Just then he looked up. I motioned him to follow, pointing at the dark hulk about fifty feet ahead.

It was tubular-shaped, so I was certain it was not a large predator like a shark—not that a shark would have sent me fleeing. Part of the fun of diving was meeting all kinds of sea inhabitants. Each had a role to play in the life of the sea. Each was fascinating in its own right.

Edgar swam beside me as I pointed ahead. I looked at him, and he nodded, a gesture that said he had seen the dark mass, too. The closer we came, the better I could discern its character. Though it was a shadow, it glistened. An oblong thing composed of a hundred mirrors, it flashed and reflected the sun rays penetrating the ocean's surface.

I swam harder. Edgar was watching the object, too. What could it be?

When we had approached to within twenty feet, I could recognize the dark, sparkling image.

A school of horse-eye jack. Hundreds of them, large disc-shaped relatives of the tuna, spiraling around in a column. A tube of silvery, coin-like fish, each the size of a hubcap, rotating around a watery axis in the middle of the ocean. Each individual platinum fish with its large, round, staring eye, circled another. Together they created a pillar of fish that no larger predator would dare to attack. In the tower of fish, each animal was a brick, with the water as mortar. And not much could topple it.

I looked at Edgar, and he smiled at me through his face mask. I pointed at my chest, then to the fish pillar.

I was going in.

Slowly I approached the silvery column. It reeled and churned only ten feet from me, its myriad of dark, mirrorlike eyes regarding me. I breathed slowly through the regulator, allowing my exhaled bubbles to escape intermittently so as not to scare the fish and destroy the tower. I stopped finning, went vertical in the water, parallel with the column, and just watched.

As I watched them, they observed me, cautious of my motives. But in fact I had no other motive than to enjoy their company and possibly become one of their mesmerizing community for a moment or

two. The size of the column spanned ten feet across by ten feet high. It was a soup can, the walls of individual, aluminum-colored fish swirling about a center.

As I stood suspended within the fold of the ocean, exhaling slowly, quietly I drew closer, and I could sense that Edgar was hanging farther back so as not to scatter the school. I studied the swarm, drifting alongside them as the tube of fish traveled as one through the ocean.

I discovered that the center of the column was empty. All the fish swam to the outside, leaving a perfect center of empty water. I eyed the center, assessed the fishes' comfort with me, and decided once and for all to do it.

I would take my place in the center of the column.

I would become one of them.

I carefully pushed myself back and then dived down about twenty feet. Below the spiraling tower of fish, I looked up and aimed for the empty hole. Slowly, very slowly, with bated breath, I drifted toward the center of the fish tube. The tower was getting closer, closer. I began to drift lightly into its living silver mass. With delicate, quiet movements, disturbing the water as little as possible, I rose up through the column.

I was inside, as in the eye of a hurricane, except that there was no violence to the maelstrom spinning round me. The fish regarded me with little anxiety as I floated inside, parallel their walls. All was quiet, the sound of my bubbles the only disruption to the completely mesmerizing effect of the experience. Despite my initial fears, they were unthreatened by my presence. I certainly did not wish to destroy their peace or tumble the tower. I just wanted to become a part of it, if ever so briefly.

For several minutes I floated within the beating heart of the fish pillar. I crossed my legs at the ankles and wrapped my arms around myself, almost fetuslike, so that my body would be as noninvasive as possible. I held my breath so as not to alarm the fish. Through my own fish-eyed face mask I regarded the wall of fish circling me only three feet away. The walls were thick with horse-eye jack, all polarized—moving in the same direction—all swimming one atop another, one aside the other, with very little space in between. Each one regarded me, not with fear or resentment, but with interest. Their eyeballs swiveled toward me and away from me as they swam past and behind me. When they approached again from the left, the eyes orbited forward, then straight out toward me, then back toward their tails as they swam around to the right of me.

The experience was exhilarating. They had accepted me as one of their own. I was a fish and loving it. For moments I was of fish mentality and essence. I, too, was a silvery mirror encradled by the sea.

I smiled, and a huge air bubble escaped my regulator. The wall of fish moved outward, all eyes on me. But the tower didn't break apart. I rotated in my column of fish and water toward Edgar. I clasped my hands to my cheeks to indicate ecstasy, and Edgar hung to the outside of the jack wall and nodded approvingly. He knew what I was feeling.

I am but a small piece of the larger familial puzzle. I feel a complete sense of acceptance, honesty, and trust with most creatures great and small as well as with many humans. Every day brings another animal encounter and another lesson that the world is far more complex than human life. Having lived and worked with animals finds me not alien to any life form on Earth but only momentarily surprised by it. Our life has come to include not only our parents, his brother and sisters, cousins, and in-laws as family but also the animals in the field, woods, farm, and exotic reaches of the world—ones we will never see or meet. We are a part of a larger thing: a world family. This family, not simply culturally or ethnically diverse but biodiverse as well, offers us so much more than the traditional human family. It offers us humor, sadness, spiritual growth, love, and acceptance and appreciation of all beings. It is a condition we hope to sustain and perpetuate, and it is one we think will embrace all people—in time.

My dream was interrupted by a voice. "So, where would you like to go for lunch today?" Edgar asked, as the truck dove out of the dimly-lit forest and into the sunshine. We had broken out into flat fields and pastures. I saw a gas station sign protruding in the distance above the trees.

I shook the ocean from my head, smiled, and said, "Oh, anywhere is fine. I don't even need lunch today. I'm content just taking a great ride—a really wonderful ride."

ABOUT THE AUTHOR

GAY L. BALLIET lives with her husband, Edgar, and their menagerie on a small farm in eastern Pennsylvania. Her other books include *Touched By All Creatures* (1999) and *Lowell: The True Story of an Existential Pig* (2000). These are a few of her favorite things . . .

Favorite book: The Hog Book by William Hedgepeth

Favorite food: donuts

Foods she avoids: donuts

Favorite TV personality: Jeff Corwin from *Animal Planet*

Most satisfying moment: adopting The Giants

Most exhilarating experience: scuba diving with sharks

Most important goal for humankind: preserving and fostering a bio-diverse world

Ultimate wish: That each person who reads this book gives a good and caring indoor or outdoor home to a needy animal at a humane shelter.